S0-ABZ-738

TE DUE

Resource Flows to Less-Developed Countries

PRAEGER SPECIAL STUDIES IN
INTERNATIONAL ECONOMICS AND DEVELOPMENT

Resource Flows to Less-Developed Countries

FINANCIAL TERMS AND THEIR CONSTRAINTS

Clive S. Gray

FREDERICK A. PRAEGER, Publishers
New York · Washington · London

The purpose of the Praeger Special Studies is to make specialized research monographs in U.S. and international economics and politics available to the academic, business, and government communities. For further information, write to the Special Projects Division, Frederick A. Praeger, Publishers, 111 Fourth Avenue, New York, N.Y. 10003.

FREDERICK A. PRAEGER, PUBLISHERS
111 Fourth Avenue, New York, N.Y. 10003, U.S.A.
5, Cromwell Place, London S.W.7, England

Published in the United States of America in 1969
by Frederick A. Praeger, Inc., Publishers

All rights reserved

© 1969 by Frederick A. Praeger, Inc.

Library of Congress Catalog Card Number: 68-55005

Printed in the United States of America

HG
4517
G7

This book is dedicated to
the memory of my mother,
Margaret Day Gray, 1905–65

PREFACE

This is a book about one limited aspect of the flow of financial resources from economically advanced to less-developed countries--the burden on the less-developed countries of servicing that portion of the flow which is repayable. The book considers how the terms of repayment on the resource flow affect the performance of that flow in meeting the goal of maximizing the economic growth rate of the recipient countries within a framework of political stability. From there the book proceeds to its central objective: to determine rigorously what maximum terms of repayment are consistent with achieving this goal, assuming certain economic parameters to be characteristic of less-developed countries.

More specifically, the book starts out by defining a spectrum of techniques of resource transfer to less-developed countries, ranked according to the burden on the recipient of repayment or other methods of servicing the transfer. Present-day private direct investment and bilateral and multilateral public aid are evaluated according to the criteria of the spectrum. On the assumption that the objective of public foreign aid is to maximize the economic growth rate of the less-developed countries, the book derives a set of five constraints that affect the terms on which the flow of resources takes place. These constraints consist of limits, either normative or positive, on:

(1) the time by which the less-developed countries achieve financial independence;

(2) the extent of these countries' maximum foreign indebtedness as a ratio to their national income;

(3) the ratio of their foreign debt service payments to export earnings;

(4) the availability of acceptable end-uses for resource transfer; and

(5) the gross, as opposed to net, outflows of resources that capital-exporting countries are willing to sustain.

Proceeding from these constraints, the book then constructs models by means of which the maximum weighted average terms on resource transfer can be derived rigorously for a less-developed country characterized by certain macroeconomic parameters. Values of the parameters concerned for a sample of less-developed countries and capital sources are plugged into the models. The results present a quantitative case for public resource transfer on weighted average repayment terms at least as "soft" as those presently in effect. Finally, the interrelationships among the various techniques of resource transfer are studied, the conclusion being that techniques of transfer on "soft" terms are today serving much more, on net, to complement and facilitate techniques on "harder" terms, rather than displace them, as is sometimes argued in public discussion.

Among possible misconceptions arising out of this study, the one I am most anxious to avoid is the impression that I might consider the repayment terms on resource transfer to the less-developed countries, more than any other aspect of the transfer (apart from the obvious one of the gross real amounts involved), to have a determinative effect on the net contribution that such transfer makes to the growth of the less-developed countries. Far from believing this, I attach relatively greater weight, in assessing the contribution of resource transfer, to its qualitative content. By this, I mean particularly the management accompanying the transfer, together with other forms of influence that sources exert on (1) the scope and manner of execution of the activities they aid directly as well as on (2) aspects of resource allocation in the less-developed countries that transcend these activities. A good deal has been written about this subject already, and I may one day have some observations to contribute to it. But, for the time being, this book is presented as a contribution to the discussion of terms of repayment and makes no claim to treat other, possibly more important, aspects of resource transfer. Based on, among other things, the considerable attention the subject has received in publications of the World Bank (notably in the writings of Dragoslav Avromovic and associates in the Bank's Economic Department), in reports of the Development Assistance Committee of the Organization for Economic Cooperation and Development (OECD), and in a variety of recent scholarly articles, there is good reason to believe that repayment terms are a significant aspect of resource transfer and a subject worthy of more systematic treatment than has yet appeared. This book purports to provide this systematic analysis.

The only other caveat I wish to introduce at the outset relates to the use in Chapters 5-9 of aggregative models of resource inflow to derive maximum repayment terms. The use of such models to estimate aid requirements of particular countries or the less-developed world as a whole over multiyear periods has been authoritatively criticized, most recently by Raymond Mikesell, whose comprehensive Economics of Foreign Aid appeared too late to serve as a reference work for this study. Any criticisms directed against aggregative resource inflow models carry their greatest sting against models such as those used in this study, the simplest imaginable in the present context. In the real world, long-run constancy assumptions in regard to capital/output ratios and rates of growth of income, investment, savings, imports, and exports have little relevance. Still, the actual quantitative impact of given repayment terms in a particular country over a period of time can always be duplicated by a set of simplified assumptions along the foregoing lines. There is really no alternative, in determining policy on aid terms, to projecting the trends of the main economic parameters along lines that seem most reasonable at present, perhaps within fairly broad ranges of probable outcomes.

In dealing with resource inflow to a particular country, it is always possible to abandon the constancy assumptions noted above and construct a much more sophisticated projection model, based on differentiated movements within particular sectors and even in regard to individual commodities. Jaroslav Vanek has recently carried out such an exercise for Colombia (see Bibliography). But, as far as the broad implications of alternative repayment terms are concerned, these do not change very much with such refinements in the models, unless the macro assumptions made in the simplest models are completely at variance with those implied by the more complex ones. In any case, it is perfectly possible to use simplified models to project the impact of alternative repayment terms without advocating in any way, as indeed I do not, that aid administrators should actually design the aid flow to particular countries over specific periods of time in accordance with the model results.

ACKNOWLEDGMENTS

This study grew out of a suggestion by Professor Thomas C. Schelling in the International Trade Seminar at Harvard University. The outline of the present book, and a portion of its text, was anticipated by the author's Ph. D. dissertation at Harvard, completed in 1964, entitled "The Spectrum of International Capital Transfer to the Underdeveloped Countries." However, Chapters 3 through 9 of the present work have been completely rewritten and Chapters 2, 10, and 11 have been updated and otherwise modified.

Particular acknowledgment is due Professor Schelling, who stimulated the study and furnished guidance in its initial stages; to Professor Gottfried Haberler, then director of the International Trade Seminar at Harvard, who commented helpfully on an early presentation of the material; to Gerald M. Alter of the World Bank, who shared with me some early relevant work of his own; to W. Haven North and Burton M. Gould, whom I assisted in the U.S. Agency for International Development mission to Nigeria and who provided many insights that benefited my understanding of aid theory and practice; and to Professor Wilson Schmidt, sometime consultant to AID, for whom I carried out an assignment in Nigeria that evoked some of the theoretical results of the study. General acknowledgment is also due to other personnel of AID, including the former International Co-operation Administration and Development Loan Fund; the World Bank; and the governments of Britain, Kenya, Nigeria, and, most recently, Colombia, who provided useful material at one time or another up to the completion of the book.

Finally, I record my appreciation to my wife, Ethne, for patience and encouragement during long periods of strain and for timely help with typing of drafts.

CONTENTS

LIST OF TABLES

xvi

LIST OF ABBREVIATIONS

AID	U.S. Agency for International Development
CDC	(U.K.) Commonwealth Development Corporation
CDW	(U.K.) Colonial Development and Welfare (Program)
DAC	(IBRD) Development Assistance Committee
DLF	Development Loan Fund
EDF	European Development Fund
EEC	European Economic Community
EIB	European Investment Bank
ERP	European Recovery Program
Eximbank	Export-Import Bank
FSO	Fund for Special Operations
GDP	Gross Domestic Product
GNP	Gross National Product
IBRD	International Bank for Reconstruction and Development
ICA	International Cooperation Administration
ICICI	Industrial Credit and Investment Corporation of India
IDA	International Development Association
IDB	Inter-American Development Bank
IFC	International Finance Corporation
MSA	Mutual Security Act
OECD	Organization for Economic Cooperation and Development
OEEC	Organization for European Economic Cooperation
P.L. 480	Public Law 480
SPTF	Special Progress Trust Fund
World Bank	International Bank for Reconstruction and Development

PART I

RESOURCE TRANSFER TO LESS-
DEVELOPED COUNTRIES--A RANGE
OF TECHNIQUES

CHAPTER **1** INTRODUCTION

DEFINITIONS

This study is concerned with various methods by which resources have been, are being, and can in the future be transferred to so-called "less-developed" countries in order to be invested there and contribute to increasing these countries' national income. Our organizing principle is to classify these methods according to a range or "spectrum," defined by the economic burden of the eventual refund that must be made to the sources of the capital. The right, or "hard," end of the spectrum corresponds to those techniques of resource transfer that impose the heaviest burden—i.e., the highest interest rates or other rents and amortization within the shortest period—while the left, or "soft," end of the spectrum is considered the locus of those techniques imposing the least burden. At the extreme left end, it will be seen immediately, comes the outright grant-in-aid, involving a zero repayment burden. For the purposes of this study, the spectrum is regarded as comprising four main subdivisions or points. Proceeding from left to right, these are grants, "soft" loans, "hard" loans, and private capital movements. (Later chapters produce evidence to support this ordering; this chapter discusses qualifications and ambiguities in regard to it.)

So that we may have a concrete basis for ranking the different transfer techniques, the repayment burden imposed by a particular instrument of transfer is defined initially in relation to the gross infusion of resources provided through that instrument. In other words, the location of various techniques along the spectrum is determined by ranking the ratios of required service payments to gross amounts of resources to which these obligations apply. This condition enables us at the outset to escape the confusion arising from a comparison of a loan program on "soft" terms and one which, though its terms were nominally "harder," might be regarded as imposing a lighter repayment burden because it also provided for relending to the borrower each year for an indefinite period the full amount repayable on previous loans. Here, the debt service burden from the hard loans would in any case be less over the period during which the refinancing was taking place; and, depending on the rate

3

by which the borrower discounted future debt payments, it might be effectively less over the entire period of repayment, even though the gross debt accumulated in the process would be considerably higher than in the case of the soft finance.*

In using the required return as the numerator and the gross infusion of resources as the denominator in the various ratios to be compared, we introduce a further significant qualification into the definition of the spectrum. We ignore the extent to which a particular transfer involves assumption by a source outside the developing country of the risks accompanying the investment of the resources. The question of debt versus equity instruments in the transfer of resources may have great significance in a comparison of the effective repayment burdens arising from transfers whose nominal terms would give them an unambiguous position in our spectrum. For one thing, a fixed obligation arising from a foreign debt may impose a foreign exchange burden at a time when the earnings generated by the corresponding investment would not be sufficient to occasion any transfer of profits or dividends. Moreover, the higher rate of return normally required on an equity versus a debt investment may compensate for losses sustained on other equity investments in the economy, where the actual return has turned out to be considerably lower than the going rate for loans and possibly even negative. This would be the case if the actual risks bore a true mathematical relationship to the higher return sought on equity investment.**

Although the spectrum is defined without reference to such questions, we do not avoid them in later discussion and comparison of the main characteristics of the various transfer techniques. Our underlying concern, in which the spectrum serves merely as an

---

*A borrower would use a fairly high rate to discount future obligations if he anticipated price inflation in regard to those commodities on which he depended for earnings out of which to reimburse his creditors. On the other hand, in this case it might be argued that the effective terms of the hard loan were actually softer than they appeared to be. Ambiguities that arise in comparing debt obligations of different maturities are discussed later in this chapter.

**In other words, if the ratio of the aggregate return on all relevant equity investments undertaken during the period for which the risks were calculated to the gross value of the investments was equal to the required return on loans. Calculations of risk, uncertainty, and profit in direct investment are rarely, if ever, based on such a precise actuarial approach. Evidence on U.S. investment in underdeveloped countries (see Chapter 2) suggests that the aggregate returns more than compensate, by a substantial margin, for the losses sustained.

analytical device, is to assess the relative contributions of the various resource transfer techniques toward capital formation and economic growth in the receiving countries. And if, for example, extensive use of the "cheapest" method of financing the internal savings deficit resulted in less resources being available from other sources and in an over-all sense, one would want to take this into account in assessing its relative contributions to growth.

Apart from the questions of gross resource availability and risk-sharing, it would seem at first glance that the spectrum as defined above serves to rank the various techniques of resource transfer according to their relative contributions: A scheme that requires the beneficiary to pay less interest on capital received and gives him more time to amortize it leaves more resources at his disposal for consumption or reinvestment than a scheme with more rigorous servicing requirements. But additional qualifications must be taken into account before the spectrum can be accorded this role. First, in comparing techniques for transferring equal gross infusions of capital, we must further specify infusions <u>measured in real terms.</u> Let us suppose that two countries, A and B, are lending to Country C. Each is lending $1 million in own currency equivalents, measured at the official rate of exchange, and each requires that the money be spent on equipment purchased from firms within its borders. The interest charges and repayment terms are identical; thus, the burden of repayment, in foreign exchange, on Country C is equal in each case. But let us suppose that prices for the specified merchandise are higher in A than in B, the contribution of Country B's loan to C's rate of economic growth will be greater than that of A.

Second, it is quite possible that the relative qualitative impacts of different transfer techniques on business management and economic policy in a developing country may be such as to reverse the original ranking on the spectrum when considering their net effects on economic growth. It is frequently argued, for example, that foreign grants tend to "spoil" a recipient country, leading it to relax financial discipline and expect further contributions without limit, a situation that ultimately disrupts the growth process no matter how much aid is poured in. Hard loans, on the other hand, or better still, foreign private investment, force the benefiting country to keep its house in order, knowing that it must finance regular service payments or profit remittances and not wanting to be labeled bankrupt through reneging on these. In this more disciplined financial environment, so it is argued, the myriad happenings that comprise economic development are more likely to take place.

Third, there may be institutional factors associated with different types of resource transfer, whether generically or by present-day custom, that cause a particular scheme with nominally "harder" servicing requirements to make the greater contribution to economic growth in a particular type of investment. For example, there is evidence that direct private foreign investment normally achieves a peculiar merger of capital and technical and managerial know-how, the infusion of which is likely to make an industrial project more successful, at least in some countries, than if it is executed on a turnkey basis with a foreign loan or grant. There is good reason for saying that different types of resource transfer have maximum favorable qualitative impact when used with particular categories of projects. Very briefly, it is often argued that private foreign investment achieves the most positive results (not merely from the investor's point of view) with industrial projects; that public loans are best implemented in infrastructure projects such as power stations, harbors, communications networks, etc.; while grants are the best vehicle for underwriting pre-investment surveys and technical assistance. All these points will be examined more closely in Chapter 10. If we can admit provisionally that they have some validity, we introduce the possibility that the various techniques of resource transfer are partly noncompetitive in terms of their relative contributions to economic growth, each having its particular role to play.

This point is, in fact, one of the main conclusions of this study, insofar as it is sufficiently controversial to merit the status of a conclusion. However, considerably more space will be devoted to procedures for deriving optimum weighted average terms on public or public and private capital inflow to the underdeveloped areas on the assumption that different techniques of resource transfer, and mixes of these techniques in varying proportions, are alternative means for financing the same complexes of economic activity. This does not necessarily mean that these techniques will be regarded as equally efficient means for financing any particular projects, inasmuch as a heavier or lighter average burden of service terms can be achieved by supplying a greater or lesser amount of hard and soft finance to the different activities for which each technique is believed to be best suited. On the other hand, there are areas of overlap in which it can be argued that the technique of finance used, whether hard or soft, particularly in the category of public foreign aid, will have little impact on the manner of execution of a project. In order to ensure that this is the case, soft loan agencies generally require that, when soft loan funds are to be invested in operations of a private or public revenue-earning organization, the organization must pay service charges to the host government on hard terms, the difference between these payments and those on soft terms that the government is then required to remit to the foreign lender becoming a windfall of general revenue for the government.

In applying our particular definition of the spectrum, making use of concepts such as "burden," "hardness," and "softness," we may be inclined at times to visualize subspectra along the main path, defined in terms of other implications of these concepts. For example, a particular piece of aid may be considered more or less burdensome by a receiving country depending on the evidently

noneconomic conditions attached to it. Thus, a grant-in-aid may be
subject to that worst of all foreign-aid bogies, political "strings";
there may be a requirement of tied procurement, often time-
consuming and substantially more expensive in relation to other
supply possibilities; or the donor may insist on participating in
decisions of how the grant is to be used, in its administration, and
in the subsequent financial audit. Thinking of the colloquial back-
ground to the invention of the term "soft loan," one might be
excused for applying the phrase "hard grant" to the above type of
transaction.* However, considering the relative contributions of
different transfer schemes to economic growth, "hardness" in the
above sense may be more conducive to growth than "softness," since
the tighter the conditions surrounding use of a grant-in-aid (leaving
aside tied procurement, which has the least to be said for it of all
conditions, at least from the recipient country's viewpoint), the less
should be the likelihood of it being squandered and the greater its
positive impact on growth.

CHOICE OF DISCOUNT RATE

We have now seen that the ranking of different techniques along
our original spectrum may be disturbed by allowing other concepts
of hardness and softness to creep into the definition. Probably the
best way to handle these is to think in terms of vertical hierarchies
intersecting the horizontal line on which are arranged the different
transfer techniques according to our definition but not allow them to
influence the left-right arrangement along the main spectrum. Even
so, our own spectrum is plagued by enough ambiguities, even in
strictly quantitative matters. For example, the rate of interest on
Loan A may be higher than that on Loan B, while B's period of amortization is shorter than A's. The only way to compare the relative
burdens of service payments in the two cases is to discount the payment streams by a common factor. But the choice of the common
factor may determine whether one loan is found to be more burdensome than the other, or vice versa.

To illustrate this point, let us compare two loans of equal gross
value, A and B, such that the interest payable on A is 2 per cent and
that on B zero; the borrower has 19 years to amortize A as opposed
to 10 years for B. We assume further that the loans are repayable
on the level annual payment system (i.e., in equal annual installments
comprising declining amounts of interest and increasing amounts of
principal, with interest payable on the amount of principal outstanding at the beginning of each year). If the factor used to discount the

_____
*This phrase was coined by Prof. Thomas Schelling in a collo-
quium concerning this study.

payment streams is 4 per cent, the present value of service payments on A stands in the ratio 838:811 to the present value of service payments on B; if the discount rate is increased to 6 per cent,
the ratio becomes 712:736. In the first case, the "burden" of A is
greater; in the second case, it is less. Generally, it can be shown
that for any pair of loans amortized under the level payment system
or in equal periodic installments of principal such that one loan has
both the higher interest rate and the longer maturity (subject to certain inequalities relating the respective terms), there will be a
discount rate that equates the present value costs of the two loans;
and discount rates higher than this value will reduce the present
value cost of the higher-interest, longer-maturity loan below that
of the other, whereas lower discount rates will reverse the ranking
of the present value costs.

In the case of loans repaid under irregular amortization
schemes in such a way that larger principal installments are paid
both before and after smaller ones, and/or vice versa, the ranking of present value costs may fluctuate repeatedly as the discount
rate moves over a range of values. Such will frequently be the case
if the attempt is made to discount future service payments on private foreign investment; earnings and remittances arising out of
private investment are subject to wide fluctuations under the influence of the business cycle and many other factors.

This ambiguity in the ranking of loan "burdens" is a real one,
because the choice of a discount rate is usually a fairly arbitrary
matter. John Pincus, who has popularized the application of the discounted present value approach to assessing the cost of foreign aid,
points out:

> The appropriate discount rate for computing present
> value of repayments depends on the purpose of the com-
> putations. The marginal domestic long-term return
> on capital is appropriate if we are interested in the
> domestic opportunity cost of capital. For the sake of
> consistency among countries we might, on the other
> hand, want to discount by the international lending rate,
> which, in the virtual absence of a private long-term
> market for lending to underdeveloped countries, is
> presumably represented by the World Bank lending
> rate. Finally, we might want to approximate the rate
> that long-term private investors would have to earn in
> these areas.[1]

He then proceeds to select rates of 5, 5 3/4, and 10 per cent as
"approximately" representative of each of the three alternatives.
The Development Assistance Committee (DAC) of the Organization
for Economic Cooperation and Development (OECD), recently
introducing this technique for the first time in its regular series of
reports on resource flows, calculates the "grant element" in official

aid flows from the various OECD member countries alternatively on the basis of (1) a uniform discount rate of 10 per cent, "taken to reflect the net rate of return on capital prevailing in the economies of OECD/DAC countries," and (2) the long-term government bond yield, rounded to the nearest one-half per cent, of the particular aid-giving country whose flow is being discounted.[2] These two are, of course, alternative measures of the opportunity cost of aid funds from the viewpoint of the source country, and, since DAC is a grouping of source countries, it is natural for it to take this viewpoint.

However, this study is concerned with the comparative efficacy of different forms of resource transfer in terms of their net contribution to the growth of the less-developed areas. It is, therefore, appropriate for us to examine factors that would enter into the determination of a discount rate by a less-developed country trying to evaluate different vehicles of resource transfer from the viewpoint of maximizing its growth. The key question from the borrowing country's viewpoint is: How much money would it have to invest right now, in the most productive uses available to it at the margin, in order to repay a particular transfer entirely out of the proceeds (including the original capital)? If the only channel of investment available for this purpose is taken to be marketable securities of high quality, the rate on government bonds might be the appropriate value. (This would hold true for government as well as private borrowers; the former, while not formally "investing" in their own securities, nevertheless earn the specified return in an opportunity cost sense by redeeming them.) On the other hand, if investment channels available at the margin are deemed to include direct project undertakings, the relevant discount rate might be higher. From the viewpoint of government agencies, the argument might run that public-sector development projects should have a considerably higher return than the rate of interest on government bonds (or else they should not be undertaken.) This principle is easier to realize because a government normally feels it is justified in taking into account the benefits of a project to society as a whole, including those members who are not taxed in direct proportion to the benefits they receive.*

Moreover, a government might not feel a strong compunction to consider only the safest, fixed-return investments for our hypothetical investment, while the risk element, involving the difficulty of raising funds from one source to settle debts with another, as well as the disastrous consequences of default, would prevent private borrowers from doing anything else. If the worst happens,

---

*This is not to be interpreted as an argument for governments asserting the right to take into account "consumer's surplus" in calculating the benefits of a project. "External economies" can be carried sufficiently far toward the boundaries of reason without need of additional fuzzy concepts.

a government can always borrow money internally on the national faith and credit, or, failing even that, crank the printing presses.

On the other hand, the question of international transfer of resources, i.e., the balance-of-payments problem, is in many ways analogous to the liquidity problem of a private debtor, and it can be argued that some function of the projected rate of increase of export earnings and the marginal foreign-exchange yield of the economy's capital is the appropriate rate for discounting future international debt obligations of a country with a small reserve margin. For many of today's less-developed countries, considering the oft-cited unfavorable prospects for their export prices, this rate should probably be pegged below the nominal rate-of-return figure used in the domestic economy. However, many countries make an implicit discount calculation consistent with the opposite assumption; putting a high premium on present imports, they accept credit at very high rates for the sake of postponing payment for a few years. As can be expected, they sooner or later encounter a payments crisis, in which they must draw heavily on their political credit. When a country is on the verge of international bankruptcy, it may have to accept credits on very stiff terms, with an extremely high implicit discount rate, in order to maintain crucial imports and prevent imminent collapse.

Although caution might seem to dictate using the lowest alternative in any set of defensible discount rates, there are good reasons why a country might want to use a discount rate based on foreign-exchange considerations even if this were higher than, say, the marginal rate of return on domestic capital. The higher the debt service obligations a country must meet in the short run, the less foreign capital may be made available to it out of concern for the country's creditworthiness in relation to its current foreign-exchange earnings. In any case, the existence of such obligations will not necessarily motivate capital sources to increase the gross supply of foreign capital (and without such increase the net supply will be lower). This is because most sources of capital are reluctant to lend for the explicit purpose of enabling a country to meet obligations arising from earlier loans. Rather, they insist on lending for specific development projects and often only for the foreign-exchange components of these. The availability of such investment opportunities often puts an effective constraint on the inflow of public capital over a period of time. Finally, aid sources often face appropriation limits on the gross amounts of resources they can furnish in a specific period, and with most of them there is no guarantee that their own sources of capital will not be sharply reduced or even dry up completely at some point in the foreseeable future. All the foregoing would be reasons for putting a premium on loans with longer maturities, even though the interest rates were substantially higher.

Questions such as the foregoing are difficult to resolve in quantitative terms, and it may be advantageous to stick to customary discount rates, based on rule-of-thumb calculations, in the numerical analysis, reserving the other considerations for qualitative discussion and decision. Although it is not intended to argue that governments should allow themselves to be influenced by all the arguments cited above, these are in sufficient everyday use, explicit and otherwise, to justify raising policy questions as to how the relative burdensomeness of various resource inflows is to be measured. Nevertheless, the existence of these ambiguities does not detract altogether from the validity of our classification scheme; and there is considerable scope for establishing criteria to choose among elements with clearly defined locations along the spectrum.

SECONDARY CRITERIA: COMPARING OUTFLOW AND SERVICE PAYMENTS

Having applied the capital transfer spectrum in its simplest form to various techniques of transfer, we will attempt to refine the analysis by comparing different techniques according to a secondary criterion referred to above: namely, the relationship between gross capital outflow and reverse flow of service payments. This criterion is related to the spectrum in that, the harder the interest and repayment terms on a form of capital transfer, the faster the rate at which annual gross outflow must increase in order to maintain a given ratio of service payments to such outflow. However, ranking according to the secondary criterion is not identical with ranking along the spectrum, because a transfer technique carrying harder terms may have the capacity for a more than compensating increase in annual gross outflow. This question would be of interest to a less-developed country faced with a once-for-all decision whether to leave an economic or geographical area open to exploitation by private foreign capital or seek to develop it under public management with the help of public foreign aid. Even if the nominal terms on public aid were less than on foreign private investment, the country would want to take into account the possibility that the availability of new public capital in the future might be less than that of private capital. Chapters 2 and 9 present statistical evidence on the recent behavior of various transfer techniques according to this criterion.

Measuring a technique of capital transfer against this secondary criterion enables us to assess its contribution to filling the "resource gap" in less-developed countries. The theory behind this gap is that less-developed countries, or at least those ruled by other than Communist governments, are unable to divert sufficient internal resources from consumption to support a level of capital formation that will enable these countries' economies to grow at

politically acceptable rates (politically acceptable being defined as a
rate that will forestall Communist-led revolts). In order that the
necessary amount of capital formation may be carried out and the desired growth rate attained, a less-developed country's domestic
savings must be supplemented by foreign capital.

Now let us suppose that foreign capital has been flowing into a
country for several years and annual service payments (interest,
profits, and dividends plus amortization and repatriation) have built
up to the point where they are equal to gross new foreign capital inflow. In that event, assuming no further draw-down of past savings
(foreign-exchange reserves) is possible, gross capital formation
cannot exceed gross domestic savings, and new foreign capital inflow
is not helping to fill the "resource gap" as we have defined it. It
is, of course, helping to fill a gap defined as the sum of capital formation and service obligations on foreign capital less domestic
saving, and it constitutes a part of total investment in a national income sense (since investment comprises both a foreign and a domestic component). Moreover, part of the country's savings will
normally arise from income generated by foreign investments, and
it is arguable whether this part should be lumped together with
"domestic" saving. One might also argue that whether the service
obligations are regarded as being financed by new foreign capital
inflow or domestic saving is an arbitrary matter of attribution.
But, if it is true that satisfactory economic progress in the underdeveloped areas can be attained only by enabling these countries to
maintain levels of capital formation in excess of savings generated
by the domestic economy, then the relationship of service payments
on existing foreign investments to gross new inflow of resources
via a particular transfer technique is relevant to an appraisal of the
technique's contribution to economic growth.

ORGANIZATION OF THE STUDY

Chapters 2 to 4 of this study follow the institutional approach
in examining generic types of resource transfer, past and present,
and trying to show where they fit in the spectrum, in terms of both
the first-order definition and the secondary criterion of the relationship between gross outflow and reverse service flows.
Chapter 2 discusses private capital movements, focusing on U.S.
private direct investment in today's less-developed areas. Chapters
3 and 4 touch on selected aspects of the flow of public aid resources
to less-developed countries. The subject of public aid is now
thoroughly illuminated in detailed reports of the Development Assistance Committee, whose calculation of the "grant element" in aid
flows tells us exactly where these flows fit, in the aggregate, along
our spectrum, and it would be superfluous for this study to try to
give comprehensive treatment to it. Instead, we focus primarily
on innovations introduced into traditional loan procedures in

response to a demonstrated need to maintain a steady and even increasing flow of resources, net of the reverse flow of service payments, into the foreseeable future. We consider steps taken to "soften" the terms of hard-lending agencies without turning them into ostensible soft-lenders and pay particular attention to those categories of capital transfer in which effective rates of return and amortization periods are not clearly defined but are left to future negotiation. The prime example of this category is the loan repayable in inconvertible local currency.

Following the institutional treatment in Part I, Part II, comprising Chapters 5 to 9, seeks to establish a quantitative framework for determining optimum weighted average terms on all resource transfer to a less-developed country, or on any portion of such transfer regarded as a residual when institutional factors fix the terms on certain components of the transfer. A set of constraints--i.e., factors that place a ceiling on the "hardness" of resource transfer terms if the transfer is to achieve its objectives--is proposed, and economic models defining the resource gap and the resulting transfer requirement are built around these constraints. Parameters of the models include gross domestic product, savings, investment, exports, and imports, as well as their rates of change. Dependent variables are the rate of return on foreign-capital inflow plus, in three of the models, the rate of amortization or repatriation of foreign capital. The culmination of this analysis consists of manipulating these models to yield solutions for optimum terms. The procedures involved in this exercise are demonstrated by inserting basic economic data for several regions of the less-developed world into the models and discussing the implications of the constraints and various subsidiary assumptions for terms on resource transfer to those regions.

Chapter 5 introduces the quantitative analysis and reviews a number of constraints on aid terms that have been suggested by other observers. It selects five of these for more intensive treatment and then outlines a simple growth model that underlies the analysis of four of the constraints. Each of Chapters 6 to 9 focuses on particular constraints; Chapter 6 deals with two, one being regarded as a corollary of the other, and Chapters 7, 8, and 9 deal with one each. The concluding section of Chapter 9 also summarizes the practical implications of the quantitative analysis for the policies of today's principal foreign aid sources.

The five constraints are:

(1) A less-developed country should become independent of net foreign capital inflow absolutely or as an increasing proportion of national income, or should repay its accumulated foreign debt, by a specified future year; or

(2) The value of foreign investment--public, private, or both-- in the country should not exceed a specified proportion of its gross domestic product (both in Chapter 6).

(3) Service payments on a less-developed country's foreign debt should not exceed a specified percentage of the country's export earnings in any year or in some specified future year (Chapter 7).

(4) The sum of the annual resource gap and service obligations on foreign investment should not exceed a level at which the required gross resource inflow can be infused into a less-developed country via specific investment projects and/or specific types of imports (Chapter 8).

(5) The ratio of a capital-exporting country's (or all such countries') receipts of service payments on its (their) investments in less-developed areas to new gross capital outflow to these areas should not exceed a specified level (Chapter 9).

Up to this point in the study, Part I has measured the burden imposed by various techniques of resource transfer on a less-developed country, and Part II has furnished the means of assessing the maximum burden the country can bear, subject to various objectives and constraints. Assuming that the flow of resources to the typical less-developed country will consist of representatives of all techniques of transfer, with the weighted average burden not exceeding the foregoing limit, Part III, comprising Chapters 10 and 11, then considers two questions arising out of this juxtaposition of different techniques. Chapter 10 examines the allocation of different components of the capital flow among various economic sectors and types of activities and considers how far certain techniques are optimally suited to particular end-uses. It finds that a number of allocation criteria in current use are largely matters of convention, although this is not true of all criteria, especially those relating to techniques of resource transfer, notably private equity investment, that have a large human resource (i.e., management) element. Finally, Chapter 11 examines the question of whether vehicles of transfer carrying easy terms tend to displace those on harder terms from playing the full role that the constraints on the investment service burden would allow them to do. The conclusion reached is that, although there are situations in which such displacement has occured in the past and is generically likely to continue to do so, there are adequate safeguards to prevent the situation from getting out of hand, and the essential complementarity of the different techniques and the mutual reinforcement they give each other by and large considerably outweigh the displacement effect.

NOTES TO CHAPTER 1

1. John Pincus, "The Cost of Foreign Aid," Review of Economics and Statistics, November, 1963, p. 361.

2. Organization for Economic Cooperation and Development, The Flow of Financial Resources to Less-Developed Countries, 1961-65 (Paris, 1967), pp. 141-44 and 192-96.

CHAPTER **2** PRIVATE FOREIGN
INVESTMENT

The role of foreign (private) investment in the past
is sometimes cited as a precedent to current development assistance, but such a comparison suffers from
a number of weaknesses. To begin with, although there
is general agreement that the intangible contribution
of foreign investment to the transfer of technology was
of great importance, the quantitative role of foreign
investment in capital formation seems to have been
surprisingly small, except during very short bursts.
Even these sufficed to raise the share of debt servicing
in the balances of payments of the borrowers to very
considerable proportions, and almost every burst of
investment produced its painful aftermath of crisis.

Above all, however, it should be stressed that
the classical cases of overseas investment before
World War I did not involve a sustained transfer of
resources to the debtor countries but precisely the
opposite. The reflow of investment income to creditor countries almost from the start matched or exceeded the flow of new net investment.[1]

Because this book is concerned only with contemporary resource flows to those countries normally described as "less-
developed" at the present time, I do not attempt here to retrace the
pre-World War II ground underlying the above statement of Ohlin.
In an earlier work, I have reviewed the available evidence showing
where prewar private foreign investment in less-developed countries fits along the spectrum of capital transfer techniques defined
in the preceding chapter.[2] Following are some highlights of this
evidence:

(1) Albert H. Imlah's estimates of the U.K. balance of payments during 1816-1913 show an aggregate net balance of minus
£760 million on trade and services, excluding investment income.
Thus, on net, Britain's investment income, which Imlah shows to
have been the largest annual net credit item in its balance sheet by

the 1870's, financed the country's import surplus and provided the credit balances on current account that built up its foreign investment.[3]

(2) If Imlah's estimate of British foreign investment in 1820 is compounded at 5 per cent per annum, which is no greater than the return that the available evidence shows this investment to have been earning in most years, the result after 93 years is nearly 40 per cent greater than his estimate of actual U.K. foreign investment in 1913.

(3) Simon Kuznets' U.S. balance-of-payments data show that net U.S. payments on account of investment income were, on an average, nearly equal to foreign capital inflow during 1850-73 and significantly in excess of it during 1874-1914.[4]

BILATERAL PORTFOLIO INVESTMENT

The overwhelming proportion of the European capital that was invested in the less-developed countries of the nineteenth century moved via private purchases of bonds issued or guaranteed by public authorities in those countries. By contrast, Table 1 shows only 6 per cent of new private foreign investment in the currently less-developed countries during 1960-66 to have been in such securities.

Further DAC data show that some 20 developing countries, including dependent territories, some of whose issues were guaranteed by the metropolitan governments concerned, were able to float bonds in 6 developed countries during 1960-65--the United States, where 78.3 per cent of the issues were sold; Britain, 8.5 per cent; Switzerland, 1.9 per cent; the Netherlands, 1.4 per cent; Germany, 0.3 per cent; and Austria, a single issue amounting to only .03 per cent. (Another 9.5 per cent comprised Euro-Bond issues; information on the locus of purchase was not available to the DAC.)[5] The distribution of issues among borrowing countries is similarly skewed, with Israel (38 per cent) and Mexico (34 per cent) accounting for nearly three quarters. These two countries are, of course, uncharacteristic of the less-developed areas as a whole with respect to their creditworthiness and (in the case of Israel) special relationship to investors purchasing the bonds. Most of the other countries placing bonds have been current or former dependent territories or exceptionally close trading partners (e.g., certain Latin American countries vis-à-vis the United States) of the country of placement.

The difficulty that most less-developed countries have today in selling bonds on their own security is illustrated by an episode on the London money market in 1962-63. Nigeria, which borrowed

TABLE 1

Net Private Capital Flows to Less-developed Countries from OECD Members, 1960-66, by Type of Flow

Type of flow	$ billion	%
Direct investment	12.9	58
Trade credits (with & without public guarantee)	5.2	24
Bilateral bond flotations	1.4	6
Portfolio investment in multilateral lending agencies	0.9	4
Other[a]	1.7	8
Total	22.1	100

Note:

[a]According to the DAC, in The Flow of Financial Resources to Less-Developed Countries, 1961-65 (Paris, 1967), p. 42, "other" includes bank loans of more than one year duration; real estate transactions; "probably . . . some export credits, in spite of efforts to separate them from the rest of the category"; and direct investment by U.K. oil companies, which are not covered in U.K. direct investment figures in order to avoid disclosure of confidential information.

Sources: OECD, DAC, Development Assistance Efforts and Policies, 1967 Review (Paris, 1967), Statistical Annex, Table 2, pp. 184-85; The Flow of Financial Resources to Less-Developed Countries, 1961-65 (Paris, 1967), Table II.4, p. 40. The first of these gives a revised total for net private transfer of $21.6 billion (Table IV.1, p. 57) but provides no breakdown by type of flow before 1963. Hence, we have used 1960-62 data from the second source.

£16 million on the London market between the end of World War II
and her attainment of independence in 1960, sought to make a placement of several million pounds to finance the dredging of an ocean
channel to the terminal of a petroleum production line developed and
operated by Shell-B. P. of Nigeria, Ltd. Shell-B. P.'s international
parent company offered to guarantee the issue, but Nigeria turned it
down on the ground that such an arrangement would not be in keeping
with her sovereignty. The Nigerians were then told that it would be
very difficult to place the issue solely on Nigeria's own credit.
Finally, agreement was reached on an arrangement whereby the
government of Nigeria acted as borrower and primary guarantor,
while Shell-B. P. of Nigeria agreed to deposit periodically in London,
as advances toward future channel fees, sufficient funds to meet
interest and sinking fund charges on the loan; and, finally, the parent
company guaranteed the performance of its subsidiary in executing
its responsibility. On these terms, the issue of £4. 25 million, for
20 years at 6 per cent, was placed privately during the summer of
1963 and oversubscribed by a wide margin.

Before we take a closer look at postwar direct investment, it
may be useful to inquire briefly into the reasons for the relative
eclipse of portfolio investment in the less-developed countries.
Certainly the primary reason is the record of defaults on securities
issued during the interwar period, most of them related to one of
the three major economic and political upheavals that occurred
within a 20-year period, i.e., the Great Depression, World War II,
and the rise of international Communism. Ragnar Nurkse noted
that, even though only 15 per cent of the dollar bonds floated in the
1920's by underdeveloped countries--excluding Eastern Europe--
proved a permanent loss, American investors were not favorably
impressed.[6] The financial pages of The New York Times present
a constant reminder of these defaults by listing transactions in the
greatly depreciated securities.* Although Nurkse excludes Eastern
Europe from his above statement, the examples set by the countries
of that region in showing what happens to a country's foreign debt
obligations when the Communists take over serve as a potent deterrent to resumed portfolio lending, in view of the takeover threat
posed by the Communists in many less-developed countries. This
lesson has been taught once again by the example of Cuba, which had
bond issues outstanding in the United States. In fact, the Cuban situation magnifies the aura of risk surrounding investment in less-
developed countries by illustrating that seizure of power by the
Communists is not a realistic threat only in countries bordering on
the Sino-Soviet bloc but may occur in an area right under the nose
of the United States.

---

*As many as 20 such securities were listed in the Sunday
edition of The New York Times as late as 1963, although more
recently one finds only two or three there.

Leaders of the international financial community were aware, as they set about rebuilding world finance near the end of World War II, that the recent economic and political record would pose a serious hindrance to international portfolio investment in the postwar world. It was partly to overcome this obstacle to investor confidence that the World Bank was assigned, among other functions, the task of guaranteeing security issues placed by needy member nations in the world money markets. However, the Bank soon realized that it could ensure more orderly conditions in the financial markets, channel resources at lower cost to the borrowers, and control more closely the use of these resources by placing its own securities in world markets and relending the proceeds to developing nations. Hence, it has never implemented the guarantee function. However, through the medium of its own securities, the Bank has revived international portfolio investment in a certain form. In addition, the Bank has given strong encouragement to countries with stable political environments and strong credit ratings to offer their securities directly on the world market, thus easing the demand on the Bank's own facilities. Countries such as Australia, New Zealand, Japan, and several West European nations have made increasing use of such borrowing.

U.S. PRIVATE DIRECT INVESTMENT

The most comprehensive data available on private direct foreign investment, giving regional and country breakdowns of the value of total investment, current net capital flows, earnings, and receipts of investment income, are those collected by the U.S. Department of Commerce in regard to U.S. foreign investment. These data were first presented in the Department's report of a census of U.S. direct foreign investment concluded in 1960. [7] They have been updated in each subsequent year in an annual article in the Survey of Current Business, prepared on the basis of annual returns submitted by firms with overseas interests. [8] In analyzing this data from the viewpoint of our spectrum of capital transfer, it is important to evaluate certain ambiguities in it and determine how they would tend to bias the positioning of private investment in the spectrum. This we will attempt to do below.

The Department's 1960 census was carried out by means of questionnaires sent to all relevant business enterprises known to the Department. The condition of relevance was that "a U.S. resident person, organization, or affiliated group, owned a 25 per cent interest, either in the voting stock of a foreign corporation, or an equivalent ownership in a nonincorporated foreign enterprise." [9] Also included were "associated foreign enterprises in which there was direct U.S. ownership of from 10 to 25 per cent of the voting stock." In some instances, nonassociated foreign companies were included of which U.S. interests owned "slightly" less than 25 per cent of the stock but were known to have strong management connections. If there was no single controlling U.S. interest, a publicly held foreign company was included only if U.S. ownership was 50 per cent or more.

Response to the questionnaires was mandatory under a provision of the Bretton Woods Agreement Act. The following estimate of coverage is contained in the census report:

> The coverage is believed to be virtually complete, at least as far as major investors are concerned. Omissions are limited to relatively small business enterprises and individuals whose foreign investments were not known to the Department; even a large number of such enterprises would not seriously affect the totals. Any such omissions are most likely in Canada and, to a lesser extent, in Mexico, other nearby countries, and a few European countries.[10]

For the purposes of this study, we have sought to extract from the census and subsequent reports data pertaining to U.S. investments in the less-developed areas (as defined heretofore). This can be done quite conveniently, inasmuch as nearly all data are presented in the form of tables containing subtotals for each continent and the main countries in it. We have used without modification the following geographical classifications in the report: Latin American Republics, Western Hemisphere Dependencies (from 1963, "Other Western Hemisphere"), and Middle East. In addition, we have used the Far East minus Japan and Africa minus South Africa. Only in these two cases was it always necessary to obtain arithmetically results not given in the tables, inasmuch as the latter give subtotals for the Far East and Africa including the two excepted nations. The only problem that arose in eliminating Japan and South Africa from their respective continents was that the tables failed to give individual country totals in regard to certain industries, notably petroleum, so that revised totals for the industries involved could not be obtained directly from the report. In some cases, it was possible to infer the correct totals by reconciling row and column subtotals; occasionally the author relied on a "guesstimate" as to the share of the continent's total in a particular industry that should be attributed to Japan or South Africa. In Table 2 we have indicated where an industry figure is subject to error arising from these procedures. Figures for all industries taken together, whether by single continent or all underdeveloped areas, are not subject to such error, but only to minor discrepancies arising from the fact that the commerce tables round off all figures to the nearest million dollars, and it was not possible for us, in subtracting entries for Japan and South Africa, to adjust for whatever rounding had taken place in each case.

TABLE 2

U.S. Private Direct Investment in Less-developed Areas, 1957-66

Industry	(I) Average annual % increase in value of investment, 1950-66	1959-66	(II) Weighted average earnings, 1957-66, as % of value of investment, 1956-65	(III) Weighted average income receipts, 1957-66, as % of value of investment, 1956-65	(IV) Cumulative absolute net capital outflow, 1957-66: income receipts, 1957-66 ($ millions)
Latin American Republics[a]					
Petroleum	5.7	--[b]	16.0	15.1	818:4,313
Other industries	6.3	6.5	10.3	6.7	1,739:3,472
All industries[c]	6.1	4.7	12.3	9.7	2,466:7,780
Other Western Hemisphere					
Petroleum	14.1	7.5	8.4	6.9	277: 279
Other industries	19.4	13.7	19.7	13.3	497: 717
All industries[c]	17.0	11.3	14.8	10.6	796: 996
Africa, excluding South Africa					
Petroleum	17.0[d]	21.4[d]	n.a.[e]	n.a.	n.a.
Other industries	13.4[d]	9.3[d]	n.a.	n.a.	n.a.
All industries[c]	15.5	16.4	12.3	9.6	915: 722

Middle East

Petroleum	5.5	4.2	63.6	607:7,522
Other industries	9.5	16.5	3.2	63: 45
All industries[c]	5.7	4.7	62.0	673:7,639

Far East, excluding Japan

Petroleum	12.5[d]	6.5[d]	n.a.	n.a.
Other industries	9.6[d]	10.4[d]	n.a.	n.a.
All industries[c]	10.6	8.7	11.3	522:1,040

Total, above areas

1. Petroleum	7.4[d]	4.3[d]	n.a.	n.a.
2. Mining & smelting	6.0	2.5	15.0	538:2,293
3. Manufacturing	10.3[b]	14.1[f]	4.9	1,487:1,006
4. Public utilities	—[b]	neg.[f]	n.a.	n.a.
5. Trade	11.1	10.2	n.a.	n.a.
6. Other	8.1	8.0	n.a.	n.a.
Subtotal, 2-6[g]	7.5	7.7	n.a.	n.a.
Subtotal, 1,4,5,6[h]	7.0	4.7	17.8	3,343:14,799
All industries	7.5	6.4	15.3	5,372:18,174

Notes:

[a]The treatment of Cuba, where U.S. private direct investment in 1959 was valued by the Department of Commerce at $956 million, presents some obvious problems. We have eliminated Cuba from the compu- tations in Column I by netting out data for that country from 1950 and 1959 investment totals. Estimates of earnings and income receipts underlying the computations in Columns II and III include Cuba. In summing investment levels, we have excluded Cuba from 1960 on; thus, Cuban investment is included in one year (1959) whereas corresponding earnings and income receipts figures for the following year (1960) are zero.

(Continued)

TABLE 2 (Continued)

b Rate of increase is below 1 per cent.

c Figures for all industries are computed from revised totals published by the Department of Commerce one year after publication of preliminary data giving industry breakdowns. The revised figures do not give industry breakdowns. Hence, there are minor discrepancies between results computed for petroleum and other industries on one hand and all industries on the other; these are evident in Column IV, where the figures for petroleum and other industries usually do not add up to the total figures.

d The Department of Commerce sources do not give figures for the value of direct U.S. investment in the petroleum industry in South Africa and Japan in either or both of the terminal years of the period in question, but include the relevant amounts in residual totals for several industries. By comparing other values in the source tables, it is, however, possible to "guesstimate" the values in question within fairly narrow limits, so that the margin of error in estimating compound annual growth rates of investment in Africa and the Far East excluding those two countries is unlikely to exceed one tenth of a percentage point.

e N.a. denotes "not available."

f Neg. denotes decrease.

g All industries other than petroleum.

h All industries other than mining and smelting and manufacturing. Petroleum represents 75 per cent of the investment in this category.

Sources:

Increase in value of investment. Compound average annual rate of change between 1950 or 1959 and 1966 levels, respectively. All 1950 data and 1959 data for petroleum and other industries taken from U.S. Department of Commerce, Office of Business Economics, U.S. Business Investments in Foreign Countries

24

(Washington, D.C.: Government Printing Office, 1960), pp. 89–91; all other data from U.S. Department of Commerce, Office of Business Economics, Survey of Current Business, September, 1967, p. 42.

Earnings as per cent of investment. Earnings comprise profits of branches of U.S. corporations and the U.S. share in earnings (or losses) of partly or wholly U.S.-owned subsidiaries, after foreign taxes but before U.S. taxes (against which foreign taxes are, of course, allowed as a credit by U.S. tax law), and before depletion charges, if applicable. Data for 1957–59 were taken from U.S. Business Investments, pp. 125–28; for subsequent years, from 1961–67 annual surveys of U.S. foreign investments appearing in the Survey of Current Business. To calculate the weighted average annual percentage, cumulated earnings over the entire period were divided by a summation of the value of investment as at the end of each year from 1956 to 1965. Sources of investment value figures are as indicated above; in addition, for our 1956 estimate, not given directly in the Commerce sources, we subtracted from the 1957 investment figure net capital outflow (from the United States) and the U.S. share in undistributed subsidiary earnings in 1957. Since the value of investment is also affected by exchange rate and other adjustments not figuring in these two measures, our 1956 estimate is subject to a margin of error, which becomes insignificant in cumulating values over the ten-year period.

Income receipts as per cent of investment. As defined in the Survey of Current Business, "income is the sum of dividends and interest, net after foreign withholding taxes, received by, or credited to, the account of the U.S. owner, and branch profit after foreign taxes but before U.S. taxes." Such income may be reinvested abroad; the Commerce sources count this form of reinvestment in net capital outflow from the United States. The bulk of reinvestment of branch earnings during 1957–59 took place in the petroleum industry. (Clive S. Gray, "The Spectrum of International Capital Transfer to the Underdeveloped Countries" [unpublished Ph.D. dissertation, Department of Economics, Harvard University, 1964], pp. 87 and 105–6.) It would, therefore, appear that income receipts in industries other than petroleum are virtually the same as income remittances to the United States. To calculate percentages, we cumulated income receipts over ten years and summed the value of investment as in the preceding exercise. Income data taken from U.S. Business Investments, pp. 130–31, and 1961–67 Survey of Current Business articles.

Net capital outflow and income receipts. Net capital outflow excludes undistributed subsidiary earnings. Sources are U.S. Business Investments, pp. 136–37, and 1961–67 Survey of Current Business Articles.

To relate private capital movements meaningfully to our transfer spectrum, we must take account of certain aspects in which direct private investment is not comparable with public lending. In the latter case, interest and amortization payments are automatically remitted, on a fixed schedule, to the foreign lending agency, whereas in the case of private investment, depreciation allowances and profits may be retained in the foreign country and reinvested there. Of course, remittances of interest and amortization payments on public loans may be offset, from a balance of payments viewpoint, by new lending. Similarly, remittances of profits may be offset by new investment. Following the procedure outlined in Chapter 1, we will focus our attention first on the payments burden associated with a single unit of capital investment, postponing to a later point the comparison of different transfer techniques in the context of the total resource flows associated with them.

The direct payment burden associated with a unit of private foreign investment, net of capital repatriation, consists of that portion of the earnings on it which is remitted abroad, as opposed to being retained locally. To assess this burden, it is relevant to compute ratios of income remittances to the value of invested capital, and this is done in Table 2. At the same time, total earnings/investment ratios are also of interest, for two important reasons. First, they are a measure of the contingent liability that private foreign investment represents vis-à-vis domestic resources in the host country. Second, depending on which capital flow series--i.e., gross or net of retained earnings--exhibits the most stable growth rate, one could defend use of either one, together with the corresponding total earnings or income remittances series, respectively, for analytical purposes. We content ourselves in Table 2 with presenting data on all relevant aspects, including changes in total investment value, net capital outflows, earnings, and income receipts.

Specifically, Column I in the table computes average annual percentage increases in the total value of U.S. direct investment in different regions and industry categories (i.e., petroleum and "all other") over two periods, 1950-66 and 1959-66. The bulk of changes in the value of investment comprises net new capital inflows as well as retained earnings. However, book revaluations resulting from exchange adjustments also figure here. The significance of these figures will be reviewed below in discussing secondary criteria of the capital transfer spectrum.

Column II gives weighted average earnings during 1957-66 as a percentage of the book value of investment at the end of the preceding year. Although complete data on petroleum are not available, it is clear that this industry, with its peculiar pattern of very high earnings rates over-all, offset only to a limited degree by negative earnings in areas where petroleum exploration and development are comparatively recent, imparts a heavy bias to the

aggregate earnings ratio of 18 per cent at the foot of Column II. Of
particular interest is the 10.3 per cent figure for other industries in
Latin America, which is the locus of over 60 per cent of U.S. private
direct investment in less-developed areas, excluding all European
countries (for data on the geographical distribution of U.S. private
direct investment in less-developed areas, see Table 24, Chapter 10.)

Column III gives ratios of income receipts of U.S. investors to
the book value of investment, the same denominator as figured in
Column II. As defined by the Commerce Department, income receipts comprise the sum total of earnings of foreign branches of U.S.
companies plus earnings of foreign subsidiaries declared as dividends to U.S. investors. This measure is not identical with income
remittances, since an unreported share of such income, especially
branch profits, is retained abroad. But, as maintained in a footnote
to Table 2, there is evidence that income receipts are an adequate
measure of income remittances apart from the petroleum industry.
The ratios of income remittances to investment are, of course, less
than the corresponding earnings/investment ratios. In the petroleum
industry, the difference is small in every area; but, in other industries in Latin America, the 10.3 per cent earnings ratio falls by 35
per cent to a 6.7 per cent income receipts ratio.

Finally, Column IV of Table 2 compares absolute cumulative
net capital outflow, from the United States to less-developed countries, with absolute total income receipts, both during 1957-66.
Net capital outflow excludes locally retained earnings, as do income
receipts, but likewise includes any branch profits or dividends of
subsidiaries that are reinvested abroad. As with Column I, the
interpretation of this column is left to a later section of this chapter.

PROBABLE BIASES IN U.S. INVESTMENT DATA

In order to lay a basis for assessing the two ratios given in
our tables, the question must be asked whether any of the figures
on which they depend are likely to be subject to systematic bias. In
other words, is either the numerator in the ratios (earnings or income receipts) or the denominator (total capital investment) likely
to be over- or understated in relation to its true economic value?
To answer this question, it is useful to ask first under what circumstances such over- or understatement would be in the financial
interest of the reporting firms. It would appear that two general
types of considerations are likely to figure in this determination,
one being the burden of taxation, the other being the safety of capital and earnings from economic and political pressures in low-
income foreign countries.

Table 3 presents some evidence regarding the burden of local
taxation on U.S. foreign investments in 1957, the focal year of the

TABLE 3

Ratios of Foreign Taxes Paid by Foreign Branches and Companies Wholly or Partly Owned by U.S. Interests to Pretax Earnings, 1957 (All nondecimal figures are in millions of U.S. dollars.)

Industry	Latin Am. Republics	Western Hemisphere Dependencies	Africa excluding So. Africa	Middle East	Far East excluding Japan	All Under-developed Areas
Petroleum						
Income taxes (T_I)	283	14	n.a.[a]	445	n.a.	n.a.
Other taxes	344	7	n.a.	61	n.a.	n.a.
Total taxes (T_T)	627	21	n.a.	506	n.a.	n.a.
Total earnings (E)	625	37	n.a.	610	n.a.	n.a.
$T_I / (E + T_I)$	.312	.275		.422		
$T_T / (E + T_T)$	.501	.362		.453		
Manufacturing						
Income taxes (T_I)	84	..[b]	..	1	14	99
Other taxes	75	..	..	.	11	86
Total taxes (T_T)	159	..	.	1	25	185
Total earnings (E)	150	..	1	1	22	174
$T_I (E + T_I)$	.359	?	?	?	.389	.363
$T_T (E + T_T)$	.515	?	?	?	.532	.515

Other Industries

Income taxes (T_I)	206	14	n.a.	2	n.a.
Other taxes	88	1	n.a.	.	n.a.
Total taxes (T_T)	294	15	n.a.	2	n.a.
Total earnings (E)	336	86	n.a.	-4	n.a.
$T_I / (E + T_I)$	.380	.140		?	
$T_T / (E + T_T)$	.467	.149		?	

All Industries

Income taxes (T_I)	575	33	448	77	1161
Other taxes	508	33	61	126	736
Total taxes (T_T)	1083	66	509	203	1897
Total earnings (E)	1111	50	607	132	2023
$T_I / (E + T_I)$	.341	.398	.425	.368	.365
$T_T / (E + T_T)$	.494	.569	.456	.606	.484

Notes:

a N. A. denotes not available

b signifies value greater than −$500,000 and less than $500,000.

Explanation and Sources:

Earnings. These represent total earnings of foreign operations covered by the Commerce study, net of foreign taxes. Thus, "E" represents not merely the U.S. share in these earnings but also the shares of any foreign interests with partial equity in the operations concerned. Earnings figures are taken from U.S. Department of Commerce, Office of Business Economics, U.S. Business Investments in Foreign Countries (Washington, D. C.: Government Printing Office, 1960), Table 36, pp. 124-5.

Taxes. These represent all foreign taxes paid by the branches and companies in question, i.e., not only those attributable to the U.S. proportionate share in the various enterprises. Ibid., Table 32, p. 120.

29

1960 Commerce census. The ratios of foreign income taxes to before-tax earnings are, in each region for which data are available, less than the U.S. corporate income tax rate of 52 per cent (on earnings above $25,000) in force in 1957. However, the Commerce data on which the table is based show at least one case of an individual country (India) in which local income taxes took over half of pretax earnings of wholly or partially U.S.-owned operations in one branch of industry (manufacturing); with income tax payments given as $7 million, and after-tax earnings as $5 million, the percentage tax take amounts to 58 per cent with a possible margin of error of $\pm$ 4 per cent due to rounding.[11] Comparison of the ratios in our table with the then U.S. tax rate of 52 per cent is not wholly valid, for multifirm ratios of actual tax payments to pretax earnings are almost always less than the legal tax rate owing to tax-loss carryforward from previous years. The Commerce study notes, for example, that U.S. manufacturing concerns paid income taxes in fiscal 1957 equal to 48 per cent of their pretax earnings.[12]

Three other exceptions must also be noted regarding the picture of higher U.S. tax rates. First, the U.S. income tax rate on companies organized as Western Hemisphere trading corporations is only 38 per cent, which also happens to be the over-all effective local rate given in our table for "other industries" in Latin America. Second, where U.S. income is received in the form of capital gains, it is taxed at no higher than 25 per cent. Companies with foreign interests frequently take advantage of this situation by selling their subsidiaries' used capital equipment at prices that represent capitalized value rather than depreciated book value, the latter being considerably lower. Exaction of such prices reduces present and/or future income of the foreign subsidiaries while raising that of the U.S. companies, who need pay only capital gains taxes on the extra income. Third, in some foreign countries, various types of indirect taxes serve as a means of raising total tax collections to a certain percentage of a company's income.[13] The second series of ratios in Table 3 sets an upper limit on this process, although we do not mean to imply that these ratios are comparable with U.S. income tax ratios.

The evidence we have seen thus far suggests that, insofar as U.S. foreign investors have need of funds for investment in less-developed countries where they operate, tax considerations alone would motivate them, on net, to maximize earnings declared and retained locally as opposed to arranging for these earnings to be attributed to U.S. operations. If such were, in fact, the intent of the "representative firm" in this situation, the firm would have several channels open to it by which it could even shift earnings from the United States to the less-developed country and pay the lower tax there. (The nature of these is suggested by our discussion below of channels by which, as we shall argue, the opposite happens, i.e., earnings are shifted out of the less-developed areas.)

But there are other aspects of the many-faceted tax business that would lead to understatement of earnings in less-developed countries. For one thing, tax administration is much weaker in most less-developed countries than in the United States, a situation that opens up many possibilities for disguising earnings even when the firm has a policy of shifting these into the less-developed country. And certainly the earnings a firm reported on a questionnaire for the U.S. Commerce Department would not be higher than those it reported for tax purposes to the government of a foreign country. On the other hand, the stronger tax administration in the United States makes it more difficult to transfer income surreptitiously to another country, whether high or low income. For example, the U.S. Internal Revenue Service tries to enforce strictly its "arm's-length" criterion to ensure that purchases of U.S. companies' products by affiliated foreign concerns do not occur at lower prices than would prevail in transactions between unaffiliated companies.

The existence of tax havens creates another major incentive to understate earnings in most foreign countries and have them appear, if at all, on the books of affiliated companies in such places as the Bahamas, Panama, or Switzerland. It is a frequent practice for a U.S. firm to place licensing and other rights in the hands of a tax-haven subsidiary, which then sells or leases these rights for lucrative fees to subsidiaries in other foreign countries. Insofar as the earnings are actually declared in the Bahamas or Panama, earnings of the two regions concerned (other Western Hemisphere and Latin American republics) and of the less-developed areas as a whole are not reduced; however, such reduction does occur when the earnings are attributed to Switzerland or any other country outside the less-developed areas. It is interesting to note that earnings ratios for other Western Hemisphere and Panama are relatively high. From Table 2 we see that the percentage of the U.S. share in net earnings of U.S. direct foreign investments in nonpetroleum industries to total book value of such investments in the Western Hemisphere dependencies has been substantially higher than the corresponding percentages in other areas for which it is available. The average earnings rate for nonpetroleum investment in Panama has been 16.3 per cent, which compares with the value of 10.3 per cent for Latin America as a whole. Although the 1962 U.S. tax law amendments tightened up considerably on the relief from U.S. tax law liability received by American firms operating in tax havens, the amendments excepted from additional liability income earned through operations in underdeveloped areas.

If it is not entirely clear how tax considerations affect the nominal as opposed to true economic earnings/investment ratios for U.S. operations in the less-developed areas, there is no ambiguity in connection with the second series of factors referred to above, i.e., the safety of capital and earnings from economic and political pressures in low-income foreign countries. U.S. investors are aware that there is virtually no independent or soon-to-be independent low-income country in which high earnings/investment ratios, particularly where foreign-owned enterprises are concerned, do not arouse jealousy, resentment, and opposition in various forms on the part of powerful local interests who may be in a position to apply measures of expropriation, limitations on convertibility, additional taxation, price controls, minimum wage levels, etc., in order to appropriate a larger share of the earnings for local interests. Although the governments of most underdeveloped countries pay lip service to the contribution private foreign investors have made, are making, or can make in the future to their economic development, there is a general belief, even among leaders who are convinced of the great value of this contribution, that ratios of earnings to investment in foreign-owned enterprises should be maintained below certain maximum levels and that, if the ratios exceed these levels, then the enterprises are probably "milking" more from the host country than they contribute to its development. A graphic demonstration of this thesis was offered when the government of Brazil, host to the second largest amount of U.S. private investment in any less-developed country in 1966 (after Venezuela), decreed in 1963 that foreign investors would not be allowed (i.e., allocated the necessary foreign exchange) to remit home each year earnings greater than 10 per cent of their net investment. Moreover, net investment was defined in terms of capital furnished from abroad and excluded foreigners' share in reinvested profits.

Following is a description of several methods by which earnings attributable from an economic standpoint to operations of U.S. investments in underdeveloped countries appear on the books of the U.S. parent companies or affiliated organizations in third countries, often tax havens:

(1) A large part of U.S. direct foreign investments comprise a captive market for products manufactured by parent companies in the United States or their subsidiaries in other developed countries. This is the case when the foreign investment includes a distribution outlet for the parent company's output or a productive facility that utilizes raw materials and intermediate products supplied by the parent company. In such cases, it is a frequent practice for the parent company to charge its foreign affiliate a higher supply price than might be obtainable from nonaffiliated sources. Such a procedure merely involves shifting the locus where a certain portion of the profit is taken. In some industries, charging an uneconomically high supply price to the distribution outlet is an industry-wide practice. ("Uneconomical" is understood to mean here that the return explicitly attributed to the resources invested in the outlet is below the level that would be dictated by theory; however, the effect on an integrated company's over-all profitability may be nil or even positive.) This is indicated by the following statement in the Commerce 1960 census report:

It should be noted that some industries, particularly the petroleum industry, derive much of their earnings from international shipments of basic commodities or other products, with earnings and income receipts generally allocated mainly to enterprises in the countries where basic production takes place.[14]

Officials of less-developed countries occasionally complain about such practices. For example, in 1963, Brazil's minister of health charged publicly that foreign drug companies were sending profits abroad illegally by overinvoicing the value of raw materials purchased from parent companies.[15]

Apart from shifting profits by simultaneously raising the overseas affiliate's costs and the parent company's direct return, the same end result is often achieved by shifting costs from the parent company to the overseas affiliate. In discussing companies that reported net losses on their overseas investments, the Commerce census report states:

A considerable number of the losses reported in the trade and miscellaneous industries reflected the establishment of foreign purchasing or servicing organizations which had operating costs but charged little or nothing for the services performed. Essentially, these losses represented part of the operating costs of parent organizations in the United States.[16]

Such practices are not confined to the trade and miscellaneous industries, but occur also in manufacturing. For example, where, as is often the case, a U.S. company has overseas affiliates producing only a fraction of the parent company's product line, the affiliates frequently maintain local selling organizations designed to promote the entire line, with the local producing facilities absorbing the entire cost of these organizations.

(2) The second factor by which returns are understated is the opposite side of the coin with respect to the first. Where an integrated operation is organized such that the overseas facility performs services or produces raw materials or intermediate products for the facility in the United States or a subsidiary in another developed country, the parent company may decide to take the bulk of its profit outside the underdeveloped country by a monopsonistic pricing policy. According to the Commerce report, of over 300 U.S. companies that reported on foreign operations with neither earnings nor losses, some "functioned primarily to furnish certain services to the parent company," while

. . . another large group sold their output at cost to parent or affiliated companies, so that they had no earnings on their own books. Although an effort was

made to determine whether sales to the United States
parent companies were at prices reasonably close to
market prices, there probably remains some degree
of understatement of foreign earnings, either as a
whole or in certain countries, because of sales at
cost to affiliates.[17]

(3) A significant share of what are, from an economic point of
view, parent company earnings are treated as costs under the heading of management fees and royalties. Commerce Department data
give the following six-year series for U.S. parent company receipts
of royalties and fees from direct investments in Latin America
and "Other Western Hemisphere." (The data are not broken down
for other less-developed areas.)

TABLE 4

U.S. Parent Company Receipts of Royalties and Fees
from Direct Investments in Latin America and
"Other Western Hemisphere," 1961-66

(All figures are $ millions.)

Industry	1961	1962	1963	1964	1965	1966	Total, 1961-66
Petroleum	24	27	29	33	29	24	166
Manufacturing	43	49	47	64	81	86	370
Trade	13	16	17	17	23	24	110
Other	24	31	31	34	40	42	202
Total	103	123	124	148	174	176	848

Source: Survey of Current Business, August, 1964 & September,
1965-67.

The effect of treating royalties and fees as earnings rather
than costs is shown in Table 5.

This table suggests that the current effective minimum earnings rate of U.S. direct investment in nonpetroleum industries in
Latin America and "Other Western Hemisphere" is closer to 15
than to 10 per cent and that effective income remittances approxi-
mate 10 per cent of investment in such industries.

TABLE 5

Effect on 1966 Rates of Earnings and Income Receipts
in Latin America of Including Royalties and Fees

(All figures are percentages.)

Industry	1966 percentages of 1965 value of investment		Royalties and fees, 1966, percentage of 1965 value of investment	Percentages including royalties & fees	
	Earnings	Income receipts		Earnings (I + III)	Income receipts (II + III)
Petroleum	14.4	14.0	0.7	15.1	14.7
Manufacturing	11.4	5.0	3.0	14.4	8.0
All non-petroleum	12.8	8.4	2.1	14.9	10.5
All industries	13.3	10.2	1.7	15.0	11.9

Source: Calculated from data in Tables 2, 3, and 4.

In order to prove conclusively the existence of a bias one way
or the other in earnings/investment ratios computed on the basis of
evidence such as we have used here and to assess the bias quantitatively, one would have to probe deeply into the financial pictures of a
large number of companies. Even if one were permitted access to
the data, it would be a herculean task to analyze and amalgamate it
into broad conclusions. However, I am satisfied that the considerations we have described impart on net a substantial downward bias
to the earnings ratios given in our tables. In part, this is because
I have been assured of the existence of the bias by persons with
long experience in the field of international private investment and
close acquaintance with the practices of individual companies. For
my own part, I had frequent opportunities during a two-year tour
in Nigeria in 1961-63 to ascertain the estimates of prospective U.S.
private investors of what they considered an acceptable return on
pending investments. To some extent, this information was gleaned
directly from would-be investors; to a larger extent, it was provided by persons, in and outside government, whose duties brought
them into continuous contact with such investors, often in negotiations over exactly such questions as what the rate of return would
or should be. The upshot of the information obtained in this way was
that American investors in a variety of different industrial fields
did not hesitate to state to any responsible and interested source

that they would not make their proposed investment in Nigeria unless they were confident to a high degree that the investment would have a pay-out period of not longer than, and often less than, five years. In other words, the minimum acceptable rate of after-tax profit seemed to be 20 per cent, and in many cases it was as high as 25 or 33 1/3 per cent.

In assessing the implications of this for the return to U.S. private investment on a world-wide basis, two factors must be taken into account. First, the investors in Nigeria were setting an advance target for earnings on a future investment. No doubt there is frequently a degree of slippage between advance intentions and actual results in foreign investment. Moreover, there would be strategic advantages, especially vis-à-vis the local government, in winning acceptance for a projected rate of return higher than the investor actually expected to earn. Second, the investors whose announced intentions are relevant here were all approaching Nigeria for the first time, i.e., they could not have the familiarity and confidence associated with successful operation of an earlier investment in the country. Moreover, there was as yet relatively little American investment in a country that had been for many years almost exclusively in Britain's financial domain.* Even when these qualifications are taken into account, however, it seems unlikely that new American capital is now flowing into underdeveloped areas to support operations that earn it a return as low as the 10 per cent given in Table 2 for nonpetroleum industries in Latin America.

We will not attempt to draw specific quantitative conclusions from the foregoing analysis but will content ourselves with stating that the earnings and income receipts ratios given in Table 2 should be regarded as minimum values.

NON-U.S. PRIVATE DIRECT INVESTMENT

In the absence of comparable data on European private investment in the underdeveloped areas, it is not possible to make a comparative analysis of European and American investment with respect to rates of earnings and income remittances. It appears, however, that in areas with which particular metropolitan countries have had close association over a number of years, business

---

*In 1961, U.S. investment in Nigeria was estimated very roughly by the American Embassy at $20 million. By contrast, a single European trading and investment company (United Africa Company) had a total investment there in 1962 of about $112 million.

interests from those countries often see a lesser element of risk in making investments and are consequently willing to invest in the face of prospects for lower profit margins than would be required to induce investors from other countries, notably the United States. This is particularly true of metropolitan investors who are already established in such underdeveloped areas. Instances are known in certain African countries where parallel investment proposals in the same industrial lines have been advanced by long-established metropolitan interests on the one hand and newly arrived U.S. investors on the other; the Americans have sometimes demanded sufficient concessions to assure themselves of a rate of return up to twice as high as that implied in the concessions requested by the metropolitans. On the other hand, it is quite possible that the shoe is on the other foot in parts of Latin America where U.S. interests are better established than European.

U.S. PRIVATE DIRECT INVESTMENT AND THE BALANCE OF RESOURCE TRANSFER

We have now come as far as we shall attempt to go in relating private foreign investment to the first-order definition of our capital transfer spectrum. By way of evaluating its contribution to the net balance of resource transfer between the United States and less-developed areas, we now turn to comparisons of (1) the rate of change of the value of investment with the earnings ratio, and (2) absolute net capital outflows with income receipts of U.S. investors. Under (1), we compare Columns I and II in Table 2, and, under (2), we look at Column IV. On the whole, the table shows that, in any comparison including the petroleum industry on a world-wide basis, earnings rates and income receipts exceed the annual increase in the value of investment and cumulative net capital outflows (from the United States), respectively, by wide margins. On the other hand, in the Western Hemisphere apart from Latin America, capital outflow and income receipts in respect of petroleum during 1957-66 were virtually equal. If South African data could be netted out of the African petroleum picture, this would probably look much the same, as new capital investment and operating losses in Libya during the early years of the period were of the same order of magnitude as income receipts that poured in during 1964-66.

The earnings rate also exceeded the rate of growth of investment in nonpetroleum industries in Latin America, which is the one less-developed area where U.S. direct investment has been around the longest and can thus be described as being the most mature. Income receipts in this category were just about double new capital investment. In other Western Hemisphere areas, while nonpetroleum investment, some of it seeking the tax havens referred to above, grew very rapidly from a small base in 1950, its growth rate slackened in the latter half of the period, and the extraordinarily high earnings rates outweighed new investment during 1957-66. Looking at the world totals by industry, we see that investment in one category--manufacturing--increased its growth rate in the latter part of the period, with net capital outflow exceeding income receipts by close to 50 per cent, while net new outflow in mining and smelting was less than 25 per cent of income receipts.

The data suggest that American private equity capital is available to move into limited sectors of industry, given reasonable though not extraordinarily high earnings prospects (earnings in manufacturing appear to have been in the lower part of the range for all industries), at a sufficient rate to maintain a balance of resource transfer that is favorable from the less-developed country's viewpoint, over a period of up to 20 years and perhaps even longer. On the other hand, as the Commerce Department's 1960 census report notes,

> Over time [income receipts] are likely to exceed capital outflows from the United States, partly because the rate of return on investments will probably remain above the rate of growth of annual capital flows, and partly because of the possibility that the use of parent company funds for capital expenditures may decline relative to other sources of such funds abroad . . . . On the other hand, the proportion of earnings reinvested abroad is about 50 per cent, and may go higher if investment activity increases.[18]

The report goes on to point out that a simple comparison of new capital investment and income receipts is not a sufficient basis on which to evaluate the net balance-of-payments impact of foreign investments. Instead, one must also take into account export earnings generated by the investments, as well as the import-substituting effect of production for domestic consumption. With additional data, the report shows that much of U.S. foreign investment generates more than enough export earnings to pay for income remittances to the United States. Although this point is very important for an understanding of the net impact of U.S. foreign investment, it is not relevant to our present discussion, which seeks to rank private investment along our capital transfer spectrum on the initial assumption that the various forms of transfer are alternative vehicles for similar investments.

NOTES TO CHAPTER 2

1. Göran Ohlin, Foreign Aid Policies Reconsidered (Paris: The Development Centre of the Organization for Economic Cooperation and Development, 1966), p. 91.

2. Clive S. Gray, "The Spectrum of International Capital Transfer to the Underdeveloped Countries" (unpublished Ph.D. dissertation, Department of Economics, Harvard University, 1964).

3. Albert H. Imlah, Economic Elements in the Pax Britannica (Cambridge, Mass.: Harvard University Press, 1958).

4. Simon Kuznets, Capital in the American Economy--Its Formation and Financing (Princeton, N.J.: Princeton University Press [National Bureau of Economic Research],1961.)

5. OECD, The Flow of Financial Resources to Less-Developed Countries (Paris, 1967), Tables II.5-6, pp. 43-44.

6. Ragnar Nurkse, "International Investment Today in the Light of Nineteenth Century Experience," Economic Journal, December, 1954.

7. U.S. Department of Commerce, Office of Business Economics, U.S. Business Investments in Foreign Countries (Washington, D.C.: Government Printing Office, 1960).

8. U.S. Department of Commerce, Office of Business Economics, Survey of Current Business, August, 1961-64, September, 1965-67.

9. U.S. Department of Commerce, U.S. Business Investments, p. 76.

10. Ibid. Additional refinements on the matter of coverage are given in the same passage.

11. Ibid., Tables 32 and 36, pp. 120 and 125.

12. Ibid., p. 46.

13. According to the United Nations Department of Economic and Social Affairs, Foreign Capital in Latin America (New York, 1955), p. 25, this is true of such arrangements as the Venezuelan "50-50" tax law.

14. U.S. Department of Commerce, U.S. Business Investments, p. 55.

15. The New York Times, October 28, 1963, article by Juan de Onis datelined Rio de Janeiro, October 27. According to the article, the charge was publicly denied by the drug companies.

16. U.S. Department of Commerce, U.S. Business Investments, p. 75.

17. Ibid.

18. Ibid., p. 67. The 50 per cent figure is on a world-wide basis and is thus largely determined by parameters of U.S. investment in Canada and Western Europe.

CHAPTER **3** OFFICIAL RESOURCE
TRANSFER--I

This and the succeeding chapter will consider a limited aspect
of the flow of official resources to less-developed countries: namely,
the development of institutional techniques for minimizing the burden of such flows on the benefiting countries' balance of payments,
i.e., techniques that shift official resource transfer toward the grant
end of our spectrum of transfer techniques. Any attempt to analyze
official aid more comprehensively in the context of this book would
be redundant in view of the thorough, continuous reporting the subject now receives from the Development Assistance Committee of
the Organization for Economic Cooperation and Development,
notably via its annual review entitled Development Assistance
Efforts and Policies as well as via occasional publications in two
series entitled The Flow of Financial Resources to Less-Developed
Countries and Geographical Distribution of Financial Flows to Less-
Developed Countries.* Also worthy of mention as a comprehensive
survey of those aspects of public resource transfer relevant to
this book is the volume International Aid by I. M. D. Little and J. M.
Clifford.[1] Much of the data used in this and later chapters on actual
aid terms comes from the DAC sources. Despite this excellent
coverage, however, the author believes that there is scope for a
fresh review here of the historical and logical development and
economic impact of different approaches to softening the burden of
servicing official resource transfer.

------

*All reports are published by the OECD in Paris. Develop-
ment Assistance Efforts and Policies has appeared annually since
1962, beginning its coverage with the year 1961. The Flow of
Financial Resources . . has appeared in 1961, covering 1956-59;
in 1962, covering 1960; in 1963, covering 1961; in 1964, covering
1956-63; and in 1967, covering 1961-65. Geographical Distribution . . has appeared in 1966, covering 1960-64; and in 1967,
covering 1965.

Bibliography.

POSTWAR "HARD" LENDING

The point of departure in this analysis is the development, during and immediately after World War II, of institutions designed to fill the gap created by the disappearance of the pre-World War I and (to the extent it existed) interwar international bond markets, insofar as these markets effected the transfer of private debt capital from richer to less-developed countries. The immediate imperative behind this transfer was to reconstruct war-torn Western Europe; however, the authorities responsible for establishing the International Bank for Reconstruction and Development (World Bank or IBRD) and expanding the activities of such national export-financing bodies as the Export-Import Bank (Eximbank) of Washington, D.C., were aware that, for a variety of political and commercial reasons, it was in the interest of the powers they represented to ensure a flow of capital to the poorer countries outside Western Europe. They were also aware that the repeated convulsions to which international financial markets had been subjected since the outbreak of World War I would make it impossible to revive these markets on their earlier pattern of risk-bearing, with the private investors' stake being secured only by the faith and credit of authorities in the borrowing countries. It would take nothing less than the guarantee of the governments of the richer countries themselves to induce private interests in those countries to provide the necessary funds.

Hence, apart from the small portion contributed in cash by its member governments, the World Bank's initial authorized capital of $10 billion was subject to call from them in proportion to members' shares in the Bank in order to meet obligations arising either from the Bank's own borrowing in the money markets or its guaranteeing the securities of borrowers in member countries. The Export-Import Bank, on the other hand, was reorganized in 1945 along essentially its present lines with an authorized capital stock of $1 billion to be paid in by the U.S. Treasury as required plus authority to borrow additional amounts from the Treasury within a prescribed ceiling. The Treasury has financed its investment in the Bank as an indistinguishable part of its total obligations; but it is reasonable from an economic viewpoint, considering the end-use to which the funds are put, to attribute financing of the Eximbank entirely to U.S. public debt operations. Thus, the Bank can be viewed as an intermediary between U.S. financial markets and overseas borrowers, attaching the U.S. Government's guarantee to such movement of capital.

From the viewpoint of our spectrum of resource transfer techniques, the principal characteristic of these two institutions, and most other bilateral public or quasi-public export-financing bodies analogous to the Eximbank, which became active in the early

1950's, is that they are structured to more than cover all direct costs by charging sufficient interest on loans to meet both administrative costs and the expense of borrowing and to accumulate reasonable reserves against losses to boot. (For the Eximbank, effective borrowing costs comprise an annual dividend--in recent years equal to 5 per cent--on the Treasury's $1 billion capital stock plus interest on each note placed with the Treasury "at a rate determined by the Secretary of the Treasury, taking into consideration the current average rate on outstanding marketable obligations of the United States as of the last day of the month preceding the issuance of the obligation of the Bank."[2]) Before the end of 1967, both the World Bank and the Eximbank had accumulated reserves of more than $1 billion each. In the World Bank's case, the total of $1,183 million was net of $210 million which the Bank had felt in a strong enough position to transfer on a grant basis to its soft-lending affiliate, the International Development Association.[3]

The fact that institutions such as the World Bank and Eximbank have always operated at a nominal profit does not necessarily mean that their activities have involved no real cost to the countries supplying and/or guaranteeing their funds, above and beyond the opportunity cost of investing the resources involved abroad rather than domestically. Theoretically, borrowing operations on behalf of these institutions may have exerted a marginal upward impact on market interest rates, thus raising the costs of other borrowers. Moreover, the contingent liability assumed by guaranteeing governments may have diminished marginally their creditworthiness for internal borrowing, thus raising their over-all borrowing costs.

Finally, a case could be made for saying that the charges levied on the loans in question do not cover the true risks of lending to the less-developed countries of today. It is true that the World Bank has thus far not experienced any defaults on service payments in respect of its loans--or at least any of sufficient duration to warrant mention in notes to its annual financial statements; administrative inefficiencies on the part of borrowers frequently lead to delays of a few days in meeting payment dates--and losses written off plus "protracted defaults" on Eximbank loans are minimal in relation to the Bank's regular annual earnings and accumulated reserves. But, as noted in detail in Chapter 8, there have been a number of instances when debt rescheduling exercises, either explicit or implicit, have been necessary to forestall probable defaults, and world events pose a continual if unquantifiable threat of massive future defaults. Nevertheless, the fact that the institutions in question here have always covered their financial costs and maintain a hard and fast policy of doing so by charging borrowers enough to meet their own borrowing costs, administrative expenses, and allocations to reserve funds, serves to place the corresponding capital flows at a particular location on our capital transfer spectrum in accordance with the first-order definition stated in Chapter 1. Moreover, it is a location implying a repayment burden that

Chapters 5-9 show to be very substantial indeed, compared with that implied by zero-interest, long-term (e.g., 40-year) loans, when account is taken of the economic parameters of the less-developed countries and the magnitude of the capital flows required to attain certain objectives.

SOFTENING THE BURDEN OF AID REPAYMENT

Even before the end of the Marshall Plan, it was clear to many authorities that the needs of the less-developed countries, measured in accordance with those parameters and objectives, could not be wholly satisfied by capital transfers on the foregoing "hard" terms without running afoul of one or more of the constraints summarized in Chapter 1, which form the subject matter of Chapters 5-9. In early 1951, World Bank President Eugene R. Black was stating, "We must frankly face the fact that these countries cannot perceptibly accelerate the rate of their development if the only capital which they receive is in the form of loans which have a reasonable prospect of repayment."[4] The principal topic of this chapter is the process by which aid agencies have adjusted the terms on their capital flows to the less-developed world in accordance with this "fact." Conceptually, there are three principal ways in which a capital source can operate on the weighted average repayment burden associated with the resources it is providing:

(1) by adjusting the proportional mixture of different institutional forms of capital transfer, carrying different explicit repayment terms, in its total aid flow;

(2) by adjusting the explicit terms on specific institutional forms of resource transfer--this is actually a special case of a completely general statement of (1); and

(3) by transferring resources on undetermined repayment terms, leaving the effective terms to be decided in the light of future conditions (notably the rate of economic progress of the beneficiary) and then interpreting the applicable conditions flexibly.

All three of the foregoing modes have been applied at one time or another in the postwar flow of public resources to less-developed countries. In a sense, mode 1 was applied even before World War II by Britain and France insofar as they extended simultaneously grants-in-aid and official loans--the latter at interest rates determined by the metropolitan money markets--to their respective colonies, and inevitably the mix of loans and grants varied from year to year. However, in the case of Britain, at least, variations in the loan/grant mixture were not the result of policy decisions in any way related to the constraints relevant to this study. Until 1929, all official British resources spent in aid of the colonies were transferred in the form of grants-in-aid to meet budgetary deficits, a process said to have been initiated as early as 1878, and any additional external resources the colonial governments needed for investment purposes had to be raised via loans on the London market. The official contribution to these borrowings consisted of the Colonial Stock Acts, which facilitated such loans and made them cheaper than they would otherwise have been by assigning them trustee status, meaning that the U.K. Government undertook to use its authority over the colonies to ensure repayment of the debts. The Colonial Development Act of 1929 provided for the first time for U.K. Government grants- and loans-in-aid of specific development activities (although education was specifically ineligible), but loans under it comprised only a small part of a total of £6.6 million spent under the Act during 1929-39, compared with £2 million spent in the same period under the older budgetary grant-in-aid system and over £100 million raised by the colonies on the London money market during 1919-39. During the interwar years, France provided considerably greater amounts of official loan and grant aid to her colonies than Britain; perhaps a close study of her performance in this period would show some sensitivity of the loan/grant ratio to debt-servicing capacity.[5]

A combination of modes 2 and 3 was practiced by the United States during World War II in the form of the lend-lease program. Under it, the Allies were supplied with large quantities of war material on credit, the terms being either long maturities and low interest (in comparison with then Treasury borrowing rates), or these plus only partial repayment of principal, the amount repayable being left to subsequent negotiation. Of relevance here, in view of this book's focus on the less-developed areas, is the fact that then British India received $161 million in "lend-lease silver credits."[6] These are probably the very first "soft" loans of direct relevance to our present study, although the use of submarket-interest and/or very long-maturity loans to subsidize economic development within the United States has a history going back at least as far as the railway expansion in the late nineteenth century.* Lend-lease was followed by a program in which the United States transferred part of the residue of its war machine to the former occupied territories of Western Europe. A price was agreed upon which represented only a fraction of the original cost of the items concerned, and the Eximbank established 30-year credits at 2 3/8 per cent interest in the corresponding amounts.

---

*In Congressional debates on the now defunct Development Loan Fund, the Fund's proponents used to cite some twenty-odd federal agencies involved at one time or another in the business of extending soft loans for irrigation, rural electrification, and other activities.

The Marshall Plan represented an application of both modes 1 and 2 for adjusting the burden of capital flows. On one hand, it was financed by a mix of 87 per cent grants and 13 per cent loans, and, on the other hand, the $1.14 billion in loans was provided on terms of 2 1/2 per cent interest and final maturities of 18 to 45 years, with the majority repayable in 35 years.[7] From 1948 through 1950, the yield on long-term U.S. Government bonds was below 2 1/2 per cent--kept down by Federal Reserve intervention-- and it is conceivable that this spread was sufficient to pay the United States' administrative costs in the first half of the European Recovery Program (ERP). However, during 1951, when the last $24 million of ERP loan funds was obligated, the average long-term bond rate was above 2 1/2 per cent.[8] Throughout the Marshall Plan period, the Eximbank was charging 3 per cent to 4 1/2 per cent on its loans. On a 1951 ERP loan to Belguim, whose financial condition was then the soundest of all Marshall Plan countries because of income from the Congo, the United States charged 3 1/4 per cent; and, on a separate loan program for Spain, the rate was 3 per cent. Apart from the question of the interest rate, the length of the maturities on the ERP loans, for the most part considerably exceeding that of the longest-term U.S. Government bonds, implied a substantial subsidy rate. As in the lend-lease case, some of the Marshall Plan aid went to less-developed countries--specifically, Greece (which received only grants), Indonesia, and Turkey, both of the latter receiving loan funds.

The next major step in the development of subsidized U.S. resource flow to less-developed countries was the $190 million, 2 1/2 per cent, 35-year wheat loan to India authorized by special act of Congress in 1951. The act provided that interest payments received in the first 5 years of the program, up to a maximum of $5 million, could be spent by the U.S. State Department on programs of academic exchange between India and the United States, as well as on shipments of U.S. books and "laboratory and technical equipment" for higher education and research in India. In 1958, responding to Indian pleas citing the intervening virtual depletion of the country's foreign-exchange reserves, the United States agreed to postpone interest and principal payments on the loan for 10 years and lengthen the final maturity to 45 years. Thus, what was an example of mode 2 became, retroactively, an illustration of mode 3 as well.

Clearly, aid transfers representing mode 3 are the most difficult to handle in terms of our spectrum of transfer techniques precisely because the real burden they represent is determined only at some undefined future date. Quantitatively, by far the most important type of such aid transfer has been the "loan" serviceable at the borrower's option in local means of payment, the lender agreeing not to exchange these funds for other currencies or to use them to export goods and services from the borrowing country except by subsequent agreement of the latter. The Development

Assistance Committee reports this aid under a special category of "grant-like transfers," and the World Bank excludes it from its statistics on external public debt. Both treatments imply a judgment on the extent to which the aid in question is likely ever to be repaid in the form of real resources--i.e., that such repayment will be minimal. This judgment differs from the formal understanding on the part of the aid-giving agencies that the aid will eventually be repaid, although the U.S. Congress' recognition of the dim prospects for real repayment of agricultural surplus "sales" for local currency under Title I of Public Law 480 has resulted in amendment of the law to call for a complete shift to dollar-repayable loans by December 31, 1971.[9] Despite its implied judgment on the over-all repayment prospects, however, the DAC does take account of real repayments of this aid in its statistics on annual aid flows by netting out encashments, for the U.S. Government's own uses, of local currency holdings resulting from loan repayments and current or previous Title I "sales." On the other hand, the World Bank's manner of treating external debt does not anticipate any real repayments of local-currency repayable loans.

From the viewpoint of reviewing the historical and logical development of different approaches to softening the burden of aid repayment, the most interesting issues are those which arose in the use by the U.S. Government of local-currency repayable loans, starting in U.S. fiscal 1955 under both P.L. 480 and the regular aid program; the consideration and ultimate rejection by the World Bank of such loans as a technique to be used by the International Development Association (IDA); the acceptance conversely, of this technique by the Inter-American Development Bank and that institution's continued use of it, without apparent reservations, up to the time of writing; and, finally, the U.S. Government's decision, under a new administration in 1961, to drop local-currency repayment in its regular aid program, switching to dollar-repayable loans on near-IDA terms, followed six years later by the Congressional directive, already cited above, to eliminate local-currency payment under P.L. 480 in another five years. Because of the interest these issues present, Chapter 4 is devoted to them entirely.

First, however, inasmuch as some of the main sources of capital to less-developed countries not involved in our subsequent discussion of local currency repayment were making loans at less than the direct financial cost to themselves before the first U.S. local currency-repayable loans appeared on the scene, and nearly all did so at some time before the end of the process analyzed in Chapter 4, it is appropriate to summarize the techniques these other sources have utilized to alleviate the burden of servicing their aid. Following this source-by-source summary, data from three of the DAC's latest published summary tables on weighted average aid terms of OECD members are presented in Table 6, and the steps taken by the DAC itself to encourage its members to soften their aid terms are summarized.

REVIEW OF SELECTED DONORS' AID TERMS

The following summary by bilateral and multilateral aid donors is alphabetical.[10]

AUSTRALIA--The DAC chairman's 1967 report notes that "one of the distinctive features of the Australian (aid) programme is that all contributions are in the form of grants."[11] During 1945-65, two thirds of Australian bilateral aid comprised capital and technical assistance and budget support for the Territory of Papua and New Guinea.

AUSTRIA--The bulk of Austrian aid consists of official export credits, financed partly through drawings from the ERP counterpart fund and partly through borrowings from Austrian private banks. Interest rates are generally 5 1/2 per cent, which happens also to be the minimum rate governing the use of the ERP funds. However, because the standard rate which the private banks charge the government is higher than 5 1/2 per cent, the national budget contains an allocation for subsidizing the interest on these credits--in 1965, this amounted to $400,000. By virtue of this subsidy, Austrian export credits technically meet the definition of a soft loan, although 5 1/2 per cent is not very soft by the standards of most aid donors (or recipients), and the weighted average maturity on Austrian loans--less than 9 years in all but one (1963) of the years 1962-66-- is distinctly "hard." Table 6 shows Austria to have provided the lowest "grant element" of all OECD member countries in its official lending in 1966. In fact, the subsidy in question is more an attempt to increase the competitiveness of Austrian exports to less-developed countries vis-à-vis other industrial countries than it is an aid contribution. (On occasion, the Austrians provided special government-to-government loans on easier terms, as in the case of a $1 million loan to Turkey in 1965 at 3 per cent, 20 years' maturity, and 7 years' grace period.)

BELGIUM--During 1956-59, the Belgians experimented with a form of aid representing mode 3 defined above. During this period, $40 million worth of budget support "loans" without specified repayment terms were made to Ruanda-Urundi. The OECD's 1961 report on aid flows treats these transactions as outright grants.[12] Belguim has also participated with most other West European governments in extending consolidation credits to Greece and Turkey at below-market interest rates--rates in 1959 were 2 1/4 and 3 per cent. In the last few years, Belgian aid has consisted almost exclusively of grants to the former African colonies. In 1965, about 60 per cent of Belgium's total bilateral aid comprised unrequited payments on outstanding Congolese obligations-- external debt and pensions, etc.--which had been guaranteed by the metropolitan government. The proportion spent on Congolese obligations dropped to about 40 per cent in 1966.

CANADA--Up to 1964, Canadian aid consisted either of out-right grants or of official export credits at interest rates based on the current yield on Canadian Government bonds. For example, 1957-58 wheat and flour loans to India and Ceylon bore 4 1/2 per cent interest and had 7-year maturities including 3-year grace periods, while more recent credits have carried 6 per cent interest and maximum 20-year maturities. These credits have been fi-nanced out of the government's long-term capital account (Consoli-dated Revenue Fund). However, in 1965, Canada introduced a new program of development loans, financed out of the current budget and carrying IDA-type terms (3/4 per cent interest, described as a service charge; 50-year maturities; and 10-year grace periods). In 1966, the service charge was abolished and an intermediate category of loans was introduced for countries with above-minimum debt servicing capacity (3 per cent interest, 30 years' maturity, and 7 years' grade period). The terms on Canada's longer-maturity loans are the most favorable available on any loans to less-developed countries, other than those repayable only in part or in local currency, from any source in the world today.

DENMARK--Having contented itself for a number of years with relatively small programs of technical assistance, guaranteed private export credits, and participation in the Greek and Turkish debt consolidation exercises, Denmark decided in 1964 to extend development loans at 4 per cent interest (compared with an average yield of 6.24 per cent on Danish Government bonds in 1964, accord-ing to International Financial Statistics), 20-year maturities, and 6-year grace periods. In 1966, before this program had made much headway, the Danish Government decided to abolish interest on these loans and raise their normal maturity to 25 years.

EUROPEAN ECONOMIC COMMUNITY--Two financial institu-tions of the European Economic Community (EEC)--the European Development Fund (EDF) and the European Investment Bank (EIB)--have provided assistance to less-developed countries associated with the Community. Through 1966, all EDF disbursements, amounting to nearly $450 million, were in the form of grants, al-though it had been planned for the Fund to provide, through 1968, some $50 million in loans with maturities of up to 40 years, in-cluding grace periods of up to ten years, and subsidized interest rates (the actual rates are not indicated in the latest DAC re-ports). EIB loan commitments to less-developed associate mem-bers, amounting to $143 million through 1966, have carried a maximum maturity of 25 years, but interest rates have been sub-sidized up to a maximum of 3 per cent through special contribu-tions of EEC members.

FRANCE--As noted earlier in this chapter, France was in the business of extending grants and loans to her overseas territories long before World War II. In 1947, she inaugurated what can be called the world's first regular soft-loan program for the benefit of less-developed countries, consisting of 1 1/2 per cent interest, 25-year credits to public authorities in the African territories through two organisms known by their French initials, FIDES and CCFOM.[13] By 1959, successor agencies, established to service the budding French Community of independent nations, were lending at 2 1/2 per cent from 10 to 20 years. The interest rate increased further after the Community members gained their independence, over half of the 1965 loan commitments to franc-area countries being made at rates between 3 and 4 per cent, and only 17 per cent at less than 3 per cent. Development loans to nonfranc-area countries, normally made at 3.5 per cent interest and 15-20-year maturities, are usually combined with supplier credits, which makes the weighted average terms for the entire transaction more burdensome. Some nonfranc countries receive guaranteed private export credits on officially subsidized terms. Notwithstanding France's sizable loan program, the proportion of grants in her gross official bilateral aid disbursements has been close to or over 70 per cent in all of the 11 years, 1956-66, for which OECD data are available at the time of writing.

GERMANY--As a result of indemnification payments to Israel and, to a lesser extent, Greece, the proportion of grants in Germany's gross aid disbursements during 1950-58 was nearly two thirds. However, with the completion of these payments and the rapid expansion of development lending activity dating from 1959, this proportion fell to 20 per cent in 1966. Up to about 1960, the interest on German development loans was based on current German Government borrowing costs except insofar as the funds were drawn from ERP counterpart accounts, bearing lower interest rates from the time the corresponding resources were originally provided by the United States. (Loans at these rates were being subsidized in an opportunity cost though not direct financial sense.) As late as 1961, according to the OECD, the German Government was worried that "loans at soft terms may impair the role of private capital, distort competitive positions and weaken the function of interest rates in allocating scarce capital among competing uses."[14] Subsequently, Germany has provided loans for "infrastructure" projects with interest rates generally between 2 and 3 per cent and maturities of up to 30 years, but it has held strictly to the principle that the terms of loans to a project should be determined according to the lifetime of the facilities to be constructed and their commercial (vs. social) character. The Germans have made relatively limited use of the so-called two-step lending procedure as a way of softening the balance-of-payments burden of loan repayment without relaxing financial discipline on the borrowing entity. (For a breakdown of average terms on German loans to four different categories of projects in 1965, see Chapter 10.)

IBRD--Most of the World Bank's easy-term lending activity is channeled through the International Development Association, discussed in Chapter 4. However, in the Bank's fiscal year 1963-64, its Executive Directors decided, according to the year's annual report,

... that the Bank itself may vary some terms of its
lending [i.e., out of funds borrowed on the private
capital markets] to lighten the service burden in
cases where this is appropriate to the project and to
the debt position of the country. It may, for instance, agree to an extended grace period, as it did
in a road loan made to Liberia in January 1964; or it
may set a longer term, as it did in February 1964 for
a 35-year loan made in Colombia for the big Nare power
project.15

The 8-year grace period on the Liberian loan was based on the fact
that Liberia's debt-service obligations were heavily concentrated
in the ensuing few years. At the same time, the 18-year final
maturity was not a particularly favorable term for a road loan;
presumably, it reflected a view on the Bank's part that Liberia's
rapidly developing iron-ore industry endowed it with very considerable debt-servicing capacity over the somewhat longer run.
From the start of 1964 through June 30, 1967, the Bank granted 7
loans with grace periods of 8 or more years for repayment of
principal. Five of these loans also had maturities of 30 or 31
years; and, during the same period, the Bank granted 5 additional
loans with maturities of 26 or more years (two at 26, one at 30,
and two at 35).16 With the exception of one issue of 30-year bonds
in 1951, the Bank has not sold any of its own bonds at longer than
25-year final maturities.

When an institution lends money for a longer term than applies
to the availability of the funds to itself, it is automatically assuming
the risk that it will have to refinance the final maturities of the loan
at an interest rate higher than that charged on the loan. Thus, the
very long-term loans made by the Bank contain a definite element
of "softness," even though its interest rate has always been above
current borrowing costs. Nevertheless, even in regard to its
interest rate, the Bank decided in 1964-65 to charge differential
rates on loans to more-developed, "market eligible" countries--
i.e., those "able to cover the bulk of their requirements for external capital from market sources"--as opposed to the less-
developed countries. The former category, comprising such
countries as Japan, Italy, Australia, New Zealand, South Africa,
Norway, and Finland, has been required to pay rates "roughly
comparable to those they pay when borrowing in the market,"17
up to 1 per cent higher than the rate payable by other borrowers,
which was 6 per cent from February, 1966, through June, 1967.
The higher rate paid by the market-eligible borrowers, who are,
of course, far more creditworthy by traditional standards than the
others and would therefore merit lower rates on strictly commercial criteria, in effect assigns them a larger share in meeting the
Bank's operating costs, including accumulation of reserves against
losses, and allows the Bank to charge less-developed countries
lower rates than it would otherwise have to collect from them.

This can be viewed as another element of softness in the Bank's regular lending operations.

INTERNATIONAL FINANCE CORPORATION (IFC)--Consideration of the World Bank's private investment affiliate, the International Finance Corporation, in the present context raises the question of how far the provision of capital at the donor's explicit risk, i.e., in equity instruments or in loans without the host government's guarantee, at interest rates and/or profit expectations considerably above World Bank interest levels, can be regarded as easy-term finance in the light of the true risks and uncertainties facing private investment in today's less-developed world. Without trying to settle this issue here, we will merely note that the riskiness of IFC's operations had already materialized by June 30, 1967, to the extent of one complete write-off of a $300,000 investment; book losses on sales of investments amounting to $158,000 (far outweighed, however, by gross book profits of $2.9 million from such transactions); temporary default, as of that date, on $130,000 in payments due the IFC on three investments; and a more or less forced refinancing operation, in which the IFC converted part of an outstanding loan to equity and took additional equity in lieu of interest due while new management sought to resuscitate an operation. On the other hand, by June 30, 1967, the IFC had accumulated a reserve of $34.7 million against losses on $107.9 million of (cost value) effective loan and equity investments held by it, giving strong reason to believe that the Corporation was surmounting its risks and finding business quite profitable.18

ITALY--As shown by Table 6, in recent years, Italy has occupied the last or second-to-last position among all OECD members with respect to the grant element in her total aid and the loan portion of it, and the weighted average maturity of her loans. Some public funds are lent at rates below the government's borrowing cost, mainly in connection with transactions where the government, through Mediocredito, finances parts of export credits granted by the private sector, the remaining parts being financed privately at the financial market rate, recently over 7 per cent.

JAPAN--Like Germany, though in lesser proportion to its total aid, Japan has provided substantial grant aid via indemnification payments. As shown in Table 6 in regard to its loans, Japan has recently charged the highest or second-highest weighted average interest rate of all OECD members. Nevertheless, because of high money market rates in Japan, these rates still involve a sizable subsidy element from the government budget. (Thus, for example, the Japanese representative at the April, 1963, High Level Development Assistance Committee meeting on terms of aid argued that the financial cost of capital assistance extended by Japan was then 8 per cent.) On occasion, especially in response to political factors, Japan has provided loans on demonstrably soft terms--e.g., an interest-free consolidation credit to Korea in 1965.

NETHERLANDS--During the first reporting period of the Organization for European Economic Cooperation (OEEC; forerunner to OECD), i.e., 1956-59, about 60 per cent of gross Netherlands aid disbursements consisted of grants, mainly to the country's overseas territories. This proportion has declined in recent years but was still over 40 per cent in 1966. The Netherlands has experimented with several different sets of soft terms on loans to its Western Hemisphere dependencies. In the 1956-59 period, it contributed to Surinam's 10-Year Plan (which began in 1955) charging 3 per cent simple interest for the first 10 years, after which the total amount of principal and accumulated interest was to be converted into a loan of 25 years' additional maturity at the then current Netherlands market rate of interest. A rice development project in Surinam received support in two different ways--(1) via zero-interest loans, and (2) via Dutch Government guarantee of a public bond issue on which the government has been required to make good some interest and amortization payments (and apparently considered it likely from the outset that it would have to do so). More recent loans to Surinam and the Netherlands Antilles have been interest free during the disbursement period, carrying maturities of 25-30 years. The Dutch also participated with other West European countries in the early Greek and Turkish consortium exercises, extending consolidation credits at interest rates of 2 3/4 to 3 1/4 per cent. In more recent consortia--e.g., India and Pakistan--the Netherlands has responded to the 1965 DAC recommendation regarding terms of aid (see later section on the DAC) by lending at 3 per cent interest and 25 years' maturity including 7 years' grace.

NORWAY--Norwegian bilateral assistance has consisted largely (in 1966, 100 per cent) of grants. A 1965 loan to Turkey carried 3 per cent interest and a final maturity and grace period of 17 and 7 years respectively.

PORTUGAL--The terms on Portugal's bilateral loans, which go exclusively to her overseas territories, have been based on the economic circumstances of the territory receiving them. In the early OEEC reporting period, some loans were interest free and without specific repayment terms. Recent policy in regard to loans from the central government provides for 5-year grace periods on all such loans, maturities of up to 24 years, and zero interest for Cape Verde and Timor, 4 per cent for all other territories.

SWEDEN--Apart from special credits to Greece and Turkey in the late 1950's, Sweden's bilateral loan program was inaugurated in 1963, standard terms being 2 per cent interest, 20 years' maturity including 5 years' grace, and amortization at 5 per cent per annum during years 5 to 15 and 10 per cent per annum for the last 5. In 1967, the normal maturity and grace periods were lengthened to 25 and 10 years respectively. The Swedish Government also provided that IDA terms could be applied in exceptional cases.

U.S.S.R, ETC.--This section applies generally to all Communist countries. According to the United Nations' 1966 World Economic Survey, credits from "centrally planned economies" carry an interest rate of 2.5 to 3 per cent and are repayable over 8 to 15 years, with a grace period of up to 1 year after completion of a project or delivery of equipment, as the case may be. The predominant form of repayment is via the debtor country's traditional exports or, in some cases, goods produced by the new facility financed by the aid. The U.N. report says that "the lack of adequate information concerning specific projects, quality and prices of goods delivered for their construction and other conditions prevent any quantitative assessment of the value of (the aid terms)."19 Although we have abstracted from differences in quality and prices throughout this study, it is appropriate to note the problem in passing here because of the substantially lesser degree of competition and thus, comparability, between capital goods produced by the Communist countries on one hand and the industrialized Western world on the other, as opposed to the competition and comparability that exist within the latter.

The U.N. report quotes two Soviet studies of the alleged savings that have accrued to the less-developed world by virtue of the difference between repayment terms on Communist loans and those at which the borrowers would have had to service loans of the same face value from Western sources. These sources compute the "savings" at up to 20 per cent of the principal value of these loans. As the U.N. authors point out, this computation takes into account only the hardest terms offered by certain Western sources and ignores the fact that the weighted average terms on all Western aid are considerably softer than these. As shown in Table 6, on the basis of a discount rate of 10 per cent, the total grant element in Western bilateral commitments in 1966 was equivalent to 79 per cent of such commitments. Applying the same discount rate to a 2 1/2 per cent, 12-year Communist loan yields a grant element of only about 25 per cent.

Communist China has frequently provided aid on terms nominally softer than the range cited in the U.N. study. Apart from capital grants, such as a £1 million independence gift to Kenya in 1963, the Chinese have extended a number of interest-free loans.

It should be noted that the typical provision for repaying Communist loans by means of traditional exports is not comparable with the Western "loan" repayable in local currency, since only in the former case is payment made in real resources. To a limited extent, it is possible that the Communists' debtors have gained by being permitted to repay in goods they would otherwise not have been able to export at the same nominal value.

UNITED KINGDOM--The main vehicle of U.K. bilateral aid up to the late 1950's was the Colonial Development and Welfare (CDW) Program, over 90 per cent of which was financed by grants (although in March, 1960, $4 million of interest-free loans and another $5 million of 2 1/2-3 1/2 per cent interest loans were outstanding under CDW. Additional soft loans were extended under the Colonial Services Vote to balance colonial budgets or meet various types of emergencies in the colonies. Under this program, $101 million of loans were outstanding in March, 1960, broken down as follows by interest rates: interest-free, $64 million; 3-4 1/2 per cent, $22 million; current market rate, $15 million. Under the Foreign Office Grants and Services Vote, interest-free loans were made to Libya in the early 1950's and have been extended to Jordan as a regular annual procedure; also during the 1950's, Libya and Argentina received one loan each at 2 and 3 1/2 per cent respectively, in years when the cost of money to the British Government was considerably higher. Up to 1958, the United Kingdom occasionally made loans at current market rates under the Export Guarantee Act, but, in general, it regarded the provision of development capital, other than to countries for which the United Kingdom had special political responsibility and which were in serious financial straits, as a burden to be carried mainly by the World Bank.

In 1959, the United Kingdom introduced a Commonwealth Assistance Loan program, financed through the Export Credit Guarantees Department at current market rates, with amortization and grace periods related to the type of project being financed and/ or the balance-of-payments position of the borrower. Over the next few years, the maturity of these loans varied from 5 to 30 years and the grace period from 2 to 8 years. A smaller program of so-called Exchequer loans to colonial territories was also introduced in 1959 under the CDW Act; these loans similarly carried a current market rate of interest and maturities of 25 years. For several years, the U.K. Treasury resisted internal and external pressures to lower the interest rate on its Commonwealth Assistance Loans, believing, according to a 1962 OECD report, that "lending at soft rates might have repercussions on the terms of treasury lending to domestic borrowers, such as the national industries."[20] However, in 1963, the British adopted a policy in respect to borrowing countries with severe debt service burdens of waiving interest payments during the grace period for repayment of principal; and, in 1965, it decided to drop interest charges altogether for such countries. As shown in Table 6, the weighted average interest rate on U.K. loan commitments fell from 5.8 per cent in 1962 to 1 per cent in 1966.

TABLE 6

Average Financial Terms and "Grant Elements" of Official Bilateral Aid Commitments,
DAC Member Countries, 1962–66

| | (1) Weighted average financial terms | | | | | | (3) Grants and grant-like transfers ÷ total aid | | (4) Loans less contracted service payments discounted at 10% ÷ loans | | (5) Total "grant element" [= sum of numerators in (3) and (4)] ÷ total aid | |
| | Maturity period (years) | | | Interest rate (%) | | | | | | | | |
Country	1962	1965	1966	1962	1965	1966	1965	1966	1965	1966	1965	1966
Australia	--	--		--	--		1.00	1.00	a	a	1.00	1.00
Austria	5.0	7.7	6.5	6.0[b]	5.5	5.7	.14	.16[c]	.18	.13	.29	.27
Belgium	--	16.2	13.9	--	3.0	2.8	.98	.95	.43	.40	.99	.96
Canada	11.6	32.9	34.3	6.0	3.4	2.4	.54	.77	.54	.62	.79	.91
Denmark	--	13.7	18.7	--	5.3	0.0	.70	.62	.25	.65	.78	.87
France	17.0[b,c]	17.6	15.3	4.0[c]	3.8	3.6	.80	.83	.36	.33	.87	.88
Germany	15.2	16.9	21.2	4.4	4.2	3.3	.43	.42	.34	.47	.62	.69
Italy	5.8	6.3	8.0	6.1	4.3	3.7	.21	.13	.16	.21	.33	.32

56

Japan	10.0	12.0	14.1	6.0	4.4	5.2	.37	.42	.25	.29	.53	.58
Netherlands	26.5	23.9	23.6	4.0	3.5	2.0	.71	.76	.44	.60	.84	.90
Norway	--	16.0	--	--	3.0	--	.96	1.00	.50	a	.98	1.00
Portugal	18.9^c	21.5^c	25.9^c	4.0^c	3.8^c	3.6^c	.29^c	.23^c	.42	.44	.59	.54
Sweden	--	20.0	20.0	--	2.0	2.0	.89	.73	.54	.55	.95	.88
U.K.	24.3	22.2	23.9	5.8	3.3	1.0	.55	.50	.44	.68	.75	.84
U.S.A.	28.6	27.9	29.3	2.5	3.3	3.0	.62	.61	.51	.55	.81	.82
Total DAC Countries	24.5	22.3	23.5	3.5	3.6	3.1	.60	.60	.42	.48	.77	.79

Notes:
a not applicable.
b denotes DAC Secretariat estimate.
c based on gross disbursement date.

Source:

OECD, DAC, Development Assistance Efforts and Policies: 1967 Review (Paris, 1967), Tables V.3, V.4, and V.6, pp. 76–77 and 81.

DEVELOPMENT ASSISTANCE COMMITTEE ACTIONS

When the Organization for Economic Cooperation and Development came into being in September, 1961, as the successor agency to the Organization for European Economic Cooperation, one of its specialized bodies was the Development Assistance Committee. The DAC's stated purpose is to provide a framework for its members to "periodically review together both the amount and the nature of their contributions to aid programmes, bilateral and multilateral, and consult each other on all other relevant aspects of their development assistance policies" in order to "secure an expansion of the aggregate volume of resources made available to less-developed countries and to improve their effectiveness."[21] The newly formed DAC, responding in large part to pressure from the U.S. Government, which was seriously concerned about the growing burden of less-developed countries' debt service payments and wanted to influence other DAC members toward offering softer terms comparable with those then current on U.S. aid, accepted the question of aid terms as one of the most important objects of the Committee's coordinating efforts. In 1962, it established a working party on aid terms, on the basis of whose report a so-called High Level DAC meeting in April, 1963, recommended inter alia as follows to the member governments:

(i)   that they relate the terms of aid on a case-by-case basis to the circumstances of each underdeveloped country or group of countries;

(ii)   where aid is on a project basis and where the terms appropriate to the project differ from the terms appropriate to the country, that they should consider whether they can apply one of the following methods: to provide an appropriate "mix" of hard loans and soft loans or grants; to lend under a "two-step procedure" providing for soft loans to governments and on-lending on hard terms to projects; to lend to projects on hard terms and provide separate financial aid for balance of payments relief;

(iii)   that they make it their objective in principle to secure a significant degree of comparability in the terms and conditions of their aid, and so far as possible to eliminate or reduce discrepancies between them. While this would not necessarily entail standard terms and conditions from all donors, it would involve a liberalization of the terms adopted by some members, whether in their individual aid programmes or in concerted aid operations.[22]

The DAC chairman's 1967 report cites the generality of this recommendation and notes that "it soon became clear that a more specific target was desirable."[23] On the basis of yet another working party report, the DAC recommended at a High Level meeting in July, 1965, that members should either

(a) provide 70 per cent or more of their commitments in the form of grants; or:

(b) (i) provide 81 per cent of total commitments as grants or loans at 3 per cent interest charges or less;

(ii) provide 82 per cent of total commitments as grants or loans with repayment periods of 25 years or more;

(iii) attain a weighted average grace period of 7 years.[24]

The resolution further specified that members should use their "best efforts" to achieve these targets within three years.[25] The figures of 81 and 82 per cent and 7 years in the recommendation represented actual weighted averages achieved in respect of all DAC member official bilateral and multilateral aid commitments in 1964. However, these highly concessionary levels resulted from the performance of a few member countries providing aid on considerably more lenient terms than the others, and the object of the recommendation was to bring the lagging members at least up to the 1964 average performance levels, thereby leading to improved average levels in future. The 70 per cent grant figure in point "a" reflects an implied judgment that as long as a country is giving 70 per cent of its aid in the form of grants, it doesn't much matter on what terms the remaining 30 per cent loan element is provided.

Since the adoption of the 1965 recommendations, the DAC has continued to stress the dire straits in which less-developed countries are finding themselves with their heavy debt service burdens; it has pointed out that the weighted average terms of 1965 commitments turned out to be harder than those of 1964; and it has applied pressure to lagging members by measuring their performances against the terms of the recommendations and publicizing the results. Thus, a table in the DAC chairman's 1967 report shows 7 countries (Australia, Norway, Belguim, France, Canada, Netherlands, and Sweden) meeting the 70 per cent grant test in 1966, with none of the remaining eight satisfying all 3 provisions of alternative "b" above, although 2 countries (the United States and the United Kingdom) satisfy 2 of the provisions--all except the 7-year average grace period, and 2 (Denmark and Germany) supplied more than 81 per cent of their aid as grants or loans at 3 per cent interest or less. On the other hand, Japan, Portugal, Austria, and Italy met none of the provisions of alternative "b" in 1966.[26]

NOTES TO CHAPTER 3

1. I. M. D. Little and J. M. Clifford, International Aid (London: George Allen and Unwin, Ltd., 1965).

2. Export-Import Bank Act of 1945, as amended, quoted in Export-Import Bank of Washington, 1934-59: Twenty-Fifth Anniversary Review, 1934-59 (Washington, D.C.: Government Printing Office, 1959), p. 199.

3. International Bank for Reconstruction and Development/International Development Association, Annual Report, 1966-1967 (Washington, D.C., 1967), pp. 19-20.

4. Eugene R. Black, address given in Chicago, January 10, 1951. Reprinted in "Economic Development," comprising statements by officials of the IBRD (Washington, D.C.: IBRD, 1951).

5. All data in this paragraph are from Little and Clifford, op. cit., pp. 30-32.

6. U.S. Agency for International Development, U.S. Overseas Loans and Grants and Assistance from International Organizations: Obligations and Loan Authorizations, July 1, 1945-June 30, 1966, March 17, 1967, p. 11.

7. U.S. Agency for International Development, Office of the Controller, Status of Loan Agreements as of June 30, 1967 (Report No. W-224), p. 145.

8. See U.S. country pages, International Monetary Fund, Interational Financial Statistics (Washington, D.C., 1948-51).

9. U.S. House of Representatives, Agricultural Trade Development and Assistance Act of 1954 and Amendments (Washington, D.C.: Government Printing Office, 1966), p. 41.

10. In lieu of footnoting each item in the following text with a detailed reference, we note here that, unless otherwise indicated, the sources of the information are as follows:

   (a) IBRD, Annual Report (Washington, D.C., 1949-50 through 1966-67).

   (b) United Nations, Department of Economic and Social Affairs, World Economic Survey, 1965 (New York, 1966), pp. 100-121, especially pp. 104-6.

    (c) OECD, The Flow of Financial Resources to Less-
Developed Countries, 1956-1963 (Paris, 1964), pp. 135-
49; and 1961-1965 (Paris, 1967), pp. 65-99 and 131-35.

    (d) OECD, The Flow of Financial Resources to Countries
in the Course of Economic Development, 1956-59
(Paris, 1961), pp. 37-125.

    (e) OECD, Development Assistance Efforts and Policies,
annual reviews, 1963 through 1967 (Paris, published
annually); especially 1967 Review, pp. 74-83.

    (f) OECD, The Flow of Financial Resources to Countries in
Course of Economic Development in 1960 (Paris, 1962).

    (g) OECD, Geographical Distribution of Financial Flows
to Less-Developed Countries, 1960-64, 1965 (Paris,
1966 and 1967).

11.   OECD, DAC, The Flow of Financial Resources, 1961-65,
p. 65.

12.   OECD, DAC, The Flow of Financial Resources, 1956-59,
p. 39.

13.   Government of France, Ministry of Foreign Affairs,
French Economic Assistance in West and Equatorial Africa, 1948-
1958--A Decade of Progress (New York: French Embassy Press
and Information Service, 1958), pp. 6-7.

14.   OECD, DAC, Development Assistance Efforts and Policies
in 1961 (Paris, 1962), p. 23.

15.   IBRD, Annual Report 1963-64, p. 8.

16.   Tabulated from IBRD, "Statement of Loans, June 30,
1967" (Washington, D.C., 1967; mimeograph).

17.   IBRD, Annual Report 1964-65, p. 10.

18.   All information in this paragraph is taken from International Finance Corporation, Annual Report 1966-67 (Washington, D.C.).

19.   U.N., op. cit., p. 105.

20.   OECD, DAC, Development Assistance Efforts and
Policies in 1961, p. 23.

21.   OECD, Development Assistance Efforts and Policies: 1967
Review, p. 2.

22.   OECD, Development Assistance Efforts and Policies: 1964 Review, pp. 97-98.

23.   OECD, Development Assistance Efforts and Policies: 1967 Review, p. 78.

24.   A paraphrase of the resolution from ibid., p. 80.

25.   OECD, Development Assistance Efforts and Policies: 1965 Review, p. 120.

26.   OECD, Development Assistance Efforts and Policies: 1967 Review, Table V.6, p. 81.

CHAPTER **4** OFFICIAL RESOURCE
TRANSFER--II

LOANS REPAYABLE IN LOCAL CURRENCY:
THE INITIAL STAGES

The two major U.S. programs for transfer of resources repayable in local currency, which functioned side by side until one was terminated in 1961, came into being at roughly the same time, via acts of Congress passed in 1954, albeit in different forms and motivated by considerations that overlapped only in part. Thus, the local currency-repayable development loans under the Mutual Security Act (MSA) of 1954 represented a form of economic assistance pure and simple, an outgrowth of the foreign aid activities originating with the first Mutual Security Act of 1951, which, in turn, can be viewed as an extension of the Marshall Plan, both in time (since most Marshall Plan countries received some MSA economic aid, although the accent of the program in Europe was on military assistance) and geography, the emphasis being shifted to less-developed countries in and outside Europe. The Agricultural Trade and Development Act of 1954, on the other hand, or Public Law (P.L.) 480 as it is commonly known and will be referred to here, "started out," according to Congressman Harold Cooley, chairman of the House of Representatives Committee on Agriculture and one of the prime movers in the whole exercise, "to be a surplus disposal program--an international trade program--a program through which we thought we would be able to expand our foreign markets."[1]

The main difference in form between the local currency-repayable Mutual Security loans and assistance under the relevant title of P.L. 480--i.e., No. I--was that the former was a straight-forward loan program in which, once an agreement was signed specifying the uses to which the resources being financed were to be put, all that remained was for the borrower to meet certain documentation requirements in order to obtain the resources, submit to U.S. audit procedures in regard to the relevant expenditures, and deposit service payments on the loan into local U.S. accounts, normally over a 40-year period. With P.L. 480, on the other hand, the transaction started out as nominally a sale in which, shortly after the arrival of each shipment of commodities, the full value of that shipment at agreed "export market" prices was credited in local currency to U.S. Government accounts in the importing country. The "sales" agreements negotiated prior to such shipments specified the proportions of the proceeds that were to be used for various purposes, including both local uses of the U.S. Government itself and loans or grants for development in the receiving country. However, during at least the first five years of P.L. 480, there was normally a considerable lapse of time, often running more than a year, before the conclusion of further agreements covering the specific uses to be made of any development grants or loans to the host government out of the local currency proceeds. Such further agreements did not, of course, represent any new infusion of aid resources to the host country, such infusion occurring already with the entry of the imported commodities into distribution. This fact naturally detracted from the eagerness of host government officials to conclude the new agreements, which represented a partial exercise of U.S. control over development expenditures not necessarily involving any direct imports of U.S. goods and services. Meanwhile, the proceeds, which eventually reached immense proportions in some countries, piled up in U.S. accounts.

THE MUTUAL SECURITY PROGRAM AND
DEVELOPMENT LOAN FUND

Local currency-repayable loans came into existence under the Mutual Security Program as the compromise result of a controversy about the relative merits of grants and loans as the proper vehicle for resource transfer to less-developed countries in Asia and Africa. (In general, Latin America did not figure in these considerations, as the U.S. Administration at that time regarded the Export-Import Bank and the IBRD as adequate supplements to private foreign capital in that area.) Some people argued in favor of continuing the Mutual Security Program on the virtually 100 per cent grant basis on which it began in 1951 and continued through fiscal 1954; they reasoned that the recipient countries were too poor to make any net repayments on the aid at any time in the foreseeable future. Furthermore, the stakes involved in keeping the less-developed areas out of Communist hands were too high for the United States to worry about recovering its financial investment.[2] The administration, on the other hand, was facing rising Congressional sentiment against foreign "giveaway" programs not dictated by immediate military and strategic requirements. Moreover, in both the legislative and executive branches, there was concern that making of capital grants for development was not consistent with promoting financial discipline on the part of the borrowing governments and that it tended to bring about an unhealthy relationship of dependence by the recipient on the donor, leading to resentment by the latter over his moral and political obligation to the former. By contrast, loans were thought to promote both financial discipline and a businesslike relationship between aid-giver and receiver. Another consideration was that, if the less-developed countries could be helped to become financially strong, there was no reason why they should not repay their creditors, just as the United States had once done vis-à-vis Britain and as the European powers were about to do in regard to the United States.

On the other hand, the administration recognized that meeting the financial needs of the less-developed countries exclusively with "hard" loans would result in a rapid build-up of their debt service obligations in relation to export earnings and would eventually bring about situations in which the only alternative to defaults on such obligations would be more or less open refinancing of them by the creditor nations and institutions such as the World Bank. Apart from being bad business practice, such transactions, it was feared, would resemble grants in creating an unhealthy political relationship between aid-giver and receiver. Thus, the administration was looking for a vehicle of capital transfer that would combine the disciplinary and "business" aspects of a loan while placing the least possible burden on the less-developed countries' balance of payments. The latter constraint called for a very low interest rate; but this was objected to on the ground that "cheap money" would spoil the market for loans at "hard" commercial rates, lead to misunderstanding of the economic function of interest, and thus encourage misallocation of resources.

The solution that finally emerged was to make loans at moderate interest rates, with both principal and interest repayable in means of payment of the borrowing country. The United States would agree not to encash the service payments for foreign exchange or use them to purchase goods for export without the borrowing government's approval. What this amounted to, economically, was an indefinite grace period on real payment of both interest and principal. The United States would revolve its local currency receipts within the borrowing country, so that, in principle, the loans would earn compound interest until such time as the United States and the developing country agreed that the latter was in a strong enough position to effect repayment in real resources. Ultimate repayment to the United States would thus be commensurate with the original investment; projects that received the loan funds would have an actual interest expense to meet (since for most economic endeavors all costs are denominated in local currency anyway); and the loans would impose a zero burden on the borrower's balance of payments until such time as it could afford the transfer.

Between the passage of the Mutual Security Act of 1954 (the first loans under it were authorized in calendar 1955) and June 30, 1960, the United States obligated $834 worth of Mutual Security loans in economic assistance to Asia, the Near East (including Greece), Africa, and Latin America, not including credits from the Development Loan Fund, established in 1957.3 Some of the loans were repayable in dollars at an interest rate of 3 per cent, with maturities ranging from 20 to 30 years including grace periods of up to 5 years. The borrowers in these cases were principally countries with stronger-than-average foreign-exchange earning power--e.g., Iran and some Latin American countries. But 87 per cent of the loan funds were repayable in local currency or optionally in local currency or dollars. In most such cases, an interest rate incentive of 1 or 2 per cent was offered for the payment in dollars; however, compared with the relief offered a country's balance of payments by being able to forego payment in foreign exchange, the incentive was practically meaningless. During the first 3 years of the program, the interest rate on all optional-repayment loans was 3 per cent if repaid in dollars, and 4 or 5 per cent if repaid in local currency. In fiscal 1959 through 1961, interest rates of 3 1/2, 4 1/2, and 5 3/4 per cent were occasionally applicable to local currency repayments. As a rule, the maturity on the optional loans was 40 years, although a number were made for shorter terms, ranging as low as 18 years. If the borrower exercised its local currency-repayment option, it was usually required to maintain the value of the service payments by adjusting them to any changes in the exchange rate. However, since this provision did not apply to funds transferred to United States accounts prior to such changes in the exchange rate, it could not prevent U.S.-held balances from declining in value. Moreover, the maintenance of value provision was not applied to about $108 million worth of loans funded out of the local currency proceeds of sales of U.S. agricultural surplus commodities under Section 402 of the Mutual Security Act, a program very similar to but administratively separate from P.L. 480.

Under the impact of the Mutual Security loan program, the proportion of loans in U.S. capital assistance obligations to all areas except Europe--capital assistance being defined to include an aid category formerly known as "defense support" plus all other nonmilitary aid except technical assistance--rose from zero in fiscal 1954 to 22 per cent in fiscal 1957 (50 per cent in that year not including the Far East, where the United States was still financing the economic needs of its military allies largely on a grant basis).[4]

Starting in about 1956, the United States reacted to such developments as the build-up of Soviet and other Communist aid to less-developed countries, the appeal of rapid economic development on the Chinese model, and the concretization of measures of the aggregate "resource gap" facing the less-developed world by undertaking a searching reappraisal of the aid program, both in regard to the amount of aid and its institutional framework. One of the results of this exercise was the establishment of a Development

Loan Fund (DLF) whose purpose was to channel the bulk of U.S. capital assistance to less-developed areas as far as possible via specific project loans. The principle of repayment in local currency was extended to this new institution, which obligated loans in the amount of $1.9 billion during its 4 years of existence, only 20 per cent of this amount being payable in dollars.[5] Most DLF loans carried an interest rate of either 3 1/2 per cent or 5 1/2 to 5 3/4 per cent, depending on whether they were extended for infrastructure or directly productive activities. The interest rate on loans to development banks and other intermediate credit institutions was determined according to the margin deemed to be necessary to provide the institution in question with a reasonable margin for operating costs in lending to local enterprise at locally prevailing rates.

As already noted, allowing a transfer of resources to be repaid in local currency leaves for decision at an indefinite future date the question of how much of the transfer will be repaid and at what effective interest rate. Throughout the Congressional hearings on the 1957 Mutual Security Act, administration spokesmen assured Congress that it was the executive branch's intention that all the loans in question should eventually be repaid in real resources together with interest compounded annually over the intervening period at the announced rates. At the same time, it was clear that the realization of this objective required machinery to keep the local currency service payments in circulation, earning interest. Such machinery had not been explicitly provided for in earlier Mutual Security Acts. The first use which the new act provided was to sell the local currency to U.S. Government agencies, in exchange for dollar appropriations, to finance authorized programs in the countries concerned. In such cases, the agency concerned would have exchanged dollars for the other currency in the local market in the absence of DLF holdings, which would have been tantamount to the borrowing country's exporting an equivalent amount of services. Thus, the effective repayment burden in such cases would be no different from what it would have been had the relevant loan installments been repayable in dollars, although the United States would be fulfilling the terms of the loan agreement by not purchasing goods for export from the country concerned. The economic effect of these transactions is correctly recorded by the DAC in, as we have already noted, subtracting in full the sums involved from new inflows of local currency-repayable resources.

Nevertheless, it was not anticipated that a major share of the DLF repayments could be wiped off the books in this way. To handle what the United States expected to be the larger part of such repayments, the act provided for them to be reinvested in the development of the same country, principally via new DLF project loans. One proposal was that the DLF might use the local currency to meet part of the local costs of specific projects for which it was also making dollar loans. The administration recognized that these loans, extended in local currency from the start, would not make new real resources available for development and would, therefore, not be greeted with the same enthusiasm by the governments concerned as new dollar loans. Nevertheless, it was expected that such governments would agree to facilitate the DLF's local currency operations in the knowledge that maintenance of the funds in interest-earning investments in development projects was a condition of DLF's over-all operations, the initial phase of which-- extending loans in dollars with indefinite grace periods for real payment of interest and principal--was very much in the borrowing countries' interest. The administration also felt that, in some countries that were not making as enlightened use of local resources, according to U.S. tenets, as they might do in order to maximize the rate of development, DLF could improve the situation by making its local currency proceeds available to activities that the local government would not support with its own funds. It was not intended that DLF would assert the right to make local currency loans over local government objections, but it was expected nonetheless that the DLF's position as a major aid source would give it considerable bargaining power to make whatever local currency loans it chose to.

By the time DLF's functions were transferred to President Kennedy's new Agency for International Development (AID) on November 3, 1961, it had collected $45.1 million worth of local currency payments of interest and principal. Of this amount, $5.8 million had been sold to U.S. Government agencies in exchange for appropriated dollars, and $1.1 million had been obligated for a total of three projects, including an airport in Israel and highway construction in Ecuador and Paraguay.[6] (A 1967 AID report makes no reference to the Paraguayan loan, which thus appears to have been transferred to some other account, but lists an agricultural resettlement project in Brazil as recipient of the third of three DLF loans out of local currency proceeds, with a total value of $2.3 million.)[7] A separate dollar loan for the same purpose accompanied the local currency credit in Ecuador; this was not the case with the Israel transaction. On November 3, 1961, the DLF had $39.1 million worth of repayments deposited in various foreign commercial banks.[8] The real resources corresponding to these repayments were thus available for allocation by the banks in the form of loans.

Maintaining the DLF repayments in local bank deposits may have had any of several possible economic effects. In countries where U.S. banks had branches, DLF policy was to deposit local currency repayments in such branches. In these cases or in other countries where DLF used branches of foreign banks, the DLF deposits may have displaced some short-term hard currency reserves, since U.S. and other foreign banks frequently have difficulty attracting local deposits to finance the loan business

they would like to carry on and, unless the exchange risk is pro-
hibitive, borrow additional funds on foreign markets. On the other
hand, if a bank used DLF funds to expand its local investments on
net, the impact would be different. If the bank purchased securities
of the local government, actual allocation of the resources would
fall to the government. If it lent to private borrowers who could
not otherwise obtain funds, the effect would depend on what such
borrowers did with the money, which includes the possibility of expanding investment or consumption or even exporting funds surreptitiously. If the DLF deposits were effectively sterilized--as by
the bank using the DLF deposits merely to increase its reserves
over what they would otherwise have been--the government could
appropriate the corresponding resources by deficit financing. Only
a government with relatively poor command over the monetary and
fiscal powers at its disposal would allow any real resources corresponding to DLF local currency holdings to remain idle until the
Fund agreed to some particular use of them.

In any case, the commercial bank accounts in which DLF kept
its funds paid much lower, if any, interest rates on such deposits
than the rates at which the dollar loans were originally made.
DLF's inability to keep its local currency funds revolving quickly in
interest-bearing investments represented already one source of
loss of value as compared with the theoretical long-run return from
keeping the original dollar funds invested at the initial rate.
Another, far more significant, source of "leakage" from the DLF
investment is depreciation of the currencies of repayment. While
DLF's dollar loans all had maintenance-of-value provisions, there
is no obligation on anyone's part to maintain the value of repayments once they are deposited to DLF's account in foreign banks,
and it was accepted from the start that any relending of such repayments would not carry maintenance of value, as the three outstanding loans do not. Thus, to the extent that U.S. agencies do not
buy up and use DLF repayments quickly, these funds are subject
to the risk of devaluation. AID data through June 30, 1967, show
that minor exchange devaluations have caused loss of value
amounting to $61,601 on the $2.3 million worth of loan payments
lent out again without maintenance of value. (The 14.3 per cent
Israeli devaluation in November, 1967, will have increased that loss
of value by close to $100,000.) However, the data ignore the far
greater loss of value on cash holdings of DLF service payments not
sold to U.S. agencies or re-lent; a rough estimate of this loss up to
the end of 1967 is $80-85 million, amounting to roughly 15 per cent of
total amortization and interest payments received on DLF's local
currency-repayable loans through June 30, 1967.[9] This figure does
not include losses on pre-DLF Mutual Security loans, which form
a greater proportion of payments received on those loans insofar
as they have been outstanding longer and subject to more depreciation. (It should be noted, however, that roughly 80 per cent of the
foregoing loss is attributable to the Indian devaluation of 1966,
which, of course, affected equally all U.S. rupee balances in existence at that time.)

Another possible form of leakage of the DLF investment is by means of outright grants by the United States of balances built up with local currency repayments. The enabling legislation for DLF made no provision for such grants under any conditions, but the Foreign Assistance Act of 1961, which established AID, provided that such balances, insofar as they exceeded official U.S. requirements in a country as determined from time to time by the President, would be available for the different economic assistance programs under the new act --on condition, however, that such uses were provided for in appropriation acts. But the appropriate Congressional committees have taken the attitude of refusing to increase aid appropriations, at least in the grant categories, to enable AID to supplement current levels of dollar aid with grants of excess local currency holdings; and, with AID expenditures increasingly tied to purchases of U.S. goods and services, there has been relatively little scope for the purchase of such holdings with aid appropriations. Thus, for the time being, it appears unlikely that DLF loans will be turned retroactively into explicit grants, as opposed to unintended ones via currency depreciation.

When the World Bank's soft-loans affiliate, the International Development Association, was formally inaugurated in September, 1960, the Bank officials who were to formulate its policies had already decided, partly on the basis of close observation of the United States' experience with local currency repayment, to steer completely clear of this technique. Similarly, President Kennedy's Task Force on Foreign Economic Assistance came to the conclusion in 1961 that the new Agency for International Development's loans should carry long maturities and virtually no interest but be serviced in dollars. The authoritative conclusion of these two bodies did not, however, represent a definitive judgment of failure on the approach taken by the Development Loan Fund and the predecessor Mutual Security loan program. Rather, the DLF was swamped by the mass of local currencies accumulated under P.L. 480, Title I, and never really had a chance to show how effectively it could revolve its local currency receipts. Explaining the reason why local currency repayment was abandoned with AID, the DLF's Terminal Report states: "U.S. accumulations of local currencies taken in payment for surplus agricultural commodities reached the point in some countries and promised to reach the point in others where it was considered inadvisable to add still further sums from loan receipts."[10] From another point of view, it made little sense to invest considerable U.S. administrative resources in selecting viable projects on which to spend DLF's local currency proceeds when it was proving impossible to dispose suitably of balances many times larger acquired under P.L. 480.

At the very best, DLF would have found it burdensome administratively to operate its revolving local currency fund along pseudo-banking lines that would have satisfied Congress and the Budget Bureau. It would also have faced (and probably already did,

toward the end of its four-year life) serious obstruction in this area
on the part of key government agencies in the less-developed countries, as well as vocal political complaints about the U.S. Government operating a credit institution with strictly local resources.
Through the marvelous workings of compound interest, DLF might
ultimately have found itself saddled with more local currency than
it could possibly invest other than in long-term securities of the
host government.

Whatever the merits of DLF's own operations, in 1961, its
corporate identity was taken away; accumulated local currency repayments on its loans were transferred to "miscellaneous receipts"
of the U.S. Treasury (still in local accounts, of course); it was ruled
that future such payments were to be similarly credited; and both
were to be disposed of, as rapidly as possible, through sales to
U.S. agencies against appropriated dollars. However, it was clear
that such disposal would take many years. As of 1967, some $1.14
billion worth of DLF local currency-repayable loans, amounting to
76 per cent of all DLF's local currency-repayable loans, had been
made to 15 countries where the Treasury Department considered
current (1967) U.S. holdings of the local currency, acquired mainly
through P.L. 480, Title I, operations, to be "excess" or "near-
excess."[11] (An "excess currency" country is one "where the
supply of a nonrestricted currency substantially exceeds the normal
operating requirements of the U.S. Government"; a "near-excess
currency country" is one where U.S. holdings, "although in no case
sufficient to be designated an excess currency, are above our immediate needs.")[12] Moreover, $544 million, equal to 75 per cent of
the pre-DLF Mutual Security loans repayable in local currency and
carrying maintenance-of-value provisions, had likewise been lent
to such countries. A 1964 study shows annual service payments
during the 1960's on DLF loans in four "excess" or "near-excess
currency" countries as amounting to four to nine times the estimated total requirements of U.S. agencies for the currencies in
question in fiscal 1961.[13]

Thus, unless Congress undergoes an unanticipated change of
heart and allows the executive branch to grant local currency loan
repayments outright, the bulk of them will remain locked in local
U.S. accounts for many years after they are received, steadily de-
preciating as a result of foregone interest and foreign devaluations.
The corresponding real resources will be appropriated by other
parties as described above, and the undiscounted real repayment
burden of the original loans, to say nothing of the burden discounted
at a rate reflecting the opportunity cost of capital, will turn out to
be a fraction of their nominal value, probably less than 50 per cent
for Mutual Security-DLF local currency-repayable loans as a
whole. Conversely, with regard to the remaining 25 per cent of
local currency-repayable loans made to countries where U.S. local
currency holdings are not excess, the repayment burden will nearly
equal that of dollar-repayable loans on the given terms, qualified

only to the extent that currency depreciation takes place between the receipt of a loan service payment and its expenditure by a U.S. agency.

PUBLIC LAW 480

It is possible to distinguish four separate elements of economic assistance, either provided for explicitly in the law or arising from the way in which it has been executed, in that portion of the P.L. 480 program which consists of "sales" of surplus U.S. agricultural products for foreign currencies. These are: (1) delays in spending sales proceeds allocated to U.S. uses and accumulated in local commercial bank accounts, allowing the real resources corresponding to such proceeds to be appropriated temporarily by factors in the local economy; (2) expenditures by the U.S. Government on local goods and services which it would not purchase in the absence of large holdings of local currency, thus in effect enabling the countries concerned to generate special exports exclusively for the purpose of financing retroactively imports of agricultural commodities; (3) outright grants of sales proceeds; and (4) loans of sales proceeds. Each of these is analyzed in turn below.

Delays in Spending Sales Proceeds Allocated to U.S. Uses

Because the original Public Law 480 (passed in 1954) applied the Supplemental Appropriations Act to at least 10 per cent of the sales proceeds, thus prohibiting the expenditure of such 10 per cent except under specific appropriations by Congress, and the executive branch considered it inadvisable to seek appropriations authorizing the use of this 10 per cent for foreign aid purposes, nearly all P.L. 480 sales agreements have reserved at least 10 per cent of the proceeds for expenditure by the U.S. Government on its own activities within the foreign countries concerned.* This "U.S.-use" proportion averaged 23 per cent in the sum total of P.L. 480 agreements signed through fiscal 1966. The original

---

*Perusal of the various semiannual and annual reports of the President to Congress on P.L. 480 indicates that a multiyear agreement with Pakistan signed in fiscal 1961 is the only exception to this rule (Congress appropriated part of the sales proceeds for aid to the Indus Basin project), although an ex-post diversion, with Congress' approval, of U.S.-use funds in Yugoslavia to Skoplje earthquake relief resulted in ex-post net U.S.-use reservations falling below 10 per cent for several years in that country.

idea behind the U.S.-use element was to enable the United States to recoup an immediate, partial quid pro quo from the P.L. 480 transaction whose negative impact on the host country's balance of payments, while equal to the full amount of the expenditures in question, would nonetheless be relatively invisible. In theory, the amount of the U.S.-use portion in each agreement was to be based on projections of expenditures by U.S. agencies, beginning with the embassy itself, in the country involved during the next year or two. However, in some countries, the P.L. 480 program mounted up so rapidly that an amount no greater than 10 per cent of the sales proceeds far exceeded the U.S. Government's normal requirements-- by 1960, special consultants appointed to consider "The Problem of Excess Accumulation of U.S.-Owned Local Currencies" (this being the title of the report they delivered) noted that current holdings for U.S. uses exceeded U.S. requirements in Turkey for 8 years, in Indonesia for 12, in India for 19, and in Yugoslavia for 36 years, based on estimated needs for fiscal 1961.[14] In an effort to diminish these balances, the list of permitted U.S. uses was continually lengthened; however, the appropriations committees of Congress have been reluctant to let official agencies expand their activities in accordance with the availability of excess local currency, insisting instead that as a general rule such activities should not exceed levels on which the expenditure of new tax dollars could be justified.

The upshot of this is that, on June 30, 1967, of $2.1 billion worth of local currency for U.S. uses collected from P.L. 480 sales to all countries excluding Poland, only $1.6 billion had been disbursed.[15] The remaining $0.5 billion constituted in effect a loan to the foreign economies concerned, subject to the same alternative real uses as were discussed in connection with DLF local currency repayments in the preceding section. These "loans" bore little or no interest, and their "maturities" depended on the ratio of the holdings to eligible annual expenditures by U.S. agencies in particular countries as well as on the extent to which such uses were offset by new deposits resulting from subsequent shipments. Moreover, the "loans" were subject to loss of value through currency depreciation. Thus, unspent accumulations of Indian rupees for U.S. use under P.L. 480 were worth on the order of $300 million just before the rupee devaluation of June, 1966; the devaluation reduced their dollar value by roughly $100 million.

U.S. Local Purchases Stimulated By
Excess Currency Holdings

A few U.S. uses, most of them subject to ceilings fixed either in P.L. 480 itself or in other authorizing acts, have at one time or another not been subject to appropriation procedures. These are educational activities under the Fulbright Act, translation of books and periodicals by the U.S. Information Agency, development of

American-sponsored schools and centers, purchase of goods for third countries under the aid program, and local travel expenses of Congressional committees.[16] Through fiscal 1965, $181 million worth of U.S.-use local currency had been spent on such activities. However, the 1966 annual report on P.L. 480 assumes that these programs "would have been carried on at the same level had there been no U.S. foreign currency holdings."[17] Such a statement is unavoidably based on speculation regarding the past intentions of Congress and the administration. Moreover, it is made in the context of a section in the report attempting to highlight the balance-of-payments benefit which U.S.-use local currencies have gained for the United States and may reflect a certain degree of bias.

However, the same section of the report assumes that $172 million worth of U.S.-use local currency disbursed under "special foreign currency appropriations" would not have been spent in the same amounts, and possibly not at all, in the absence of excess accumulations of such currency. This category of disbursements began in 1960 after a compromise was finally reached between, on one hand, administration and Congressional elements who wanted for a variety of reasons, mainly of a foreign policy or strictly aid policy nature, to reduce the excess holdings and/or desired to expand certain programs for which dollar appropriations were not available, and, on the other hand, the Congressional appropriations committees and fiscal purists in the Bureau of the Budget who regarded the local currency holdings as government assets which could eventually be redeemed at a consequent saving to the U.S. taxpayer. Under the compromise, the same uses that had always been subject to appropriations procedures remained so. However, government agencies were encouraged to identify, in their regular budget submissions to the Bureau of the Budget, special proposed expenditures in countries where U.S.-use local currency holdings had been identified by the Treasury as excess to U.S. needs--there being 11 such countries as of January 1, 1967, 10 less-developed countries and Poland. It would be clearly understood that these expenditures were supplemental to the regular dollar-financed activities of the agencies concerned and that the agencies proposed to carry them out only if excess local currency were made available above the level of dollar appropriations required for such regular activities. The Bureau of the Budget would then submit its recommendations to Congress, and Congress would appropriate dollars in two categories, one corresponding to regular agency activities and the other to whatever "special foreign currency programs" it chose to permit the agencies to carry out. Appropriated dollars in the second category would then be used to buy excess local currency from the Treasury, with the dollar proceeds being credited to the Commodity Credit Corporation (the object of this procedure was to deduct the corresponding amounts from the stated cost of the domestic agricultural price support program). Expenditure of the U.S.-use local currency on programs that the administration admits "may cover activities of lower priority than regular appropriations"[18] has the economic effect of boosting host country exports (counted as services in the balance of payments) specifically in order to allow the agricultural commodity imports to be paid for retroactively, and, in that sense, constitutes aid.

Outright Grants of Sales Proceeds

Sales agreements signed from the start of the program through calendar 1965 allocated 17 per cent of total projected sales of $10.5 billion to grants for economic development in the recipient country. Although the proceeds in question are not always transferred expeditiously to the intended recipients of the grants--as of June 30, 1965, AID had disbursed only 77 per cent of the $1.57 billion already transferred to it for this purpose[19]--the fact that the sales proceeds are deposited in U.S. accounts in the host countries' central banks enable the host government to appropriate the real resources in question from the outset. As a result of Congress' rising opposition to this grant program, based on hostility to the idea that part of the U.S. agricultural surpluses have to be disposed of under non-charity auspices--i.e., apart from the largely charity program operated under Title II of P.L. 480--without even a semblance of a quid pro quo,[20] the Administration has virtually stopped providing for such grants in sales agreements signed after 1964 (from January 1, 1965, through March 31, 1967, the only grants agreed to comprised $16.2 million for India).

Loans of Sales Proceeds

It is by virtue of the original Section 104(g), authorizing the President to loan local currency sales proceeds "to promote multilateral trade and economic development," that P.L. 480 has been in part explicitly a soft-loan, as opposed to exclusively sale-cum-grant, program. The theory behind this provision was similar to that which underlay the DLF's operations. The difficult economic situation of the less-developed countries warranted relieving them of the balance-of-payments burden of making real payment for the resources involved within the foreseeable future. However, to make a 100 per cent grant program of P.L. 480 would bring about the unhealthy political relationship mentioned earlier and would relax financial discipline on the part of the recipients. Also, the latter should eventually be able to afford real payment, and, as noted above, Congress refused to accept the idea of the United States receiving little or no quid pro quo for its farm surpluses. Thus, the principle was adopted of lending as large a share of the sales proceeds as the less-developed countries would accept, in lieu of having them decline the whole transaction, and keep the funds revolving and earning interest until the recipients could afford to

redeem them. In order to protect this U.S. investment, for four
years after the start of the program, maintenance of value provisions were applied to all such loans, and interest was charged at
rates varying between 3 1/2 and 5 per cent (in early years, the old
Mutual Security loan principle of giving an interest-reduction bonus
of 1 per cent for repayment in dollars was applied). The maturity
on most of the loans was either 30 or 40 years.

However, as noted early in this chapter, once the sales agreements had been signed, ensuring the arrival of the real aid--i.e.,
the agricultural commodities--the United States found itself in a
weak bargaining position to induce the recipient countries to conclude agreements for loans of their own currency, requiring negotiations over the end-uses of the funds and subjection of such end-
uses to U.S. auditing procedures. Delays in concluding the loan
agreements caused local currency to accumulate in U.S. accounts
in central banks at a rate several times higher than the accumulation of U.S.-use proceeds. By early 1959, close to $1 billion worth
of local currency was awaiting disbursement via country loans. One
of the steps taken by the administration to reduce these balances
was to drop the maintenance of value provision from such loans with
effect from fiscal 1959. Up to that time loan agreements worth
$964 million had been negotiated subject to maintenance of value
provisions; subsequently, through June 30, 1967, $3,574 million
worth of agreements without such provisions were signed. As of
that date, $746 million, or 21 per cent of the original dollar value of
the nonmaintenance of value loans, had been written off by AID
owing to exchange-rate adjustments.[21] There is no doubt that this
process will continue during the 30- or 40-year life of the loans in
question.

Loss of value in an opportunity cost sense will also result
from the fact that the loans carry submarket interest rates. By
March 31, 1962, the United States had collected $38 million worth
of interest payments in local currency on these loans, and, in June
of that year, the administration, anxious to avoid further accumulations on that account, reduced the interest rate on the loans to 0.75
per cent. However, in 1964, Congress amended the act with a requirement that the interest rate be no less than the prevailing U.S.
Treasury rate for obligations of similar maturity, although the
President was given authority to designate a different rate in specific instances.[22] Data in a 1967 AID report indicate that this
authority was used only in the cases of India, Pakistan, Yugoslavia,
and Brazil, the first three being among the four countries (the
U.A.R. coming ahead of Yugoslavia) with the largest accumulations
of unspent currency designated for aid uses.[23] Again in 1966,
Congress amended the interest rate requirement, this time to
exempt from it all countries in which the Treasury rules U.S.-use
holdings to be excessive. Recent terms in such countries have
followed the current pattern on AID's softest loans, i.e., 0.75-1.0
per cent during the first 10 years and 2-2.5 per cent during the
remaining 30.

As in the case of DLF loans, in order to assess the real payment burden of the P.L. 480 local currency loans, it is necessary to trace the service payments on these loans to their ultimate disposition. Up to 1961, the only uses authorized by law for these payments were to finance Fulbright Act activities (but only against dollar appropriations) and meet travel expenses of Congressional committees. In 1961, an amendment to P.L. 480 made local-currency payments of principal and interest subject to the same uses authorized for fresh sales proceeds; however, a 1964 amendment required that Congress be given special notice (30 days if in session, 60 if not) of any use proposed to be made of loan service payments other than for purchase by appropriated dollars.[24] This seemed to indicate a special concern on Congress' part to prevent the local currency loans from turning into delayed grants. Then again in 1966, Congress exempted all excess-currency countries from this provision. As of June 30, 1967, the United States had collected $389.9 million worth of local currency service payments on these loans. Another $63 million optionally repayable in local currency had been remitted in dollars by the economically stronger debtors.[25] Such repayments are, of course, subject to the same loss of value through currency depreciation and foregone interest that affects other P.L. 480 local currency balances. In addition, the recent exemption opens the door more widely than ever to outright grants of these holdings.

Brief mention should be made here of the so-called Cooley loan program, authorized by a 1957 P.L. 480 amendment of Congressman Cooley, under which up to 25 per cent of the proceeds of local currency sales agreements may be set aside for direct loans to U.S. business firms operating in the countries concerned as well as to local and non-U.S. foreign firms for operations that will process or sell U.S. agricultural products. Through fiscal 1966, 5.3 per cent of the total value of all sales agreements had been allocated for Cooley loans. Through fiscal 1967, $258 million worth of local currency had been disbursed for this purpose and $103 million worth collected in service payments.[26] Interest rates and maturities are supposed to be comparable to those available on the local financial markets, taking into account the nature of the investment proposed, and generally range between 5 and 15 per cent and 5 and 20 years. Interest collections of $38.3 million through fiscal 1967 were almost enough to offset the exchange loss of $39.7 million recorded up to that time, representing 14 per cent of the total value of Cooley loan agreements. The range of possible economic impacts of the Cooley program is similar to that in the case of U.S.-use deposits in commercial banks. The loans may substitute for foreign exchange that investors would otherwise bring in to purchase local currency; conversely, they may result in foreign-exchange inflow that takes place only because of the availability on moderately favorable terms of complementary local finance. In any case, they are likely to have some influence on local resource allocation.

Since the late 1950's, both Congress and the administration
have been concerned about the political and administrative implications of large U.S. holdings of inconvertible foreign currencies.
On the political front, the administration's 1960 consultants posed
the question of how Americans would feel if a single foreign power
controlled claims on internal U.S. resources to the extent of 9 per
cent or more of our gross national product (GNP), as was already
the case with three excess-currency countries in 1959.[27] Moreover, Congress in particular was concerned about the rapid
erosion of the value of U.S. foreign currency assets. In an attempt
to stem the tide, a new Title IV was added to P.L. 480 in 1959,
providing for a supplementary program of loans repayable in dollars over a term not to exceed 20 years, at interest rates not
above Treasury borrowing costs for the same maturity. To
sweeten the pill of dollar repayment, the new program permitted
the conclusion of long-term commodity supply contracts assuring
deliveries for as long as ten years. The program was slow in
getting under way, the first agreements being negotiated only in
fiscal 1962. However, it has accelerated very rapidly such that
P.L. 480 agreements signed in fiscal 1966 provided for $406
million of dollar-repayable loans as against $690 million of local
currency-repayable loans, including $50 million for Cooley loans.

Through fiscal 1966, the administration had succeeded in
shifting 15 countries formerly in the Title I category entirely over
to Title IV; another 4 signed agreements under both titles in that
year, indicating that they were probably in a transition stage; and
10 more countries (treating AID's East Africa-Regional category
as three countries) had signed agreements under Title IV without
ever participating in Title I. Of 18 developing countries where
U.S. local currency holdings were excess or near-excess on December 31, 1966, eight were either entirely on a Title IV basis or in
the above-mentioned apparent transition stage. Fifteen countries,
including such excess or near-excess currency countries as India,
Pakistan, Tunisia, and Turkey, signed Title I agreements in fiscal
1965 and/or 1966, without ever participating in Title IV; two
countries, Chile and Peru, appeared to have shifted in a perverse
direction, in the sense of signing Title I agreements two years
subsequent to their last Title IV agreements.[28] It was the trend
toward Title IV that encouraged Congress in the 1966 P.L. 480
amendment act to set a deadline of December 31, 1971, for "a
progressive transition from sales for foreign currencies to sales
for dollars," although it added the qualification that, insofar as
this was not possible even on the available dollar credit terms,
there should be a transition to sales for foreign currencies on
AID development loan terms--the implication here being to eliminate outright grants of sales proceeds--"and on terms which permit conversion to dollars at the exchange rate applicable to the
sales agreement."[29] In other words, Congress was asking for
reintroduction of the old maintenance-of-value requirement on P.L.
480 local currency-repayable loan agreements by the end of 1971.

Quite likely, the United States will find by 1971 that some countries now obtaining all their P.L. 480 supplies under local currency arrangements can stand the present 2.5 per cent, 20-year dollar-repayment terms under the former Title IV (since 1966 merged with Title I). On the other hand, there is a good chance that local currency sales to some countries will have to continue. For example, if India still requires U.S. agricultural commodities at the annual rate of about $300 million worth, which it has imported in recent years of normal weather, servicing such imports on the above terms would add about $20 million per year to its annual debt service burden. This is equivalent to about 1 per cent of gross foreign-exchange earnings in 1966. With India's debt service ratio already close to .20 in 1966 and showing signs of continuing to increase on the basis of the present relative growth rates of debt service and exports, it is doubtful whether it will be able to afford the aforementioned addition to its debt service burden on account of P.L. 480.

THE INTERNATIONAL DEVELOPMENT ASSOCIATION (IDA)

From the early stages of the discussion among and within World Bank member governments about the need for a multilateral vehicle for development finance on terms considerably easier than those of the Bank itself, one of the questions raised was that of what type of terms would be offered. Considerable attention was devoted to the possibility of repayment in local currency on the pattern then current with U.S. aid. A U.S. Senate resolution, promoted by Senator A. S. Mike Monroney and passed in July, 1958, called on the administration to consider promoting a multilateral institution that would provide "a source of long-term loans available at a reasonable rate of interest and repayable in local currencies."[30] The resolution saw another object of the new institution as being to facilitate "the use of local and other foreign currencies, including those available to the U.S. through the sale of agricultural surpluses." The Senators reasoned that, as long as IDA was involved in the business of handling local currency received through service payments on its own loans, it could relieve the United States of the burden of administering its existing P.L. 480 and Mutual Security/DLF loan repayments. It was felt that a multilateral institution, particularly one with the experience and reputation of the World Bank, would be in a much better position to work with local currencies, influencing the allocation of strictly local resources, than the government of a foreign power such as the United States. The Senators also considered that the availability of such local currencies might facilitate the execution of desirable projects for which, because of institutional obstacles, the local resources needed to supplement new foreign capital might not otherwise be forthcoming. On this basis, it was even hoped that the other members of the Bank would accord some recognition to a

U.S. contribution in local currencies in the assignment of required shares in IDA's foreign-exchange capital. In December, 1958, then World Bank President Eugene R. Black lent his authority to the possibility that IDA would operate on the basis of local currency repayment by writing that "one of the main reasons for setting up a new International Development Association . . . would be to create an international pool of capital for loans repayable wholly or partly in local currency."31

However, the articles of agreement establishing IDA, which were circulated in January, 1960, and adopted in September of that year, left the question of precise repayment terms open, stating merely that financing out of IDA's initial resources "shall take the form of loans, . . . on such terms as the Association may deem appropriate, having regard to the economic position and prospects of the area or areas concerned and to the nature and requirements of the project."32 Further flexibility is provided by a section that allows IDA, if it finds that the circumstances so warrant, to "agree to a relaxation or other modification of the terms on which any of its financing shall have been provided."33

In the two years that elapsed between the writing of Black's comment above and the inauguration of IDA, a good deal of soul-searching went on over the question of local currency repayment. The author understands from a representative of one of the developing countries who participated in these discussions that some in that category of Bank members favored local currency repayment on the unstated ground that it would result in transfers of capital that would never have to be repaid in real terms. The reasoning here was that, once local currency repayments had reached a substantial amount, it would seem logical, and involve no political obstacles, to cancel a large share of the debt or grant the funds outright to human investment or relief projects.

On the other hand, the Bank management eventually came down squarely in opposition to local currency repayment. This was not so much because it was worried about never getting its money back--from the start, it was understood that all of IDA's capital would be provided without fixed terms of repayment to the sources, and the terms eventually applied to all of IDA's lending contain a 73 per cent grant element when repayments are discounted at a moderate rate of 6 per cent. Rather, the Bank was most concerned about dissipating its administrative resources in allocating funds--i.e., local currency service payments--which represented no new injection of real resources into the developing economy. Assuming that IDA made local currency-repayable loans at 6 per cent interest and that all repayments on these loans, as well as repayments on the invested repayments, were invested at the same rate, IDA would acquire, and thus be compelled to administer, over the 50-year period that was eventually accepted as the maturity of IDA credits, an amount of local currency equal to 15 times the face value of its original dollar loans. This would make it impossible for the Bank to concentrate on ensuring the efficient execution of those projects to which it was contributing new resources, it would detract from its prestige in the international financial community, and it would involve the Bank in extensive hassles with the borrowing governments. The Bank was also bothered by the thought of having to negotiate with borrowing countries at some unspecified time in the future the question of when they could afford real repayment of the loans by allowing IDA to cash in its local currency holdings. From the Bank's point of view, it was much more businesslike for a country's creditors to decide unilaterally when the country could afford to start net repayment of its debt and then force it to do so by halting the inflow of public capital.

In all these considerations, the Bank staff had, of course, the benefit of U.S. experience in dealing with local currency repayments, and what they saw made them averse to getting involved in a similar situation. The Bank's European members felt the same way and, in addition, were anxious to avoid drawing pressure onto themselves (such as would ensue if IDA made local currency-repayable loans) to get into the same business. The upshot was that IDA adopted a policy of making "development credits" repayable in the currencies lent, with a 0.75 per cent service charge in lieu of interest and a grace period on amortization payments during the first 10 years, followed by amortization at 1 per cent annually for 10 more years and 3 per cent annually for the next 30, for a total term of 50 years. From the outset, these terms have applied, vis-à-vis the borrowing governments, to all IDA loans. When the ultimate user of an IDA credit is an entity that is required to earn a direct return on its investment, IDA applies the two-step procedure mentioned in the discussion of the OECD Development Assistance Committee earlier in this chapter. In the case of program loans for industrial imports such as the IDA has made to India and Pakistan, the user is required to pay cash down to a public agency for all or part of the goods imported, and the money is immediately invested in the national development program.

On the question of using U.S. local currency accumulations, the United States was able to have included in the articles of agreement a provision allowing members to contribute, in addition to their regular subscriptions, "supplementary resources" in the form of currencies of other members, subject to the latter's agreement. The articles also allow such contributions to be made subject to conditions regarding the use of earnings on the funds involved and the disposal of the resources in the event IDA ceases operations or the contributing member withdraws. The administration's intent here was to provide for the eventuality that Congress might want to insist on the United States ultimately redeeming its local currency contribution to IDA and thus salvaging part of the original dollar investment. However, Congress, showing its usual ambivalence toward the local currency question, failed to agree to a 1960 bill that would have authorized the transfer of P.L. 480 currency to IDA, and the administration, having "not seen any indication on the part of the IDA management, or indeed of the member countries, to utilize such local currencies," decided to leave the matter "in abeyance."[34] Meanwhile, through June 30, 1967, IDA had received $223.7 million worth of inconvertible local currency, either in cash or non-negotiable, noninterest-bearing demand obligations, as part of the subscriptions of so-called Part II (less-developed) member countries of IDA (10 per cent of these countries' subscriptions was payable and had been fully paid, in foreign exchange). These funds were subject to IDA administrative use or project lending, within the countries involved; by the same date, only $2.9 million of the funds had been spent, reflecting an extremely limited demand for local currencies on IDA's part.[35]

THE INTER-AMERICAN DEVELOPMENT BANK (IDB)

Apart from the U.S. Government, the Inter-American Development Bank, which opened its doors in 1960, is the only agency active in the foreign aid field that has used repayment in local currency as a device for softening the burden of repaying loans in foreign exchange. The Bank has applied this provision to over half the dollar lending of its Fund For Special Operations (FSO) and to all the dollar loans made out of the Special Progress Trust Fund (SPTF), which the Bank administers on behalf of the U.S. Government via a special trust agreement. Unlike the U.S. Government, however, the IDB has thus far made local currency repayment work well enough to want to continue it in the foreseeable future. To a large extent, this is because the IDB, unlike the United States, has not had to dispose of huge accumulations of local currency generated by "sales" of surplus agricultural commodities.

Through December 31, 1967, the IDB had acquired control over about $410 million worth of Latin American and Caribbean currencies, not including principal repayments on loans originally made in the same currencies, and had spent, or was committed to spend by virtue of undisbursed balances on authorized project loans, 90 per cent of this amount. Sources of these currencies and their disposition are shown in Table 7. By mid-1968, the IDB's holdings of at least one Latin American currency--the Colombian peso-- were considerably less than the amount it desired to lend to supplement its foreign-exchange loans in the country concerned.

In addition to the lower order of magnitude of the IDB's local currency holdings, there are two more key differences between the Bank and the U.S. Government in regard to their situation vis-à-vis local currencies. The first of these concerns the restrictions

TABLE 7

Receipts and Commitments of Local Currencies Acquired by the IDB through December 31, 1967
($ million equivalents)

Receipts		Commitments	
Member's subscriptions/contributions-total	334.4	Loans provided in local currency-total	331.1
Cash-total	226.7	Disbursed and outstanding-total	140.2
Ordinary Capital (O.C.)	96.3	O.C.	71.5
Fund for Special Operations (FSO)	130.4	FSO-own account	44.7
Non-negotiable, noninterest-bearing		SPTF-own account	16.1
demand notes – total	107.7	SPTF-participations in FSO loans	7.9
O.C.	20.5	Approved and undisbursed-total	190.9
FSO	87.2	O.C.	36.8
Loans-Total	75.0	FSO	154.1
Amortization of dollar loans-total	32.3	Expenditures on administration and technical	
FSO	6.9	assistance-total	35.0
Social Progress Trust Fund (SPTF)	25.4	O.C. and FSO (estimate)	10.0
Earnings-total	43.0	SPTF[a]	25.0
O.C. and FSO (estimate)	20.0	Grand Total	366.0
SPTF	23.1		
Grand Total	409.0		

Note:
[a]Includes $1.3 million of declared exchange losses on currency holdings.

Source: Inter-American Development Bank, Annual Report (Washington, D.C.) 1960 through 1967, entries in financial statements and tabulation of data in loan statements.

83

attached to the lender's use of such currencies, or, in other words, their degree of inconvertibility. Most U.S. local currency holdings are restricted to the point where they cannot even be used to buy locally produced goods for export, with the exception of books and objects of scientific or cultural value, unless the borrowing government consents. Under the IDB's articles of agreement, on the other hand, no member can restrict the Bank's or any borrower's use of any of the member's currency held by the Bank for the purchase of goods and services produced in the member's territory, whether for export or any other purpose.[36] The same provision is included in the separate SPTF agreement.

Another provision in the articles of agreement goes further to state that, unless a member specifically registers its intention to do so with the Bank, it cannot restrict the use of its currency by the IDB or a borrower of the Bank "for payments in any country."[37] This is conditioned by a further provision that gold and currencies held by the IDB "shall not be used by the Bank to purchase other currencies unless authorized by a two-thirds majority of the total voting power of the member countries."[38] The upshot appears to be that, for example, unless Member Country X registers a general reservation with the Bank, it cannot refuse to redeem its own pesos from a European supplier from whom an investor in Member Country Y has bought machinery with an IDB loan of X's pesos. Nor, except on the same condition, could X refuse one of its own investors the foreign exchange with which to buy European machinery against such an IDB loan.

In view of the potentially serious balance-of-payments repercussions of such procedures, it is surprising that only two IDB members, Mexico (in regard to both ordinary capital resources and FSO holdings of its currency) and Guatemala (part of the FSO holdings only) have entered the reservation in question. Presumably, it signifies confidence on the part of members that they will be able jointly to prevent the IDB from using their currencies to finance exports of extraregional countries. One way of doing this is to provide sufficient vehicles for investment of the currency domestically, which appears to have happened. (Another, less constructive, way might be to refuse licenses for imports under such IDB loans-- this would probably not violate the letter of the agreement.) Thus far, the IDB has more than responded to its members' interests on this point. It has made no loans to any member country in another's currency (apart from dollars) and has raised funds in Europe, Canada, and Japan to finance non-U.S. capital imports.

Apart from meeting local costs of development projects in the respective countries, the most logical function for the Bank's local currencies, and one fully in accord with its long-range objectives, would be to finance intraregional trade, especially in capital goods, which usually require more than short-term financing regardless of who the buyer and seller are. The IDB has, in fact, been financing intraregional trade in capital goods since 1964, but through 1967 it has done so exclusively with dollars, provided in eight revolving credits to six countries for a total value of $32 million. Very recently, in part because of U.S. pressure to restrict the use of dollars to direct purchase of American goods and services, Bank members have agreed that holdings of the currencies of the four Latin American countries with the largest FSO quotas-- Argentina, Brazil, Mexico, and Venezuela--will be used to finance not only capital exports from those countries but also local costs of projects in other countries.[39] Thus, for example, a future IDB loan to Paraguay may consist partly of Brazilian cruzeiros, which Paraguay will not have to spend on Brazilian goods and services but instead can use to bolster her foreign-exchange reserves--even buying gold with them initially, although, in accordance with economic principles, the effect of the expenditure of a corresponding amount of guaranies on local costs of the loan project will be to draw the reserves back down close to their former levels within two or three years.

Mention of the IDB's growing emphasis on intraregional trade leads us directly to the third major difference between the IDB and the U.S. Government in regard to the local currency problem: namely, that the IDB is a regional institution which has as its raison d'etre not only to channel foreign capital into Latin America and the Caribbean but also to participate in the allocation of the area's own resources and influence it in the direction of activities conducive to (a) maximum growth and (b) social justice. (This is not the place to consider how far these two objectives are compatible or conflict with one another.) It is true that the U.S. Government's voice in the IDB is considerably stronger than that of any other single member. At the end of 1967, its share in the total subscribed capital of all members in the Bank's two regular sections and the SPTF combined was 67 per cent.[40] Corresponding to this role, the United States has 42.2 per cent of the voting power in the IDB's Board of Executive Directors; moreover, by virtue of a requirement that decisions of the FSO and SPTF be approved by a two-thirds majority of the votes, the United States can in effect veto proposed loans from those funds. Nevertheless, Latin American influence in IDB decision-making is strong, and, in some aspects, predominating. By gentleman's agreement, the post of Bank president is reserved for a Latin American, and, since the Bank's founding, it has been headed by Felipe Herrera, a Chilean economist of considerable stature in Latin America. Latin Americans comprise a majority of the Bank's staff, including most of the economists and engineers who evaluate projects and submit recommendations to the Board of Executive Directors. On the whole, the Bank has a marked intraregional flavor, and its participation in internal resource allocation has far less of the political overtones associated with the exercise of such a role by the U.S. Government.

Whatever the reasons, it is a fact, demonstrated by Table 7, that the IDB has been able to keep its local currency moving. As the table shows, lending has been the principal means of utilizing the local currency. Of the $331 million lent, 92 per cent has accompanied IDB loans in foreign exchange. But with ten loans made exclusively in local currency, the Bank has made clear its determination to avoid the pitfalls of local currency management encountered by the United States. Rather than allow idle balances to accumulate to the point where they are too large to manage without creating serious frictions with the government concerned, the IDB will invest them in activities which it lacks time and resources to review as carefully as it does its dollar loan projects and to which it has no intention of lending foreign exchange.

Another demonstration of the IDB's intention here is given by the fact that, in 1967, when it could not find suitable project vehicles under SPTF auspices to make prompt use of some $8 million of local currency proceeds of earlier SPTF loans, the Bank used this money to buy participations in the local currency portions of 13 existing FSO loans. The Bank's executive directors have authorized it to continue to do this with SPTF local currency proceeds, "provided (the FSO) loans are in substance in compliance with the provisions of the Trust Fund."41 The effect of the foregoing transaction was merely to increase the FSO's local currency balances by the same amount that it reduced the SPTF's. However, as the Bank's own conditions for spending FSO money are somewhat easier than those imposed in the Trust Fund Agreement with the United States, the transaction will make it easier to keep the local currency in question revolving.

Looking in greater detail at the IDB's two soft-lending operations, we find that, since 1965, the Bank no longer publishes data showing whether FSO dollar loans are to be serviced in dollars or local currency,* so this information is not available for 1966 or 1967, years in which dollar loan approvals more than doubled from a level of $310 million at the end of 1965 to $768 million on December 31, 1967. Table 8 shows the extent to which service in local currency was permitted in regard to dollar loans approved as of December 31, 1965.

As the table shows, the application of local currency repayment to amortization of FSO dollar loans has been considerably greater--through 1965, about 50 per cent more--than its application to interest payments. Many loans require interest to be paid in dollars, whereas amortization may be paid in local currency. (Through 1965, there was only one case of the reverse arrangement:

---

*Even the monthly loan statements available on request to member governments do not show this information with regard to loans made after 1965.

TABLE 8

Currency of Service Payments on IDB/FSO Loans
Through December 31, 1965

(percentages)

Percentage of total value of FSO loans which may/must be serviced in:	as to:	Principal	Interest
(1) Local currency (at borrower's option)		58	39
(2) Dollars (obligatory)		26	50
(3) Part local currency, part dollars:		16	11
(a) Portion to which local currency option applies		6	5
(b) Portion to which dollar requirement applies		10	6
(4) Total		100	100
(5) (1) + (3a)		64	44
(6) (2) + (3b)		36	56

Source: Tabulated from "Statement of Approved Loans as of December 31, 1965," IDB 1965 Annual Report (Washington, D.C., 1966), Appendix II-8, pp. 92-107.

namely, a loan to Ecuador that required amortization in dollars but permitting payment of interest in local currency.) Item 3 in the table refers to loans in which a portion of the amortization and/or interest payments--usually those due during the first half of a loan's maturity--are repayable in local currency, while those due in the remaining years must be paid in dollars. The U.S. Development Loan Fund earlier tried out a similar pattern on a number of its loans.

The author understands from IDB staff members that the last two years have seen a considerably higher proportion of local currency repayment in FSO lending than is shown in Table 8. This results from the fact that the U.S. Government has been willing to contribute dollars to the FSO at an annual rate--$250 million for three years from early 1965 and $300 million during 1968-70-- considerably higher than the Fund's initial dollar endowment of $146 million. Accordingly, there appears to be less need for dollar repayment as a means of replenishing the FSO's foreign-exchange resources than was originally believed.

The FSO has also used the interest rates and maturities on its loans as a vehicle of payments relief. Interest rates have varied according to a project's revenue-earning capacity within the limited range of 2.25 to 4.0 per cent, with a 0.75 per cent service charge being added in some cases. Maturities have taken into account project lifetimes, with technical assistance/preinvestment loans occupying a shorter range of 5 to 15 years and infrastructure projects running from 15 years to 30.

All dollar loans carry maintenance of value provisions, although loans of local currency do not. Nevertheless, in the event a member currency undergoes formal devaluation or, "in the opinion of the Bank, depreciate(s) to a significant extent," the member is required to "pay to the Bank within a reasonable time an additional amount of its own currency sufficient to maintain the value of all the currency of the member held by the Bank . . ., excepting currency derived from borrowings by the Bank."42 This provision in effect requires the member governments to maintain the value of future loan service payments on loans provided and payable in local currency (and at the same time enables the IDB to carry on its books at original dollar equivalent value most-- since early 1963, all--of the ordinary capital and FSO local currency loans, even in cases where the currency has already depreciated to such an extent as to reduce the current dollar value of such loans appreciably). Apart from political risks "a la Cuba" or commercial risks which the Bank bears to the extent that it uses its authority to lend to private enterprise without government guarantees, the only potential loss of value of FSO or ordinary capital local currency assets derived directly or indirectly from members' contributions and paid-in subscriptions arises from the opportunity cost of holding any short-term local currency balances in central bank accounts paying little or no interest. But this is insignificant compared with the leakages affecting U.S. local currency holdings.

A stringent maintenance of value requirement is logical for the IDB, given the chronic inflation and devaluation to which many of its members are subject. The comprehensive insurance against currency depreciation which the FSO enjoys by virtue of its maintenance of value provisions provides the foundation on which it can survive and make a success out of local currency repayment and relending over the long run. The Bank's ability to impose these provisions is also in itself a measure of the stronger bargaining power it has as a participant in the internal resource allocation process as compared with that of the U.S. Government. The latter, as we have already noted, felt obliged to forego maintenance of value on local currency loans out of P.L. 480 "sales" proceeds after March, 1959, and never felt itself in a position to insist on maintenance of value in regard to further uses of Mutual Security/DLF dollar loan service payments in local currency.

As of the end of 1967, 92 per cent of the SPTF's $525 million endowment had been committed, with all service payable in local currency on terms of either 3.5 per cent (on loans for water supplies and sewage systems) or 2 per cent (all other loans), both including a service charge of 0.75 per cent, and maturities ranging from 7 to 30 years, the great majority being 20 years or more. In 1964, after the United States' second capital contribution to the Fund, it was agreed that new resources would henceforth be channeled through the FSO, which would supplement its existing functions with the SPTF's former role in aiding social development. Once its dollar resources were exhausted, SPTF's activities would be limited to relending its local currency proceeds. Through 1967, apart from the $7.9 million participation in FSO loans, the SPTF had re-lent $16.1 million of its local currency proceeds by substituting them for part of the dollars allocated to cover local costs under the original loan agreements.[43] It had not yet made any direct loans exclusively in local currency.

While the SPTF's dollar loans require maintenance of value by the borrower, no such provision applies to its local currency proceeds, in contrast to those of ordinary capital and FSO, once they are paid over to the Fund. In other words, the SPTF is in the same situation as the U.S. Government with its Mutual Security DLF loans. Loss through currency depreciation as it affects local currency assets of the SPTF is an annual item in the Bank's income and expense statement. Through 1967, such losses had amounted to about $1.3 million on loan service payments totaling $48.5 million.[44] This "leakage" from the dollar value of the Fund's assets may be expected to continue indefinitely, unless and until the money is refunded to the United States or invested at interest rates high enough to compensate for exchange depreciation.

Given the objectives of the IDB, effective repayment of local currency-repayable loans does not mean the same thing for the Bank as it does for the U.S. Government. For the United States, it means, very simply, repayment in hard currency. The Bank, on the other hand, is intended to be a permanent regional institution channeling resources to and within Latin America and the Caribbean to further certain economic and social objectives. As a matter of form, the Bank's articles of agreement provide for a member's right to withdraw, followed by repurchase of its capital stock (though on terms dictated by the IDB), as well as for termination of the Bank by a two-thirds majority of the Governors representing three quarters of the voting stock. Moreover, the SPTF agreement allows the United States, in effect, to terminate the Fund unilaterally if it finds it to be "no longer necessary or that the purposes of the Fund can no longer be appropriately or effectively carried out."[45] It also provides that, upon termination, the Fund's net assets, including outstanding loans, revert to the United States.

Nevertheless, the present U.S. Administration and influential sections of Congress entertain no thought of getting any of the United States' cash contributions back into the Treasury in the foreseeable future. Instead, the United States would be only too happy to see the IDB act indefinitely as a stimulus to sound economic and social development in Latin America by applying regional direction, with U.S. participation, to the promotion of intraregional trade and movement of resources as well as the efficient execution of development projects. By and large, this would be acceptable to the Bank's other members as well. Thus, for the IDB, getting repayment of a loan to a country in the country's currency is already a meaningful form of repayment in that it permits the Bank to pursue its principal objectives in the country and, as we saw above, finance capital exports from that country to other Bank members. From the Bank's viewpoint, the ultimate effective repayment will have occurred when Latin America's economic position permits the Bank to use any of its local currencies to finance capital imports from outside the region.

THE AGENCY FOR INTERNATIONAL DEVELOPMENT (AID)

Since we earlier reviewed the process by which the new Kennedy Administration decided to shift from local currency-repayable project and program loans under the Development Loan Fund to dollar-repayable loans under the new AID, in this concluding section, it remains only to summarize developments in regard to AID terms since the agency was established.

The AID enabling legislation gave the administration considerable flexibility with regard to loan terms, providing merely that development loans were to be "payable as to principal and interest in United States dollars on such terms as (the President) may determine."[46] It is interesting to note, in view of the traditional banker's approach in Congress which was later to force AID to raise its interest rate, that a more populist, anti-usury attitude prevailed in the passage of the original (1961) Act for International Development, resulting in a provision which required that interest rates not be "excessive or unreasonable for the borrower and in no event higher than the applicable legal rate of interest of the country in which the loan is made."[47]

Only in the Kennedy Administration's second year, after a lengthy discussion of the question of loan terms, did AID finally adopt formal guidelines on the subject. Most countries would receive their development loans at 0.75 per cent interest, with a 10-year grace period for principal repayment and 40-year final maturity. The few countries nearing self-sustaining growth, or enjoying a favorable balance-of-payments position because of a strong export sector (e.g., petroleum), would pay 0.75, 3.5, or 5.75 per cent with grace periods not exceeding 5 years and final maturities, including grace periods, of 15 to 25 years. Serious consideration had been given within AID to having yet a third category, comprising the economically weakest countries, who would get AID loans on IDA terms (see section on IDA above). However, it appears that AID may have decided 50 years was stretching the concept of a repayable loan a bit too far and that it would be in the interest of harmonious relations with Congress to fix slightly harder terms than IDA. On the lower end, 30 years was only a little longer than what is usually regarded as the upper end of the hard loan scale--i.e., 25 years. Amidst these considerations, it is quite likely that 40 years emerged as a compromise solution.

Despite AID's attempt to mollify Congress by holding down the loan maturities, the 0.75 interest rate was a red flag to a number of members of both houses, who applied continual pressure to have Congress step in and specify minimum terms, thereby curbing the flexibility permitted by the original act. In January, 1964, Congress fixed a minimum rate of 2 per cent after the 10-year grace period; and, in October of the same year, it set minimum rates of 1 per cent during the grace period and 2.5 per cent thereafter. In November, 1967, it nibbled again, raising the minimum rate during the grace period to 2 per cent. The psychology behind these moves is revealed in a letter written by the promoter of the latest change, Senator Peter H. Dominick, to The New York Times after the paper had published an editorial criticizing it. After noting that the weighted average interest rate on DAC member countries' loans in 1966 was 3.1 per cent, Dominick wrote, "The current pressures of our economy unfortunately have dictated cutbacks in both domestic and foreign spending. Under these circumstances, it is my feeling that U.S. citizens should not have to pay at least twice the interest rate a foreign nation must pay in order to borrow funds from the United States Government."[48]

Through June 30, 1967, AID had applied 0.75 per cent, 40-year terms (or, after January, 1964, 40-year terms with the minimum interest rates established from time to time by Congress) to 93 per cent of the total of $6.4 billion worth of development loans obligated by then. Some 47 loans worth a total of $433 million had been extended on other than the most favorable terms, the weighted average maturity of these being 22.4 years (range: 8 to 30) and their interest rates varying between 0.75 and 5.75 per cent.[49] Although obvious candidates for harder-than-minimum terms such as Iran, Israel, Greece, Thailand, Venezuela, and Taiwan were among the recipients of these loans, a number were made in countries to which most AID loans were going on the softest terms. In many such cases, the borrower was a revenue-earning entity that would be expected to pay harder terms. Normally, in lending to such entities, AID has used the two-step procedure; in fact, nearly half of all AID development loans have been of the two-step variety. However, in some cases, there have been administrative obstacles to making a loan through the government concerned to the end-user.

Another aspect of AID loan terms is the insertion in all loan agreements with effect from May 8, 1962, of a renegotiation clause according to which the borrower agrees to negotiate, any time after six months prior to the scheduled date of the first amortization payment, acceleration of the loan maturity. There are two standard versions of the clause, one for Latin America, stressing the partnership aspect of the Alliance for Progress, and another for all other countries. The clauses stipulate criteria to be used in determining whether acceleration is called for; these comprise judgmental factors such as "significant improvement" and "favorable trends" in key economic parameters, the "success" of projects and extent to which they have created capital for reinvestment elsewhere, etc. In insisting on these clauses, the United States has in mind the example of the Marshall Plan countries, some of which have voluntarily accelerated their repayments to the United States even in the absence of renegotiation clauses in the Marshall Plan loan agreements. Nevertheless, given the fact that the discrepancies in living standards between, on one hand, the United States and those Marshall Plan countries that have accelerated their loan repayments, and, on the other, the United States and the less-developed countries it is now aiding, are of an entirely different order of magnitude and that the latter discrepancies are unlikely to decrease in the foreseeable future, there is a strong chance that the United States and the countries in question will interpret the renegotiation criteria rather differently in practice. The case of Japan is relevant here. By the standards of most less-developed countries, Japan is very well off, yet the Japanese Government points to the country's low per capita income relative to other industrial nations--according to AID data Japan's per capita GNP was $922 in 1966 compared with $1,150 for Italy, the next lowest DAC member--in justifying its failure to offer soft terms on its aid.*

In addition to its development loans, as of June 30, 1967, AID had lent 606 million appropriated dollars under other titles of its act, notably "supporting assistance" and "contingency" funds and a special authority called the Inter-American Social and Economic Program. The President was authorized to furnish "supporting assistance" "on such terms and conditions as he may determine, in order to support or promote economic or political stability."[50] The section governing contingency assistance was even more vague, specifying merely that it was to be

*For example, this was the position of the Japanese representative at the April, 1963, High Level DAC meeting on terms of aid.

used "in accordance with the provisions applicable" to the economic assistance part of the act.[51] "Supporting assistance" largely replaced earlier categories of general budgetary and balance-of-payments aid which had been extended primarily on a grant basis, and the Kennedy Administration promised Congress that it would use these funds exclusively for loans. Included in $430 million which AID had lent through fiscal 1967 under "supporting assistance" was $60 million in local currency-repayable (3.5 per cent, 40-year, with maintenance of value) loans to Morocco, AID's only local currency-repayable dollar loans. Morocco had insisted on a continuation of the pre-AID terms on this aid as part of the price for U.S. base rights in that country. Other "supporting assistance" loans carried interest rates of 0.75 to 4.5 per cent and maturities of 10 to 40 years, the weighted averages being 2.4 per cent and 29 years respectively. Contingency fund loans totaling $46 million were made at 1.0 to 4.5 per cent interest and 10 to 40-year maturities, the weighted averages being 3.1 per cent and 25 years respectively. Of the loan funds advanced under the Inter-American Social and Economic Program, 90 per cent consisted of a $100 million loan to Chile in the wake of that country's 1960 earthquake. Terms were 0.75 per cent, 30 years.[52]

NOTES TO CHAPTER 4

1. Congressman Harold Cooley, Statement in the U.S. House of Representatives on April 26, 1961. Congressional Record (87th Cong., 1st Sess.), p. 6311.

2. As Professor Thomas Schelling noted in 1957, "getting the money back should be the least of the considerations, if the program is really as important as the President and others have implied." "American Aid and Economic Development: Some Critical Issues" in International Stability and Progress: United States Interests and Instruments (New York: The American Assembly, 1957), p. 157.

3. Tabulated from U.S. International Cooperation Administration, Operations Report, December 31, 1960, table on "Obligations against Loans Authorized under the Mutual Security Program," pp. 28-29.

4. Clive S. Gray, "The Spectrum of International Capital Transfer to the Underdeveloped Countries" (Unpublished Ph.D. dissertation, Department of Economics, Harvard University, 1964), pp. 206-207.

5. U.S. Agency for International Development, Office of the Controller, Status of Loan Agreements as of June 30, 1967 (Report No. W-224), p. 1.

6. U.S. Development Loan Fund, Terminal Report (Washington, D.C., January, 1962).

7. U.S. AID, op. cit.

8. U.S. DLF, op. cit., Schedule 3 in financial statements.

9. This figure was derived as follows. From a comparison of local currency loan service payments received up to November, 1961 (according to U.S. DLF, op. cit.), and June, 1967 (U.S. AID, op. cit.), the author estimated cumulative totals of such payments received in Yugoslavia, India, and Israel up to the dates of the devaluations in those three countries (July, 1965; June, 1966; and November, 1967, respectively). The estimated loss is the percentage of devaluation times the payments in question.
In a formal sense, some of the local currency might already have been spent on U.S. agency programs and thus escaped devaluation. However, in all three countries, the United States has large excess currency balances reserved for U.S. uses as a result of P.L. 480 operations, and whether it is these funds or DLF payments that are sold to U.S. agencies is an arbitrary matter.

10. U.S. DLF, op. cit., p. 4.

11. Tabulated from U.S. AID, op. cit.

12. U.S. House of Representatives, Committee on Foreign Affairs, Hearings on the Foreign Assistance Act (90th Cong., 1st Sess.), 1967, p. 342.

13. Gray, op. cit., p. 234.

14. Edward S. Mason et al., The Problem of Excess Accumulation of U.S.-Owned Local Currencies (Washington, D.C.: Department of State, 1960; mimeograph), p. 25.

15. U.S. Treasury Department, Fiscal Service, Bureau of Accounts, Semiannual Report of Collections under Title I, P.L. 480 Sales Agreements, June 30, 1967, pp. 1 and 75; U.S. President, The Annual Report on Activities Carried Out under Public Law 480, 83rd Congress, as Amended, during the Period January 1 through December 31, 1967, Appendix Tables 15 and 16.

16. U.S. House of Representatives, Committee on Agriculture, The Eleventh Semiannual Report on Activities Carried on under Public Law 480, 83rd Congress, As Amended (86th Cong., 2nd Sess.; House Doc. 335), 1960, p. 7.

17. U.S. House of Representatives, Committee on Agriculture, Food for Peace--1965 Annual Report on Public Law 480 (89th Cong., 2nd Sess.; House Doc. 457), 1966, p. 27.

18. Ibid., p. 26.

19. Ibid., Table 13, p. 139.

20. When he heard about a four-year $1.3 billion Title I agreement with India which provided for granting the Indian Government outright 42.5 per cent of the proceeds, Congressman Cooley, who has as much interest as anyone else in curbing surplus commodity stockpiles without loss of farm income, commented, "I hope that will not be a pattern for all the transactions hereafter to follow." Congressional Record (87th Cong., 1st Sess.), p. 6312.

21.   U.S. AID, op. cit., p. 1.

22.   U.S. House of Representatives, Agricultural Trade Development and Assistance Act of 1954 and Amendments (Washington, D.C.: Government Printing Office, 1966), p. 34.

23.   U.S. AID, op. cit.

24.   U.S. House of Representatives, Agricultural Trade Development and Assistance Act of 1954 and Amendments, loc. cit.

25.   U.S. AID, op. cit., p. 1.

26.   Ibid.

27.   Edward S. Mason et al., op. cit., Appendix I, p. 6.

28.   U.S. AID, U.S. Overseas Loans and Grants and Assistance from International Organizations: Obligations and Loan Authorizations, July 1, 1945-June 30, 1966, March 17, 1967.

29.   U.S. House of Representatives, Agricultural Trade Development and Assistance Act of 1954 and Amendments, p. 41.

30.   Quoted by Harlan Cleveland in "The Convalescence of Foreign Aid," American Economic Review, Papers and Proceedings of the 71st Annual Meeting of the American Economic Association, December, 1958, Vol. XLIX, No. 2 (May, 1959), p. 223.

31.   Eugene R. Black, "Finance for the Grcwth of India," Commerce (Bombay), December, 1958 (IBRD reprint).

32.   International Development Association, Articles of Agreement and Accompanying Report of the Executive Directors (Washington, D.C., January 26, 1960), p. 11.

33.   Ibid., pp. 11-12.

34.   U.S. House of Representatives, Subcommittee of the Committee on Appropriations, Hearings on Foreign Operations Appropriations for 1962, Part 2, (87th Cong., 1st Sess.), 1961, p. 91.

35.   Calculated from appendixes C and E to the financial statements of the International Development Association in IBRD/IDA, Annual Report 1966/1967 (Washington, D.C., 1967), pp. 58-59 and 61-62. Expenditure is taken as equal to 90 per cent of paid-in subscriptions of Part II IDA members, less currencies of those members held by the Association.

36.   Inter-American Development Bank, Agreement Establishing the Inter-American Development Bank (Washington, D.C., 1965), p. 12.

37.   Ibid.

38.   Ibid., p. 13.

39.   IDB, Proposal for an Increase in the Resources of the Inter-American Development Bank (Washington, D.C., April, 1967), p. 25.

40.   According to financial statements in the IDB's 1967 Annual Report (Washington, D.C.), the U.S. share was as follows on December 31, 1967: $761.8 million out of $1,778.8 million in the ordinary capital resources; $1,800.0 million out of $2,303.7 million in the Fund for Special Operations; and $525 million out of $525 million in the Social Progress Trust Fund, for a total of approximately $3.1 out of $4.6 billion.

41.   Ibid., p. 115.

42.   IDB, Agreement Establishing the Inter-American Development Bank, p. 13.

43.   Tabulated from SPTF loan statement, IDB 1967 Annual Report, pp. 130-139.

44.   Tabulated from Annex III-2, Social Progress Trust Fund financial statements, IDB Annual Reports for 1962-67.

45.   IDB, Social Progress Trust Fund Agreement (Washington, D.C., 1964), p. 9.

46.   The Act for International Development of 1961 (P.L. 87-195, 87th Cong., 1st Sess.), Sept. 4, 1961, Sec. 201(b), p. 2.

47.   Ibid., Sec. 201(d), p. 3.

48.   The New York Times, September 9, 1967, p. 30C.

49.   Tabulated from data in U.S. AID, Status of Loan Agreements.

50.   The Act for International Development of 1961, Sec. 401, p. 10.

51.   Ibid., Sec. 451, p. 10.

52.   Figures in this paragraph were tabulated from data in U.S. AID, Status of Loan Agreements.

DETERMINING OPTIMUM FINANCIAL
TERMS ON RESOURCE TRANSFER

CHAPTER   **5**   CONSTRAINTS ON
FINANCIAL TERMS

In this second part of the book, we will examine various
ways and means of determining quantitatively what the weighted
average terms on resource transfer to a less-developed country
or a group of such countries, or a residual part of such transfer,
should be, given certain targets to be met by the transfer and
constraints to which it is subject. The different modes of analysis
suggested below are fitted to data supposedly representing the
economic circumstances of "typical" less-developed countries;
and, from the results of these exercises, certain policy recommendations for the governments and multilateral agencies that are
major sources of capital and other resources to the less-developed
world are formulated. On the other hand, since the governments
and multilateral agencies concerned, or at least certain elements
within them, have already adopted policies along the lines of our
recommendations, or have been proposing such policies for a number of years on the basis of considerations very similar to those
on which our analysis is based, the analysis may be regarded more
accurately as providing further quantitative support for these
policies.

Any quantitative analysis designed to show what we propose
to show hereunder--i.e., what the average terms on resource transfer should be--must be made up of three principal elements. These
are: (1) one or more objectives which the resource transfer is
supposed to help achieve; (2) one or more constraints to which the
transfer is subject; and (3) a macro model of the economy or
economies benefiting from the transfer, projecting various magnitudes in the course of development and relating them to the transfer
terms via the service flows generated by these terms. In reviewing the current literature below, we will consider several alternative modes of analysis which comprise the foregoing elements,
implicitly or explicitly. In regard to the first and third elements
above, these analyses are very similar. They pose essentially
the same objective for resource transfer, namely, to supplement
domestic resources in the less-developed countries and thus help
them raise their rate of increase of national income above that
attainable solely with domestic resources. The more systematic

of these analyses go on to specify a target rate of growth that will allow for both a fast enough increase in per capita consumption to maintain political stability and sufficient investment out of domestic resources to launch the receiving countries into a self-sustaining growth process within a "reasonable" period of time.

As regards macroeconomic models, the literature treats the development of debt-servicing capacity as a function of over-all growth. Less-developed countries are assumed to start out with a deficit between attainable domestic savings and the rate of investment required to achieve acceptable economic growth, or between attainable exports and the imports required to the same end--the two deficits are equivalent ex post, but causative factors relevant to a particular country will normally dictate focusing on one more than the other. Resource transfer from abroad is then assumed to occur at a level that will cover both this basic deficit and the increment to it that arises from the benefiting country's obligation to service the transfer on specified terms. The standard model projects domestic savings (or exports) as growing more rapidly than investment (or imports), so that the need for foreign resources eventually declines and, in some variants, becomes negative, representing the stage at which less-developed countries can start to amortize the resource transfer.

It is in regard to their assumed constraints that the analyses reviewed below differ significantly. A "constraint" in this context means a set of specifications indicating how a system of quantitative relationships is to be solved for an unknown policy variable, in this case one or another aspect of terms on resource transfer. The constraint will normally direct that a particular variable in the system be minimized or maximized or that it be set equal to some value determined outside the system. In the next few paragraphs, we examine and evaluate a number of alternative constraints suggested in the recent literature, eventually selecting five as a basis for our quantitative analysis in Chapters 6 through 9. Chapter 9 summarizes this analysis by drawing the policy conclusions referred to above.

REVIEW OF RECENT LITERATURE

Our review of the recent literature begins with the two very similar papers by Wilson Schmidt (1964) and Richard Cooper (1965).[1] Their point of departure is the concept of a "grant equivalent" in resource transfer, described by John Pincus in a 1963 article.[2] A grant equivalent is the face value of a resource transfer less the discounted stream of required future service payments. The grant equivalent to the recipient is obtained by discounting the stream of service payments at his marginal rate of return on capital, and that to the source of the transfer by discounting at the marginal rate applicable in the source's country. The Schmidt-Cooper constraint is as follows:

(I) For a given grant equivalent to the recipient (a less-developed country), the grant equivalent to the source should be minimized.

If the appropriate discount rate is the same for both recipient and source, the grant equivalent will likewise be the same for both, and no manipulation of terms will alter this relationship. The interesting cases arise, therefore, when the discount rate is different. In the case where the recipient's discount rate exceeds the source's, Schmidt shows that the constraint is fulfilled by making a loan rather than a grant and by increasing the size of the loan while stiffening its terms (i.e., raising the interest rate and/or shortening the maturity). Alternatively, Cooper shows in the same case that, with the face value of the loan held constant, the constraint can be fulfilled by lengthening the loan's maturity while raising its interest rate. These points are intuitively clear when one reflects that, because of the recipient's higher discount rate, a larger volume of service payments will be discounted relatively more from the recipient's point of view, even over a shorter period of time, than from the source's viewpoint, and that (reflecting Cooper's point) this discrepancy increases as the discount period lengthens. For quantitative proofs, the reader is referred to the two papers themselves.

In the case where the recipient's discount rate is less than the source's, both writers show that the constraint is fulfilled, formally, when the source makes a grant to the recipient which the latter invests in the source country, taking home the income earned on it as desired. On the more realistic assumption that the aid proceeds will still be invested in the recipient country, Schmidt shows that the constraint is fulfilled by making a grant rather than a loan on any positive terms. As to how likely it is that the recipient's discount rate will, in fact, be less than the source's, the two writers take differing stands. Cooper's view is that "the proper application of external resources will raise output in most less-developed countries by more than the same resources will raise output in the developed countries."[3] (He does, however, qualify this by noting that absorptive capacity limits the volume of resources to which this statement applies and that " 'proper application' may involve expenditures very different from mere installation of capital goods.") Cooper also states that, if the marginal rate of return on capital is, in fact, less in the less-developed countries, "then much of the extant literature on economic development is misguided."[4] Schmidt, on the other hand, is neutral on this question in his text; and, in a footnote, he cites three authoritative references to suggest that "the real return on capital is not necessarily higher in underdeveloped than in advanced countries."[5]

I myself wholeheartedly endorse this view and take the even stronger position that the real return is, in fact, generally lower in less-developed countries. The basic reason for this is that, because of high unit costs of production arising from such factors as inefficiency of labor and management, a less-developed infrastructure, and restricted economies of scale due to a limited market, the proportion of real output, even when valued at domestic prices inflated by protection, available for allocation to capital is less at the margin in less-developed than in advanced countries. In a world where resources, including labor, were perfectly mobile, this condition would soon be corrected, but the unreality of perfect mobility is obvious to all and is as much an assumption of the Cooper argument as it is of our contrasting view.

Schmidt and Cooper consider a number of constraints on resource transfer that are either alternatives or complementary to their own. Schmidt lists seven alternatives and quickly demolishes them as having little or no economic validity. (He does not consider the question of how far the alternatives influence the actual behavior of aid sources in the real world and are likely to continue doing so. This is, of course, a different but, from many points of view, no less important question.) The seven alternative constraints are:

(II)   The poorer the recipient, the more appropriate are grants rather than loans. Schmidt's counterargument: Poverty is irrelevant "since it is always possible to provide a loan under terms that give the same net gain to the borrower as any grant which might be offered."[6]

(III)   Loans are appropriate to revenue-earning projects, while nonrevenue-earning projects require grants. Counterargument: If nonrevenue-earning projects net the economy as a whole a return commensurate with the capital invested, as they should if they are undertaken at all, then the government can appropriate, via taxes or reductions in other expenditures, as much of this return as is needed to remit service payments.

(IV)   Grants are preferable to loans "where payment prospects in foreign exchange are dim because of balance of payments difficulties."[7] Counterargument: The terms on a loan can always be adjusted so as to take the real burden of servicing it in foreign exchange into account when equating its net benefit to the recipient with that of a grant.

(V)   Loans evoke greater financial discipline than grants on the part of the recipient, and are therefore likely to be used more efficiently. Counterargument: This is true only if the recipient acts irrationally. The best allocation of funds depends on the comparative benefits derived from alternative uses, not on source or terms.

(VI) Grants are more appropriate for financing outright consumption, which yields little or no return that can be appropriated for service payments. Counterargument: Just because aid is provided for the nominal purpose of consumption and may even comprise physical shipments of consumer goods (e.g., surplus foodstuffs) does not mean its net economic impact is to increase consumption by an equivalent amount or even any significant amount at all. Such aid usually represents just another convenient vehicle for development assistance.

(VII) Loans are preferable to grants because they cost the source less. Counterargument: If cost to the source were the ruling consideration, it could be minimized by extending no aid at all. As already shown, the cost relationship between loans and grants depends on comparative discount rates in the recipient and source countries; if the rate is higher in the source country, a given grant equivalent can always be extended to the recipient more cheaply in the form of a grant than a loan.

(VIII) Grants are appropriate vehicles of aid to countries that are particularly friendly to the source country, while loans are more suitable in the case of less friendly countries. Counterargument: The basis for this constraint is entirely noneconomic.

I acknowledge the validity, on economic grounds, of all of Schmidt's counterarguments. Yet, in my view, he has set up and demolished a straw man. Several of these alternative constraints are applied in practice more to effect a division of labor between different types of resource transfer within a package of aid to a particular country than as indicators of the weighted average terms suitable for transfers to any country, which is the central problem that Schmidt and we are concerned with. In Chapters 6-9, we discuss models based on five alternative constraints, none of which Schmidt even mentions and all of which I will try to show are of much greater importance to our central problem than any of the above alternatives II through VIII or even constraint No. I, on which both the Schmidt and Cooper analyses are based. Cooper, on the other hand, introduces two alternatives closely related to our fifth constraint below. These are, in Cooper's words, that:

(IX) "Donor governments may place a ceiling on the total gross flow of capital, public and private, to the less-developed countries, regardless of the grant element"; and

(X) "Donor governments may place limits both on the grant element in aid to less-developed countries and on the total gross capital flow--at least the total flow from public sources."[8]

It was precisely in order to explore the implications of these constraints for U.S. aid policy that Evsey Domar published an article as early as 1950.[9] The Domar model forms the basis for our discussion in Chapter 9 of a close variant of constraint No. X. As Cooper treats them, under the first (No. IX above), the total gross resource flow required to transfer a given grant equivalent to the recipient is obviously minimized by putting as much of it as possible in the form of outright grants. Cooper shows that the optimum form of aid under the second constraint is "a perpetual loan, that is, a loan without fixed maturity."[10] This technique maximizes the grant equivalent to the recipient for given ceilings on total gross aid and on the grant equivalent from the source, the latter ceiling being reached by adjusting the interest rate on the gross outflow. It can be argued that the concept of a perpetual loan is approximated by a maturity as long as 50 years, such as applies to loans from the World Bank's IDA. The same can be said of loans repayable in the borrower's currency, where it is understood that the service payments will be reinvested in the same country until its economy is adjudged strong enough to afford repayment in convertible currency, or of other loans subject to a renegotiation provision, such as that employed by U.S. AID (see Chapter 4).

Writing in the Economic Journal, A. Qayum of the American University at Cairo has built a contribution to this analysis on an entirely different constraint, namely, that:

(XI) Loan terms should be such that the net additional savings which accrue in an economy within the period of maturity of the loan(s) in question as a result of investing the loan proceeds are no less than total required service payments, including amortization.[11] The savings effect in question is estimated by multiplying a constant marginal savings ratio, defined as unity less the "over-all marginal propensity to consume,"[12] times the net output resulting from investment of the foreign aid, which is derived from a constant capital/output ratio. Qayum further assumes that net additional savings in each year is invested in the following year and yields additional output in accordance with the same capital/output ratio, with the same proportion of output as above being saved and invested in the next year, and so on indefinitely. In effect, Qayum is, therefore, discounting loan service payments at a rate equal to the marginal propensity to save divided by the capital/output ratio. Since there is no direct relationship between this parameter of Qayum's and the marginal return on capital by which Pincus, Schmidt, Cooper, and others discount loan service payments, the two parameters will normally give different quantitative results. Thus, looking at the same less-developed economy, there exists a wide range of loan terms such that Qayum would advise less-developed countries to accept loans on these terms (assuming them to be the best available) whereas the others cited would consider the terms too onerous, and, of course, vice versa. The question therefore arises: Who is right?

In my view, Qayum's thesis suffers from basic confusion arising out of partial equilibrium analysis of phenomena that have to be examined in a more general equilibrium context. Thus, if one is considering the aggregate debt service payments, including amortization, generated by a single loan or loan package, as Qayum is doing, then one must also take into account at least two other factors. These are (1) the gross and net availability of additional foreign capital, and (2) the comparative net contribution to national product of (a) investments for whose execution the loan is responsible, i.e., which would not have been carried out in the loan's absence, not necessarily the investments with which the loan is nominally associated, and (b) future investments which must be foregone in order to direct savings not generated by the investments under (1) into service payments on the loan. Thus, if the loan's maturity is so short as to require diversion of savings not generated by investments resulting from the loan, the otherwise foregone investments may, nevertheless, be carried out with the help of new foreign loans, and it will not be true, as Qayum says, that "it is harmful . . . to borrow foreign capital from the very long-term point of view."[13] Admittedly, if the country refinances cumulatively at short term, it is likely to find itself sooner or later in a credit squeeze, but this is quite a different problem from what Qayum is talking about. Moreover, even assuming no new foreign loans are available, if the projected net national product created by the foregone investments is no greater than that of the investments undertaken with the help of the foreign loan, accepting the loan and undertaking these latter investments will not reduce national income below the level that would otherwise have prevailed. In fact, the reverse is likely to be true, because the net national product foregone by diverting a relatively small quantum of savings resulting from the investments in question will normally be small in relation to that created by the investments.

On the other hand, under the Qayum formula, it is also possible to approve a foreign loan whose acceptance and use will make the borrowing country worse off. To demonstrate this, let us assume--something which is not only conceivable but frequently happens--that the uses available at the margin for additional capital are too inefficient to generate any profits or interest on invested capital, although decpreciation charges are covered. It is still possible for the factors employed in the projects in question to have a marginal propensity to save comparable with that of the economy as a whole. Now let us assume that the net additional savings generated directly and indirectly by the investment are exactly equal to required loan service payments in each successive year and are appropriated by the government to meet these obligations. In practice, the government will not be able to catch all such savings in the hands of those whose savings have risen because of the investment in question--many of these will be channeled directly into new investment. However, in theory, the government can appropriate the required amount of savings in the economy at large, either by taxation or borrowing. If it does so by taxation, then there will have been no net additional private savings as a result of the investment, since a private party's taxes are not his savings. Instead, the increment will have occurred in public savings. However, if an investment recoups for the government in taxes an amount equal to service charges on the capital required to finance it, then it is no longer unprofitable, contrary to our earlier assumption. For this assumption to hold, it is necessary for the government to appropriate the savings increment via borrowing. But, in order to borrow, the government, like everyone else, has to pay interest. All new resources generated directly or indirectly by the investment in question are already accounted for, so the government will have to tap additional resources in order to pay the interest. And at least part of these additional resources would have been invested to bring further growth, which must now be sacrificed. Over time, the additional value contributed by the original investment will be offset by this sacrifice; and, although the situation meets Qayum's criteria for a growth-enhancing loan, the need to pay debt service at the assumed rate on the loan will lead to a reduction in the level of national income that would otherwise have held.

In a partial equilibrium analysis of the terms of a particular loan or loan package, I do not see how one can avoid taking into account the net return on the invested proceeds or making some assumption about the future availability of gross capital inflow. The Alter model described below, which will be used extensively in the following chapters, assumes, somewhat like Qayum, that the difference between aggregate domestic savings and investment, ex post a measure of the net foreign balance, is available to finance debt service. The model makes an explicit assumption about amortization and the relationship between gross and net capital inflow but says nothing about the return on capital. In the light of what we have said about Qayum's analysis, it would be fair to state that the Alter model makes the implicit assumption that the marginal return on capital is at least as high as the return on foreign loans. Otherwise, the model's assumptions about the relationship between investment and growth would sooner or later be nullified.

We conclude our review of the literature by referring to an analysis that has been developed over a number of years in the World Bank and is described comprehensively in Economic Growth and External Debt, by Dragoslav Avramovic and associates in the Bank's Economic Department.[14] The model on which this analysis (and most of our own in Chapters 6-8) is based was first elaborated by Gerald M. Alter, now director of the World Bank's Western Hemisphere Department, as long ago as 1953 in an unpublished Bank paper,[15] the following year in his Ph.D. dissertation at Harvard,[16] and in 1957 in a paper delivered at a roundtable of the International Economic Association, proceedings of which were published in 1961.[17] A broader version of this model was developed in the Bank in 1956 and used implicitly in two studies of debt-servicing capacity written by Avramovic and Ravi Gulhati and published in 1958 and 1960, respectively.[18]

Underlying this Bank analysis are two concepts of how to appraise the debt-servicing capacity or "creditworthiness" of less-developed countries. From a slightly different viewpoint, both of these concepts, as well as a third which the Avramovic book hints at briefly, may be regarded as constraints on the terms of resource transfer. Couched in language appropriate to this use, the three constraints, listed in the order in which we consider them in Chapters 6-8 and numbered in the series starting with Schmidt, are as follows:

(XII) The weighted average return on resource transfer to a less-developed country should be no greater than will enable the country to maintain a reasonable economic growth rate independently of such transfer within a specified period of time, "independence" being defined as meeting one of the three following alternative criteria: (1) the country's foreign liabilities increase at no higher rate than its national income; (2) the liabilities do not increase at all; or (3) the liabilities are fully refunded and thus reduced to zero. (This will be referred to below as the "independence constraint.")

(XIII) The weighted average terms (including amortization of principal) should be no more severe than will enable the benefiting country to maintain its ratio of annual foreign investment service liabilities to current foreign-exchange earnings at or below a specified level. (This will be referred to below as the "debt service ratio constraint.")

(XIV) The weighted average terms (including amortization) should be no more severe than will enable the sources of such transfer to match it with acceptable end-uses other than refinancing of existing liabilities. (This will be referred to below as the "end-use constraint.")

Yet another constraint, which is closely related to XII above and is given qualitative weight by a number of capital sources, although it is not mentioned in any of the World Bank literature, is the following:

(XV) The weighted average return on resource transfer should be no greater than will cause foreign liabilities to rise to a level where they bear an acceptable ratio to the benefiting country's national output. (This will be referred to below as the "debt burden constraint.")

Barring a rephrasing below of Cooper's constraints numbered IX and X above, this completes the list of constraints to be analyzed

in this study. The list does not purport to be exhaustive, and undoubtedly there exist constraints not mentioned above which are
currently applied or, if not, deserve to be applied by capital
sources and recipients. For example, Avramovic et al. note the
existence of "countries in which the relationship of public debt
service to public revenue portrays more accurately the liquidity
problem."[19] As the extreme example of this, they cite the case
where a country lacks control over its own money supply, as was
then (but is no longer) the case in the three territories of East
Africa. On the other hand, even where a government can create
internal credit at will by borrowing from its monetary authority,
capital sources and responsible authorities in the borrowing
countries themselves wish to avoid a situation where service payments on public foreign debt can be financed only in this manner.
Because of the rapid spillover of large-scale credit creation into
inflation and--thence, in most less-developed countries--imports,
use of credit powers would quickly bring a country up against the
familiar real resource limitations on savings and exports.

Capital sources therefore assess the creditworthiness of a
government in the light of its real resource position, with particular
reference to its revenue sources, expenditure commitments, and
access to real savings. Problems of economic backwardness that
severely limit the savings or exports which a country can be expected to reserve for future debt service, at least in comparison
with its present thirst for resources with which to strengthen its
economy, also affect its government's ability to allocate finance
for debt service by raising taxes or curbing expenditures. Factors
making for instability in less-developed countries' export earnings and rigidity in their import requirements have their analogues
in regard to government revenues and expenditures, respectively.

Since a sizable portion of resource transfer to less-developed
countries does not pass through the governments concerned, governmental creditworthiness is a less general constraint on aid
terms than the principal constraints listed above. Furthermore,
much of the resource transfer that does pass through local official
channels is on-lent to statutory organizations or private bodies
that are expected to earn a commercial return on their money.
Even so, it would be useful to analyze a model relating aid terms
to capital inflow requirements for infrastructure investments
sponsored by governments and to trends in public revenues and
expenditures. It is to be hoped that the thorough research efforts
of the World Bank's Economic Staff in the whole area of debt-
servicing capacity will soon generate data usable in such an exercise. Unfortunately, our study will have to ignore what might be
called the "government finance constraint."

RELATIONSHIP BETWEEN AID TERM CONSTRAINTS
AND CREDITWORTHINESS

Since constraints numbered XII and XIII are introduced in the literature in the context of appraising creditworthiness, and numbers XIV and XV are equally applicable to such an appraisal, it will be of interest to see how creditworthiness is defined in the context of resource transfer to less-developed countries and how this definition can be translated into constraints on aid terms. In general, the extent of a borrower's creditworthiness is measured as the probability that the repayment terms of a loan agreement, covering both interest and principal, will be fulfilled on the time schedule specified therein. This, in turn, depends on the probability that the borrower will have assets at his disposal in the future which will suffice to meet the repayment obligations. In domestic borrowing, such assets may be fixed, subject to sale if necessary to meet debt service obligations; the counterpart in international lending to fixed assets is a country's foreign-exchange reserves. Alternatively, assets for debt-servicing may be available out of current income--this is the situation preferred by creditors; or the borrower may be able to refinance his obligations by contracting additional loans. However, the traditional definition of creditworthiness rules out a situation where the borrower would be dependent on his original creditor to refinance the debt--for then the creditor is, de facto, not getting his money back. A more complete definition of the traditional concept of creditworthiness would be the probability of a creditor's being repaid in circumstances (other than, say, nuclear war) when he himself would choose not to refinance the debt. The fact that the creditor may, when the time comes, be willing to make further loans, thus retaining an income-earning investment in the borrower's enterprise, because the investment is attractive in relation to other possible uses of the money, is irrelevant to assessing creditworthiness at the time the original loan is made.

Those countries that attracted large infusions of private capital before World War I were creditworthy in traditional terms, because, although they may have depended on further infusions of capital to "roll over" their existing debt, any individual lender could expect that others like him would come forward to, in effect, refinance his loan, without his being compelled to do it himself or else see the loan go into outright default. The case of present-day lending to less-developed countries offers several contrasts with this earlier situation. In the first place, the differences in income levels between the capital sources and less-developed countries of today are of a wholly different order of magnitude from the differences between pre-World War I European incomes and incomes of the main beneficiaries of capital transfer at that time. One of the consequences of the extreme relative poverty of today's beneficiaries is that they cannot build an adequate economic base to service their foreign debts and simultaneously increase per capita incomes at rates acceptable over the long run within a non-Communist political framework if net infusions of foreign resources take place only in brief spurts, as was the case in earlier days. Rather, to attain such targets, many less-developed countries will require, as Göran Ohlin has reported to the Development Assistance Committee of OECD, "a large and sustained net inflow of foreign exchange."[20] Thus, any lender to today's less-developed countries cannot help being much more aware than the pre-World War I investor that the prospects of his being repaid depend on a continuing volume of net inflow of capital to his debtors.

Furthermore, because of the political risks involved in lending today--notably the ever-present possibility that a government will come under the control of elements who will repudiate all foreign debts--alongside the opportunities that exist for earning high returns inside the industrialized countries, private loan capital is generally deterred from the type of investment that contributed to prewar development. Instead, the main sources of debt capital today are a limited number of governments and intergovernmental institutions. Like the oligopolist in contrast to the micronistic perfect competitor, today's source can discern clearly the impact of his own activity in a limited field and is aware that his failure to refinance the maturing debt owed to him, if not explicitly then at least by maintaining a constant stream of aid to new projects, would create a severe danger of default. Thus, the concept of creditworthiness in de facto use today in lending to less-developed countries is considerably more lenient than the traditional one.

To define this modern concept, we return to the constraints in the foregoing section. The definition underlying Gerald Alter's analysis, translated by us into constraint No. XII, is that a country is creditworthy for capital inflow on given terms only if it can be expected with a reasonable probability to meet a given independence target (i.e., reduce the rate of increase of debt to that of national income, reduce this rate to zero, or reduce debt itself to zero, by a specified future date), on the assumption that any debt that matures before either of the first two targets is reached or matures more rapidly than the country can repay it enroute to the third target, will be refinanced at no higher rate of return. The alternative definition underlying the concept of a debt service ratio in our constraint No. XIII is that a country is creditworthy for capital inflow on given terms only if the inflow in question, and any additional inflow likely to take place within the relevant period, will not saddle the country with a ratio of debt service to exports that creates an unacceptably high probability of default in the event of reasonably probable short-run disturbances, once again assuming that existing debt is refinanced in an orderly manner. The phrase "orderly manner" excludes a situation where emergency debt consolidation credits are required to prevent default, since the concept of creditworthiness has no meaning at all if a borrower is considered creditworthy in the light of a reasonable probability that he will require such credits. However, we must admit that today's capital sources continue to lend to countries that have previously been the subject of emergency debt rescheduling exercises and may well be so again, so perhaps the inescapable conclusion is that creditworthiness has been debased to apply to any country to which public capital sources wish for any reasons whatever to ensure an inflow of resources, regardless of the country's prospects for servicing that inflow in future.

It remains now to see how a definition of creditworthiness is translated into a constraint on terms of resource transfer. To begin with, the terms on a particular resource transfer are a major factor in determining the beneficiary's creditworthiness to receive the transfer in the first place. A borrower who is creditworthy for a 50-year loan of $1 million at zero interest may not be creditworthy for a 5-year loan of $1 million at 6 per cent interest. But further than this, in the modern context, a constraint on terms of resource transfer is also designed to maintain the beneficiary in a state of creditworthiness for all future transfer he will require to meet the targets underlying the current transfer whose terms are under consideration. In other words, in appraising a less-developed country's creditworthiness to service a particular loan to maturity, the capital source has to take into account the future obligations that country must incur in order to maintain an orderly growth path. Otherwise, the source's objective in making the loan in the first place will be undermined.

In the following chapters, we see how Alter, Avramovic, et al., build constraints numbered XII and XIII into Alter's basic aid-requirement model; we do the same ourselves with numbers XIV and XV; and we examine the original Domar model, featuring this reworded version of numbers IX and X above: The weighted average terms (including amortization) on resource transfer to a less-developed country, or to the less-developed countries as a whole, should be no more severe than will enable sources of capital to maintain the required net outflow to such country or countries, subject to institutional and other limitations on gross outflow.

(This is referred to below as the "gross outflow constraint.") We manipulate these models, showing how they can be used to derive optimum weighted average terms on total resource transfer as well as on a residual part of the transfer, assuming the terms on one or more components to be fixed on institutional grounds. We construct variants of some of the models; run data through them representing a sample of less-developed countries; examine the comparative relevance of the different constraints in varying situations; and summarize the policy implications of the analysis. So as not to encumber the discussion with mathematical formulae, those final expressions worthy of mention in this book are given in the Mathematical Appendix.

THE BASIC AID-REQUIREMENT MODEL

To conclude this chapter, we examine the basic characteristics of the Alter aid-requirement model and certain of its variants. The model departs from the assumption that the fundamental economic objective of the leadership of an underdeveloped country, and of the developed countries that export capital to it, is to achieve a target rate of growth of per capita income. This requires a certain rate of investment, expressed as a ratio of national income. A very poor country cannot generate, at the outset, a sufficient rate of savings (also expressed as a ratio to national income) to finance this investment on its own. The difference between required investment and domestic savings represents the amount of external capital that must be provided if the investment is to be carried out and the income growth target achieved. Moreover, external capital demands a certain (average) return, which must be paid out in each year as a percentage of debt outstanding at the end of the previous year. This adds to the resources that must be available to the economy and thus to the requirement for external capital (since the latter is calculated as a residual after maximum attainable domestic savings are taken into account). As the country develops, it should be able to effect a gradual increase in its rate of savings. If this increase can be maintained, the rate of savings will eventually become equal to the rate of investment and, later on, to the rate of investment plus outpayments on account of interest and dividends on the external debt. At this latter point, net inflow of external capital is no longer required. As the savings ratio rises still further, domestic savings exceed investment plus outpayments on account of investment income; these excess savings are available to pay off the external debt, which can eventually be reduced to zero. If the country cannot increase its rate of savings, it will never be able to maintain its target rate of growth by itself but must depend indefinitely on infusions of foreign capital, which will have to increase steadily to cover interest and dividends on itself.

Alter assumes that the underdeveloped country will have a constant marginal per capita savings ratio, this being defined as the annual absolute change in per capita savings divided by the annual absolute change in per capita income. He shows that, if the foreign debt is ever to be fully repaid, this ratio must be greater than the ratio of investment to national income. He also assumes a constant rate of return on external debt, a constant rate of population growth, a constant rate of growth of national (as well as per capita) income, and a constant rate of growth of investment (this follows from the preceding assumption and from the assumption that required investment is a constant percentage of national income).

The fundamental equation in the Alter model, which gives external debt at the end of any given year as a function of the foregoing variables, may be found in the Mathematical Appendix at 2(a). By making an assumption about the size of the debt at the end of a given year--e.g., that the percentage increase during the second year is equal to the assumed rate of increase of national income, or that there is no increase at all--it is possible to eliminate the debt term from the equation and examine the relationships that must hold between all the other variables if the assumption about debt is to hold in any given year. This is the procedure Alter follows in order to evaluate the three variants of the independence constraint, which is the only constraint he is concerned with. Setting the given year equal to 25 and 50 alternatively, he solves his equations for values of the marginal per capita savings ratio, following which he computes maximum values of cumulative debt, expressed as a multiple of national income in a base year.

Throughout Part II of this book, we are interested in techniques for deriving optimum terms on resource transfer as directly as possible. In other words, we treat the expressions that represent these terms in our various formulae as dependent variables. Alter, on the other hand, treats the marginal per capita savings ratio (which he denotes by s'--we will denote it by s'' to avoid confusion with the marginal aggregate savings ratio) as his primary dependent variable, although he notes that it is possible to hold it constant together with all but one of the other variables and then solve for the remaining one. Moreover, by putting through his model several sets of data featuring alternative values for the target rate of growth, the capital/output ratio, and the return on debt, Alter does give us some scope to determine values of these variables compatible with fixed levels of the marginal per capita savings ratio. Alter justifies singling out this ratio on the ground of "our interest in the economic policies which can be used to affect the marginal savings ratio. It can be argued, furthermore, that the marginal savings ratio is more easily subjected to governmental influence than some of the other key variables."[21] Alter was writing at a time when the spectrum of techniques for transferring resources to less-developed countries was much more restricted than it is today. Hence, he allowed his variable for the return on debt to assume only two alternative values, 4.5 per cent, which was then the normal rate on World Bank loans to all borrowers, and 10 per cent, which was a somewhat notional representation of the minimum return required to attract private equity capital into less-developed countries.

It can be argued that experience gained in the past 15 years with respect to development efforts of governments in nontotalitarian societies teaches that there are upper limits to the level of the marginal per capita savings ratio which can be achieved in support of such efforts. Alter notes that India's First Five-Year Plan implied that 38 per cent of increased per capita income was

to be saved. He questions whether this is feasible, especially in
view of the fact that the implied annual increase in per capita income was to be less than 1 per cent. In the event, although per
capita income increased by close to 1.5 per cent annually, the value
of s' achieved during the First Plan period was only about .28-.29.
Before these results were in, the Indians produced a preliminary
outline of the Second Plan implying a value well over .50 for s'; the
final official Plan model reduced this to .24. Again, the data suggest
that somewhat less than .30 was actually achieved. The Third Plan
model implied a value of .28.[22] In <u>Economic Growth and External
Debt</u>, Avramovic selects a value of .20 for the marginal aggregate
savings ratio in his basic run of the Alter model; if we accept his
other data assumptions and assume a population growth rate of .02,
this is equivalent to a value of .33 for s' in the first year under
study, declining by small increments thereafter. Avramovic describes .20 as being "below what many national programs postulate
but . . . probably higher than many countries have actually
achieved."[23] While not denying that government policies can affect
savings or that it is important to impress upon those with political
authority in developing countries how much their growth prospects
depend on savings efforts, I would argue that, for the purposes of
this analysis, it is reasonable to treat the savings variable as independent.

There are at least two other savings variables that could be
assumed constant and thus given a role in an Alter-type model
analogous to that of the marginal per capita savings ratio (s'') in
the original without destroying the model's simplicity. These are
(1) the marginal aggregate savings ratio, and (2) the annual rate of
increase of aggregate savings. Although Alter does not justify his
selection of s'', it is reasonable to assume that he believed a
measure of the savings effort out of additional per capita income
would best reflect the sacrifice required at grass-roots level.
Avramovic and his associates, in their 1964 study, choose instead
the marginal aggregate savings ratio, again without justifying this
explicitly in relation to alternative possibilities. I have in earlier
work developed the formulae corresponding to an assumed constant
annual increase in aggregate savings and applied them to actual
data for a few countries.[24] The three variants of the Alter model's
fundamental equation for cumulative debt, corresponding to the
three different savings variables, are given in the Mathematical
Appendix at 2(a),(b), and (c).

Any assumption of constancy over a number of years for a
macro variable of this type is at best a crude simplification of
reality. It would make an interesting statistical project to test the
comparative stability of the three savings variables in regard to
various countries at different stages of their development. It is
not clear in advance of such a study whether any of the variables
would show sufficient stability, or at least random distribution
around a particular value, to give us much confidence in it as a

basis for a savings equation in an Alter–type model. Unfortunately, there is no scope for such an analysis in this book. Moreover, even Avramovic et al., with the extensive statistical resources available to them, shy away from making quantitative estimates of the marginal savings ratio in a table giving indicators of economic growth for 40 less-developed countries.[25]

Some suggestions as to which is the most useful assumption to make about savings may be gained by examining the effect on two of the variables of assuming the third constant. The following picture results:

(1) Marginal per capita savings ratio constant:

  (a) Marginal aggregate savings ratio increases by a declining proportionate amount;

  (b) Rate of growth of aggregate savings decreases by a declining proportionate amount.

(2) Marginal aggregate savings ratio constant:

  (a) Marginal per capita savings ratio decreases by a declining proportionate amount;

  (b) Rate of growth of aggregate savings decreases by a declining proportionate amount.

(3) Rate of growth of aggregate savings constant:

  (a) Marginal per capita savings ratio increases by a constant proportionate amount;

  (b) Marginal aggregate savings ratio increases by a constant proportionate amount.[26]

It can be argued plausibly that a country should be able to increase its marginal per capita savings ratio with time. In a near-subsistence economy, there are serious economic, political, and sheer administrative obstacles to capturing more than a small fraction of increased per capita income for investment. As the economy grows, however, a larger share of increases in per capita income occur outside the subsistence sector and are more easily translated into savings and investment. The foregoing paragraph shows that the only constancy assumption under consideration here that permits an increasing marginal per capita savings ratio is that of a constant growth rate of aggregate savings. This assumption also implies an increasing marginal savings ratio. In this connection, it is interesting to note that Rosenstein-Rodan, in his well-known analysis of international aid requirements, while assuming a constant value for the marginal savings ratio of each country within a given five-year period (his projections cover three such periods, 1961-66, 1966-71, and 1971-76), in every case assumes an increased value of this ratio for the second period and, in most cases, raises it once more between the second and third periods.[27] Moreover, as shown in my earlier study, the expression for the proportionate change in the two marginal savings variables that arises from a constant growth rate of aggregate savings is both constant with respect to time and far simpler than the corresponding expressions for proportionate change of the two residual variables when either of the marginal variables is held constant.[28] These considerations militate in favor of using a constant aggregate savings growth rate in this type of analysis. Admittedly, there are no well-known conventions indicating what is a feasible level for this variable corresponding to the implicit convention of a 20 per cent marginal savings ratio; however, considering the shaky grounds on which that convention rests, this is no real objection to using the new variable.

Setting the average savings ratio (national income over savings) at a given level in any future year uniquely determines values of our three savings growth variables, assuming each in turn to be constant over the growth period. However, each of the three describes a different growth path, so that the areas under the respective growth curves vary. The least such area is that described by a constant aggregate savings growth rate and the largest by a constant marginal aggregate savings ratio, with the savings curve described by a constant marginal per capita savings ratio falling in between the two. Accordingly, a constant aggregate savings growth rate implies the greatest investment-savings gap before a given average savings ratio is attained, whereas a constant marginal savings ratio implies the smallest gap, the least requirement for external resource transfer, and, thus, the soonest attainment of independence from such transfer, since the burden of interest and dividends on cumulative transfer is less. Conversely, it is possible to calculate values of the three savings growth variables that imply identical cumulative investment-savings gaps up to the point where a given average savings ratio is attained. However, in each case, the year in which that point is reached will differ, being soonest for the constant aggregate savings growth rate and latest for the constant marginal savings ratio.

As already noted, the import-export gap is another measure of required resource transfer which is equal to the investment-savings gap ex post, even though movements of its individual components bear a much less direct and significant relationship to the long-run growth process than is true of investment. Thus, while the absolute level of investment is a fundamental determinant of growth, a relationship expressed via the capital/output ratio, international trade parameters are basically an indication of how the country divides its buying and selling geographically. Depending on comparative advantage, a country may grow just as fast by substituting for imports as by increasing its exports. However, this formal statement of the case is partially undercut by the doctrine of foreign trade as an engine of growth, which is supported by a large body of evidence from the less-developed nations of today correlating growth of national income with growth of exports. Moreover, international trade is subject to much more accurate measurement than investment, savings, or national income, and most of the multiyear plans prepared by less-developed countries these days project imports and exports in greater detail than they do savings. Indeed, given the lack of usable data required to measure savings directly, many authorities--including U.S. AID, whose estimates we use in applying the Alter model in Chapters 6-8--estimate savings as the residual from investment less the net foreign balance (an inflow being treated as positive). Furthermore, inelastic world demand for a country's products frequently forces the planners to concentrate on allocating scarce foreign exchange and substituting for imports in the face of apparent comparative disadvantage. On all these grounds, projecting the foreign aid requirement via the import-export deficit, at least over the medium term, is often a simpler and more realistic exercise than trying to do it via the investment-savings gap.

If one is willing to make the heroic assumption that the rates of increase of imports and exports can be given simple algebraic expression similar to those of investment and savings in the original Alter model and its variants discussed above, it is a simple matter to run an Alter-type model in terms of these parameters and carry out analogous exercises in order to evaluate the constraints on aid terms. A "marginal per capita export ratio" makes little sense as the counterpart of Alter's marginal per capita savings ratio, but there is more to be said for a marginal aggregate propensity to import or, alternatively, a marginal per capita import ratio, different from the initial average ratio of imports to income. Whether the marginal ratio was larger or smaller than the initial average ratio would depend on the circumstances of the country. A country whose resource base favors increased exports of primary products or manufactures based on those products rather than import substitution is likely to have a propensity to purchase more imports out of increased national or per capita income than it presently buys in relation to current income. Conversely, a country with better comparative advantage for import substitution may reduce its import ratio as it grows. Assuming either of the marginal import terms constant would give the model a form identical to that developed by Alter or Avramovic, with the purely formal difference that in the international trade model the constant marginal variable would apply to the expenditure side of the gap rather than the resource side.

Consistent with our use throughout this study of an Alter-type model in which aggregate investment and savings increase at constant annual rates, we construct import-export variants of the model along analogous lines. The Mathematical Appendix gives, at (3), alternative expressions for debt in a given year on the alternative assumptions that:

(a) imports increase at the same rate as GDP, and exports increase more rapidly; and

(b) exports increase at the same rate as GDP, and imports more slowly.

NOTES TO CHAPTER 5

1.   Wilson E. Schmidt, "The Economics of Charity: Loans Versus Grants," Journal of Political Economy, August, 1964, pp. 387-95; and Richard N. Cooper, "A Note on Foreign Assistance and the Capital Requirements for Development" (Santa Monica, California: The RAND Corporation, February, 1965; Memorandum RM-4291-AID).

2.   John A. Pincus, "The Cost of Foreign Aid," Review of Economics and Statistics, November, 1963, pp. 360-67.

3.   Cooper, op. cit., p. vii.

4.   Ibid.

5.   Schmidt, op. cit., p. 389, footnote 12.

6.   Ibid., p. 387.

7.   Ibid.

8.   Cooper, op. cit., p. 18.

9.   Evsey D. Domar, "The Effect of Foreign Investment on the Balance of Payments," in Domar (ed.), Essays in the Theory of Economic Growth (New York: Oxford University Press, 1957).

10.   Ibid.

11.   A. Qayum, "Long Term Economic Criteria for Foreign Loans," Economic Journal, June, 1966, pp. 358-69.

12.   Ibid., p. 360.

13.   Ibid., p. 361.

14.   Dragoslav Avramovic, et al., Economic Growth and External Debt (Baltimore, Md.: The Johns Hopkins Press, 1964).

15.   Gerald M. Alter, Capacity of Underdeveloped Countries to Service Foreign Capital Inflows (Washington, D.C.: IBRD, July 22, 1953; preliminary draft, mimeograph).

16. Gerald M. Alter, "Savings and Investment Aspects of Raising Income Levels in Underdeveloped Countries" (Unpublished Ph.D. dissertation, Department of Economics, Harvard University, 1954).

17. Gerald M. Alter, "The Servicing of Foreign Capital Inflows by Underdeveloped Countries," in Economic Development for Latin America, proceedings of Round Table of the International Economic Association, Rio de Janeiro, August 18-26, 1957 (New York, 1961).

18. Dragoslav Avramovic and Ravi Gulhati, Debt Servicing Capacity and Postwar Growth in International Indebtedness, and Debt-Servicing Problems of Low-Income Countries, 1956-58 (Baltimore, M.D.: The Johns Hopkins Press, 1958 and 1960, respectively). Reference to the 1956 model is made in Avramovic et al., op. cit., p. 11n.

19. Avramovic et al., op. cit., p. 41.

20. Göran Ohlin, Foreign Aid Policies Reconsidered (Paris: Development Centre of the OECD, 1966), p. 92.

21. Alter, "Savings and Investment Aspects", p. 16.

22. Clive S. Gray, "The Spectrum of International Capital Transfer to the Underdeveloped Countries" (Unpublished Ph.D. dissertation, Department of Economics, Harvard University, 1964), pp. 404-06 and 475-82, gives the steps followed in making these computations and cites the Government of India Planning Commission documents used as sources of data.

23. Avramovic et al., op. cit., p. 58.

24. Gray, op. cit., p. 463-73 and 505-07.

25. Avramovic et al., op. cit., 1964, Table 9, pp. 76-77. The change in the ratio of savings to GDP during the 1950's and, again, in "recent years" is rated for those countries where any data are available on a scale of ++, +, 0, and -, corresponding to "marked increase," "mild increase," "no significant change," and "decline."

26. For relevant formulae and proofs see Gray, op. cit., pp. 460-62 and 499-504. All calculations assume inequalities on which the Alter model and/or variants are based, namely, that target rate of growth of national income exceeds population growth rate, rate of growth of aggregate savings exceeds target rate of growth of national income, and both marginal per capita savings ratio and marginal aggregate savings ratio exceed initial average savings ratio. Statements of a declining proportionate rate of change in cases 1 (a)-(b) and 2 (a)-(b) are based on fact that the first derivatives of the relevant expressions with respect to time are all negative, which is obvious from inspection.

27. Paul W. Rosenstein-Rodan, "International Aid for Underdeveloped Countries," The Review of Economics and Statistics, XLIII, No. 2 (May, 1961).

28. Gray, op. cit.

CHAPTER **6** THE INDEPENDENCE AND
DEBT BURDEN CONSTRAINTS

The weighted average return on resource transfer
to a less-developed country should be no greater
than will enable the country to maintain a reasonable
economic growth rate independently of such transfer
within a specified period of time, "independence"
being defined as meeting one of the three following
criteria: (1) the country's foreign liabilities increase
at no higher rate than its national income, (2) the lia-
ᴗilities do not increase at all; or (3) the liabilities are
fully repaid and thus reduced to zero.

The weighted average return on resource transfer
should be no greater than will cause foreign liabilities to
rise to a level where they bear an acceptable ratio to the
benefiting country's national income.

The application of these two constraints is closely related,
since adjusting the terms on resource transfer to ensure that debt
ceases rising faster than GDP by a particular time involves virtually the same technique as enforcing a ceiling on the ratio of
debt to GDP. We will develop the appropriate model in conjunction
with the independence constraint and then consider the debt burden
constraint separately at the end of this chapter.

DEFINITION OF "INDEPENDENCE"

To begin our analysis of this constraint, it is useful to define
five points in time along a country's growth path in line with the
Alter model:

$0 =$ the instant at which the growth path begins, i.e., the start of the first year

$t_1 =$ the year in which domestic savings first equals investment

$t_2 =$ the year in which the proportional increase in debt from the end of that year to the end of the next is equal to the rate of growth of national income

$t_3 =$ the year in which debt reaches a maximum

$t_4 =$ the year in which debt is reduced to zero

Depending on the values of other parameters in the model, t_2 may precede t_1 rather than <u>vice versa</u>, as is suggested by their subscripts. Otherwise, given positive values for all other parameters, each t is larger than any other t with a lesser subscript. Moreover, if an Alter model with fixed parameters describes a country's growth path from 0 to t_4, fixing the values of all the parameters determines a unique set of t's; and, conversely, fixing any one of the t's to solve for an unknown parameter determines all the other t's uniquely.

In line with our statement of the constraint above, "independence" may be defined, and is so defined by Alter (except that he uses no special notation for these points in time), alternatively as the attainment of t_2, t_3, or t_4. Avramovic, on the other hand, ignores t_2, defining three "major stages in the growth-cum-debt sequence"[1] which our notation can represent as follows: first stage, 0 to t_1; second stage, t_1 to t_3; and third stage, t_3 to t_4. Thus, for Avramovic, independence is equivalent to attaining either t_3 or t_4.

RATIONALE FOR THE INDEPENDENCE CONSTRAINT

Before considering the relative merits of different variants of the independence constraint, it is appropriate to examine the basic theory underlying this constraint and evaluate its relevance to the real world. In Chapter 5, we noted the following target as that assumed by the various aid models we have considered: to supplement the less-developed countries' domestic resources to the extent necessary for them to achieve a rate of economic growth that will allow for both a fast enough increase in per capita consumption to maintain political stability and sufficient investment out of domestic resources to launch these countries into a self-sustaining growth process within a "reasonable" period of time. In my view, this is

an accurate statement of the primary aid objective of those sources
of resource transfer which have the ability to direct their funds and
manipulate the terms of repayment in response to noneconomic
incentives and to which the policy recommendations of this study
are directed. Of course, additional objectives, mainly of a political nature, lie behind this one, but it is outside the scope of this
study to consider how it is that self-sustaining economic growth
is expected to build up resistance to Communist takeover attempts
within such countries, and so on.

The "reasonable" period of time in the foregoing statement
may be defined more narrowly as the shortest period of time which
parameters internal to the less-developed countries will permit,
subject to certain constraints on the terms of resource transfer.
Such constraints in this context are ones that limit the proportion
of grants and soft loans in an over-all aid programme, either by
outside fiat (e.g., votes of Congress) or by virtue of a belief on
the sources' part that too much aid on easy terms would have undesirable effects on incentives, financial discipline, etc.

Admittedly, capital-source countries might have some
reasons for favoring prolonged indebtedness of the less-developed
countries and delaying their attainment of at least the third variant
of financial independence. Such would be the case if the source
countries felt that continued indebtedness would prolong their own
political influence in the less-developed countries, on the ground
that the latter would want to retain their good will for the purpose of refinancing debt. But continued indebtedness at a more
or less constant level is not at all inconsistent with reaching the
maximum level in the shortest possible time, and, for reasons
given below, we believe that this is the objective of highest priority
for most capital sources. The long-term attitude of source
governments toward private investment by their nationals in less-
developed countries is probably more ambivalent. Although private foreign investment is often in an exposed position politically,
it offers sizable advantages, some of them direct to the country of
origin, by way of spreading commercial influence at many levels
of society that are oblivious to public aid inflow, accelerating the
development process with scarce entrepreneurial and managerial
resources (i.e., initiative and know-how) that governments cannot
provide, forestalling competitors from other countries, and
eventually reaping a return flow of payments. There are per-
suasive arguments for allowing and, indeed, encouraging private
foreign investment to increase indefinitely, although it cannot do
so at a faster pace than GDP without eventually giving rise to
political problems.

Reasons why most capital sources want to see less-developed
countries achieve independence of extraordinary resource transfer
as quickly as possible include the following:

(1) Until such time as a less-developed country has reached the stage of self-sustaining growth, where internal forces are capable of carrying the brunt of further development, the danger persists that such forces having a vested interest in seeing growth continue under non-Communist auspices will be too weak to counteract the conditions of economic stagnation and deprivation that feed unrest and provide a base for Communist agitation.

(2) As long as a less-developed country is dependent for reasonable economic progress on voluntary resource transfer from foreign powers--especially ones whose most vital interests are tied up in a world-wide power struggle, whose past record in the developing areas is one of colonial or "neocolonial" domination and and who are represented in the less-developed country by economic interests that attract jealousy and resentment--those internal forces with whom the aid sources cooperate and whose control over the country they wish to solidify are politically vulnerable.

(3) The longer net resource transfer continues, the greater chance there is that short-run economic and/or political disturbances will occur and cause the less-developed country to default, if only temporarily, with all the economic and political embarrassment that brings.

(4) Again, the longer the growth-cum-debt process continues, the greater the likelihood of governmental changes in the source countries--such as election of Congressional majorities that reflect constituencies fed up with imperceptible gains from foreign aid--which interrupt the net flow of resources and upset the process.

(5) As a corollary of (4), aid sources are sick and tired of their periodic battle to secure new appropriations that will meet a minimum proportion of less-developed countries' needs and would like to bring the process to an end as soon as possible.

(6) Prolongation of the growth-cum-debt process threatens to ingrain an attitude of dependence on subsidized foreign resource transfer in the minds of key elements in a less-developed country, thus increasing resistance to the mobilization of sufficient local resources to carry the burden after net transfer from abroad is no longer essential and making it more difficult to end the transfer.

Turning to the variants of the independence constraint, the justification for treating t_2 as an alternative condition of independence is that the burden of debt, whether incurred by private concerns, governments, or entire nations, is generally assessed in terms of its ratio to the debtor's current income. As long as debt is increasing relatively more rapidly than income, creditors must be concerned with the possibility that this process will continue indefinitely, perhaps even accelerate, and eventually lead to default when short-run difficulties make the debtor unable to meet all claims on current income. In order to prevent such an eventuality, creditors may take extraordinary steps, such as, in the present context, lightening the terms on resource transfer. Once the developing country has reached a stable ratio of debt to income and is servicing that level of debt without apparent difficulty, the creditors may feel that the danger point has passed and that extraordinary measures can be relaxed. Again, in the present context, this may mean curtailing the flow of public aid and requiring the developing country to resort instead to hard loans from export-credit institutions or even to private capital markets. We have already seen that t_2 is a more logical point than t_3 and especially t_4 by which to define "independence" vis-à-vis private foreign investment. Such investment should continue to grow absolutely, but an aid source will want to help less-developed countries reach the point where it is not continually expanding its share of the national capital, or, viewing the situation from a more constructive angle, where local enterprise is able to plow back enough money from current earnings to maintain its share of total investment.

On the other hand, there may be some situations where the inflow of resources that permitted a country to reach t_2 may have been on such easy terms that a complete return to hard terms would push the debt once more onto a more rapid growth path than income. Alternatively, the country may have reached t_2 with such a high ratio of debt and debt service to current income that creditors consider it necessary to reduce this ratio before cutting the country loose from public aid channels. Avramovic has evidently opted for the position that aid sources will not regard a developing country as being "out of the woods" prior to that point on the growth path, i.e., t_3, where continued availability of resources on the same terms would enable the country to dispense with further net inflow. Forcing the country to start refinancing its debt on harder terms after t_3 will ordinarily cause the debt to resume its upward path for a while, although, except in highly unfavorable circumstances, this rate of increase would not be "excessive."

The relevance of t_4, which symbolizes the highest degree of independence, is doubtful in present circumstances. In a world where prospects for some of the largest less-developed countries are widely regarded as hinging on the doubtful outcome of a race between population and productivity, particularly in agriculture, the vital question aid sources are asking is: "Can these countries achieve self-sustaining growth, and, if so, how?"--not "When can we expect to get all our money back?" Once self-sustaining growth is achieved, the aid sources will almost certainly allow the benefiting countries to refinance much of their debt, if on less concessionary terms, thereby being in a position to divert more resources into consumption or to invest more and thus increase the rate of growth above the level projected in the original growth model. Certainly twenty-five or even fifty years hence will see no absolute diminution of the gap between today's rich and poor countries, and it is difficult to conceive of a situation even that far ahead with the rich putting pressure on the poor to move into a net capital-exporting position in order to amortize their debts.

This assertion is made despite the precedent of European postwar recovery, during which few could foresee the rapid success of the Marshall Plan and many thought that repayment prospects for even that minor segment (roughly 25 per cent) of U.S. aid provided in the form of loans rather than grants were very dim. In the event, however, not more than ten years afterward, most of the benefiting countries were in a position to remit larger annual service payments on the aid than they were liable for, and at least one country, France, made premature repayments on its loan liabilities to assist the U.S. balance of payments. However, the discrepancy between the productive power of today's advanced and less-developed countries is of an entirely different order of magnitude from that which held between the United States and postwar Europe, particularly when the latent skills and energy of the un- or underemployed Europeans of that day are taken into account. Large-scale aid to the underdeveloped world is already more than ten years old, and, while a few countries are regarded as having "taken off" into self-sustaining growth, there is a much larger group whose requirements for resource transfer, as defined in exercises analogous to the Alter model, increase every year.

QUANTIFYING THE CONSTRAINT

If aid sources have limited discretion to provide their aid in the form of outright or quasi-grants, then minimum values for the t's of a particular country are defined within rather narrow limits by the country's growth parameters. Apart from this type of situation, assigning a value to any of the t's is bound to be an arbitrary procedure, since assessing the time limit outside which the probability of defaults and other undesirable contingencies becomes unacceptably high is a matter of speculative judgment and virtually no conventions have been established in this area. A number of projections made for t_2 or t_3 in respect of an individual country or the underdeveloped world as a whole have subsequently had to be revised upward. Thus, the Indian Third Plan, published in 1961, stated: "It is also implied that progressively external aid will form a diminishing proportion of the total investment, and by the end of the Fifth Plan [i.e., 1976] the economy will be strong enough to develop at a satisfactory pace without being dependent on external assistance outside of the normal inflow of foreign capital."[2] This projection that Alter's t_2 or t_3 (it is impossible to say which applies here, but over so short a time span they would only be 2

or 3 years apart anyway) would occur after 15 years was more con-
servative than the 10-year estimate made a year earlier in the
Third Plan Draft Outline.[3] But at the time this is written, as the
Fourth Plan is being scrapped,[4] economic independence for India
in only 8 years is a pipe dream.

On the side of an aid source, President Kennedy's new administration gave this assurance to Congress in the summary
presentation of the Act for International Development in early
1961: "Foreign aid to the less developed countries should not be
endless. The peak requirements should occur during the decade
of the sixties, and by the end of this period a significant number
of recipient countries should be capable of continuing their growth
without large amounts of extraordinary assistance."[5] The 1967
edition of this document was much more cautious, telling Congress
only that "several nations--Korea and Turkey for example--show
distinct promise of the kind of 'pay off' that has enabled AID to
end its assistance to Greece, Taiwan, and Israel."[6] In the case
of Turkey, it cited the Turkish Government's "principal economic
goal" as being to reach "self-sustaining economic growth without
foreign aid on special terms" by the end of its Second Five Year
Plan in 1973.[7]

Avramovic chooses a t_3 equal to 25 years in his one comprehensive run of the Alter-type model. As he explains it, "The
benchmark of a quarter of a century has been chosen on the
assumption that the developing and the developed countries, in
making their present decisions to borrow and lend, respectively,
want to have some idea, however hazy, of whether they can see the
light at the end of the tunnel within the lifetime of a generation."[8]

AVRAMOVIC'S RESULTS

Assuming values for the growth parameters in the model--
GDP growth target, 5 per cent; initial gross domestic savings
rate, .10; marginal savings rate, .20; and capital/output ratio,
3:1--Avramovic shows that a weighted average return of 6 per
cent on foreign debt is compatible with achieving t_3 in 25 years.
Thus, in the composite "country" represented by Avramovic's
model, resource transfer exclusively on hard terms is permitted
under that variant of the independence constraint where t_3 equals
25 years. (As we will see in Chapter 7, Avramovic's parallel
assumptions about export behavior in the same model give rise to
a peak value of over .50 for the ratio of debt service to current
exports, suggesting that the average rate of return might have to
be lower in order to meet the debt service ratio constraint.)

By virtue of the law of compound interest, the results of a model projecting growth over 25 years are extremely sensitive to small changes in the assumed parameters. We will examine this phenomenon more systematically below. Avramovic himself shows how a reduction of the assumed marginal savings rate from .20 to .16 affects the results of his model--t_1, the number of years required for domestic savings to become equal to investment, increases from 15 to 37, and t_3 and t_4 are never attained as debt increases indefinitely. The results are also affected by Avramovic's choice of a constant marginal aggregate savings ratio, rather a constant marginal per capita savings ratio or rate of growth of aggregate savings. As we saw in Chapter 5, where values for these three savings variables are chosen that lead to attainment of the same average savings ratio in a given future year, the savings growth curve defined by a constant marginal aggregate savings ratio has the largest integral, implying the lowest foreign capital requirement and hence the smallest value for debt in that year. Avramovic's value of .20 for the marginal aggregate savings ratio implies that an average ratio of .169 is achieved in year 25. Assuming alternatively (1) the rate of growth of aggregate savings and (2) the marginal per capita savings ratio to be constant, with the rate of population growth assumed at .025 in case (2), values of (1) .073 and (2) .257 respectively imply an average savings ratio of .169 in year 25. Plugged into the appropriate equations of these variants of the Alter model corresponding to 2 (a) and (c) in the Mathematical Appendix, with t_3 equal to 25, these assumptions imply an average rate of return on debt equal to (1) 5 per cent and (2) 5 7/8 per cent respectively, compared with Avramovic's 6 per cent.

Avramovic stresses that his "single generation variant" gives a more optimistic picture than applies to many less-developed countries. He therefore defines the "long-haul case," describing a country with exceptionally low per capita income, large population, and poor natural resources, where the return on capital and/or the marginal savings rate are low and/or the external accounts inflexible.[9] Although Avramovic does not mention any members of this class of countries by name, he implies that it comprises countries with parameters significantly less favorable than those chosen for his model run. It is in the long-haul cases that the "risks of debt failure must be judged considerable" and that, after qualifying his views in the manner of a proper international civil servant (if the risks "are so judged by the governments--suppliers of capital; and if these suppliers of capital consider that the case of development should be subsidized out of their tax proceeds--and this will increasingly depend on the growth record and growth prospects of the receivers of funds"), Avramovic says the need for soft-term aid arises.[10]

DERIVING OPTIMUM TERMS

Avramovic does not carry this point to the extent of plugging parameters characteristic of the long-haul case into his model and showing how far his .06 weighted average return on debt must be reduced in order for t_3 to be achieved in 25 years. We will, therefore, now proceed to carry out this extention of the analysis. The first step is to establish a procedure for solving Alter-type equations for an unknown value of such return, which we denote by "i." If all terms in i are collected on one side, we get equations of the form $(1+ai) (1+i)^n = b$, or $(1+ai) (1+i)^n + bi = c$, where a is generally different from unity and n, which represents one of our t's, is an integer normally well above 10. Such equations cannot be solved directly for i with ordinary computational methods, but an earlier study outlines a simple iterative method, involving the use of partial derivatives, and demonstrates its use in obtaining a value of i within 1 per cent of the correct value after only one cycle, starting from a trial value eight points to one side of the correct one (i.e., the difference between -.05 and .03).[11]

Any value for the independence constraint that requires debt to be maximized before savings rises to equal investment-- i.e., which requires t_3 to be achieved before t_1--implies a negative solution for i. Looking ahead to Table 9, this situation arises if t_3 is pegged below 26, 15, 6, 17, or 22 years in models based on data from Africa, South Asia, East Asia, Southern Europe and the Middle East, or Latin America, respectively. Under the most realistic interpretation possible, a negative return implies that the larger the amount of capital Source A has loaned to Less-developed Country B, the more A must grant B in addition. If the specific loans A is providing carry a positive interest rate, then A's grants must be large enough both to offset these interest payments and to provide net aid at the rate of i (absolute value) times cumulative debt. Both debt and grants will reach a maximum before t_1, but the grants must continue until the debt has been fully repaid. Although, in a formal sense, the negative i permits the less-developed country to meet its independence constraint, in real-world terms, independence cannot be said to have arrived as long as the country requires capital grants, albeit at a diminishing rate.

A situation more attuned to real-world conditions is that of a single capital source or group of sources wishing to finance as much of a country's total aid requirement as feasible (meaning as much as is compatible with attainment of independence in a "reasonable" number of years) out of funds available only on fixed, "hard" terms. This is almost universally the case, because such funds are available in far greater, indeed practically unlimited amounts on the private capital markets, requiring at most the source government's guarantee, as compared with grants and soft-loan funds, which must normally be appropriated out of tax revenues and are strictly rationed in order to meet the demands of close to 100 nations. In terms of our present analysis of the independence constraints, given a particular value for t_2, t_3, or t_4, the amount of hard loan aid that can be provided is maximized if the borrower's entire debt-servicing capacity--in the Alter-type model, the difference between his savings and investment after t_1--is reserved for hard loans. This means that if any additional resource transfer is needed because the borrower could not fulfill the given constraint if the entire transfer were on hard terms, then that supplementary transfer must bear zero return. In the Alter-type model, grants, zero-interest loans, or any mixture of the two have the same effect on a country's attainment of t_3. In other words, debt is maximized at the same time regardless of whether the supplementary transfer is in the form of grants or zero-interest loans. On the other hand, the relative proportions of grants and zero-interest loans do affect (1) the timing of t_2 and t_4 and (2) the total debt burden, defined as the ratio of total debt to income at any given time. This is because zero-interest loans are just as much part of total debt as loans at a positive interest rate.

As part of our general concern in this study for quantitative derivations of terms on resource transfer, it would be useful to have a formula indicating how much grant or zero-interest loan aid must be provided in order for a less-developed country to meet a specified independence constraint, subject to the further constraint that the amount of resource transfer at a given positive return is maximized. In deriving such a formula, it is simplest to proceed from the assumption that all grants/zero-interest loans are made in the early years of the growth-cum-debt process, and that no positive-interest loans are made until all the grants/zero-interest loans have been disbursed. This is clearly an over-simplification of the procedure that will actually be followed, since sources providing easy-term aid will normally want to encourage some participation by hard-loan and equity sources in financing the country's growth as early as possible. Their objective in this will be to share the burden, smooth the way for an increasing role of private and hard-loan public capital once easy-term aid can be phased out, and accustom the benefiting country to the discipline of servicing foreign hard-loan or equity investment from the beginning. On the other hand, it is certainly true that aid sources are less likely to provide easy-term aid once they are satisfied that a country is on its way toward self-sustaining growth, even if that stage has not yet been reached. The theory behind the special "development grant" program which the Eisenhower Administration in its final year introduced for Africa was that these newly independent countries were so far from self-sustaining growth that it made no sense to burden them with additional debt for the time being.

The Mathematical Appendix gives, at 5 (a), a formula for debt outstanding in any year up to and including t_3 on the assumption that no more debt is contracted, at a given return i, than will permit a country to stop increasing its debt after a given t_3. The formula implies that there is a year, which we will denote t_L in which the first debt is contracted and that, in all previous years (as well as, partially, in t_L), the investment-savings gap is filled by grants/zero-interest loans. Total aid on the latter terms is easily computed by summing the investment-savings deficits in all years from O through t_L and subtracting any debt contracted during t_L itself. Total aid through t_3 is simply this sum plus debt outstanding in t_3, and the proportions of aid extended in easy-term and hard-loan form, respectively, are given by simple ratios.

Assuming that grants/zero-interest loans are made to the exclusion of hard loans in the early years results in a minimum estimate of required total aid as well as of the easy-term component of aid, since capitalization of interest on outstanding debt is thereby delayed to the latest possible moment. A maximum estimate of required total aid and grants/zero-interest loans may be obtained by calculating debt in t_3 according to the original Alter formula or one of its variants on the assumption that all aid is in the form of loans with return i. For the country to proceed after t_3 without increasing its debt, savings less investment in year t_{3+1} must be no less than i times debt in year t_3. Thus, in t_3, aid sources must either forgive or convert to zero-interest loans all debt in excess of that meeting this condition. These will be maximum estimates because capitalization of interest on debt will have occurred to the maximum extent.

Before the foregoing model and its variants are applied to real-world data, it should be adjusted to take into account the fact that nearly all developing countries have already attracted foreign capital on which they are required to pay a return and will continue to have to do so until it is fully repaid. This requirement augments the set of claims on resources that have to be met out of domestic savings and foreign resource transfer and thus delays the time by which a country can achieve independence from resource inflow with a given rate of growth of savings. To allow for this factor, we begin by assuming that any amortization payments of pre-existing debt prior to t_3 are offset by new gross transfers bearing the same return--in other words, that existing debt is continually refinanced on constant terms. This is parallel to the assumption throughout the Alter-type model that net resource transfer fills the gap between savings and investment plus return on foreign debt, so that gross transfers is adequate to offset any amortization payments, and the rate of amortization is irrelevant.

We now further assume that payments of the required annual return on pre-existing debt are financed by additional resource transfer at a return equal to the weighted average rate applicable to the debt. New resource transfer is needed to finance these payments up to t_3 because future domestic savings are already fully allocated to other uses by the assumptions of the Alter-type model. Thus, pre-existing debt is assumed to increase until t_3 at a compound rate equal to its present rate of return. Moreover, t_3 will be attained only when domestic savings have increased sufficiently to cover three analytically distinct claims on resources: (1) domestic investment, (2) return payments on debt accumulated in order to fill the gap between savings and investment from year 1, and (3) return payments on the debt contracted before year 1, which increase thereafter as already indicated. In the variant of the Alter-type model, in which the early resource transfer takes place in the form of grants or zero-interest loans so as to enable the benefiting country to maximize its interest-bearing debt by a certain time, we assume, for the sake of simplicity, that all earnings on pre-existing debt are matched by equivalent net additional grants/zero-interest loans, from year 1 through t_3. In this case, the pre-existing debt, rather than growing geometrically, remains constant absolutely and declines as a percentage of current GDP. However, the requirement for grants/zero-interest loans goes up correspondingly.

The Mathematical Appendix shows at (6) how some of the earlier formulae can be expanded to take pre-existing debt into account.

To make the analysis based on an Alter-type model fully consistent, it would be desirable to include all forms of private and public foreign investment and earnings thereon in our measures of pre-existing debt and its return. The reason for this is that the model, by basing the resource transfer requirement on the gap between aggregate investment and savings, projects the net total of all forms of resource transfer, both public and private. It is, of course, possible to focus the model on the public component of transfer by assuming that fixed proportions of aggregate savings and investment relate to the public and private sectors exclusively. However, it is simpler, and more useful for our central purpose, first to examine the effects of alternative constraints on the weighted average terms of all forms of transfer to a less-developed country, and then to ascertain the required terms on that form of public transfer which plays the part of a residual, assuming various proportions of private investment and public loans on fixed terms, such as export credits financed by internal borrowing. Thus, it would be useful to incorporate data on existing nonpublic liabilities; however, the available data in this area are so fragmentary that their use would be misleading. We must, therefore, be content to regard the public debt figures as substantial underestimates of presently existing foreign-owned assets and related earnings to be remitted or refinanced throughout the growth-cum-debt process.

APPLICATION OF THE MODEL TO REAL-WORLD DATA

We now proceed to apply the model to parameters based on actual data as reported by the World Bank and U.S. AID. Data on 1960-65 values of most relevant parameters are given for selected groups of countries in five regions of the less-developed world in two World Bank documents, its 1966-67 annual report and a special report on public debt published in October, 1966.[12] The regions are Africa, South Asia, East Asia, South Europe and the Middle East, and Latin America.* Annual savings data for 1960-65 are given in AID statistical reports for a selection of countries comprising three regions, the Near East and South Asia, the Far East, and Latin America.[13] The first of these three is largely coextensive with the second and fourth World Bank regions, taken together. By a method described in the Mathematical Appendix at (7), we computed annual rates of growth from these series. The savings growth estimates (denoted by "s") for the Far East and Latin America are used in conjunction with the World Bank's data for East Asia and Latin America, respectively, with adjustments indicated below; and the single estimate for AID's first region is assumed to apply to each of the corresponding two World Bank regions. As AID had not published analogous savings data for Africa at the time of writing, we followed a different procedure to obtain a value of the savings growth parameter for use in connection with that region--namely, we determined that value of s which would bring about the same savings/GDP ratio in year 25 as would Avramovic's assumption of a constant marginal aggregate savings ratio equal to .20.

To determine the ratio of existing debt to GDP, we took the World Bank's estimates of disbursed public debt outstanding as of June 30, 1966, and divided these by AID estimates of 1966 gross

---

*Data from the following 40 countries underlie regional totals for main parameters given in Bank's annual report:

Africa--Ethiopia, Ghana, Kenya, Malawi, Morocco, Nigeria,
        Sudan, Tanzania, Tunisia, Uganda
South Asia--Burma, Ceylon, India, Pakistan
East Asia--Republic of China, Korea, Malaysia, Philippines,
        Thailand
South Europe & Middle East--Cyprus, Greece, Iran, Iraq,
        Israel, Jordan, Turkey
Latin America--Argentina, Bolivia, Brazil, Chile, Colombia,
        Costa Rica, Ecuador, Guatemala, Honduras,
        Mexico, Nicaragua, Panama, Peru.

Debt-related figures are based on a slightly different list of 49 countries. In each case, availability of data determined the selection of countries.

national product for the same groups of countries.[14] (The use of national rather than domestic product data in this exercise, on the ground that the former was more readily available, introduces a discrepancy which is minute in relation to the margin of error of the estimates of output and most other parameters here and can, therefore, safely be ignored.) The rate of return on existing debt was computed by taking the interest component of public debt service payments in 1964, as given by the Bank, and dividing it by debt outstanding on January 1, 1964.[15]

The following significant adjustments were made before these data were run through the model:

(1) World Bank data showed that the five regions had attained GDP growth rates during 1960-65 as follows: Africa--.042; South Asia--.032; East Asia--.064; South Europe and Middle East--.07; Latin America--.047. We assumed a target GDP growth rate of .050 for the three regions with the lowest recent values on the ground that any lower rate would not permit a politically acceptable rate of increase in per capita consumption. (In this way, the rate of population growth becomes an implicit though not explicit variable in our variant of the Alter model.) On the other hand, we assumed that East Asia and South Europe and the Middle East would not be able to maintain, over the length of period relevant to our model, as high rates as they had achieved in recent years in extraordinary favorable exogenous circumstances. We therefore assigned targets of .055 and .06, respectively, to these two regions.

(2) Dividing World Bank data for average gross investment rates (gross investment divided by current GDP) by corresponding average annual rates of growth of GDP, we obtained the following estimates of the incremental capital/output ratio (denoted by "K"): Africa--3.4; South Asia--5.2; East Asia--2.6; South Europe and Middle East--2.7; Latin America--4.0. We assumed that South Asia's extraordinarily high value, resulting to a sizable extent from poor monsoons in India, would be reduced to 4.0 in the future, and that the low values for East Asia and South Europe and the Middle East would rise to 3.0 over the long haul. To a considerable extent, these adjustments mirror those made in GDP growth rates above and offset them in the calculation of the average investment rate over the period of the model. (This is shown in Table 9.)

Table 9 illustrates the application of the independence constraint, based on an Alter-type model. Part I of the table gives the parameters obtained as described above, as well as another variable determined directly by our assumptions about savings and investment, namely, t_1, the year in which savings first becomes equal to investment. Part II then gives results of applying the model to illustrate the relationship between the rate of return on foreign debt; the number of years required to achieve independence,

TABLE 9

Effects of Independence Constraint

	Africa	South Asia	East Asia[a]	South Europe and Middle East	Latin America
I--Values of actual or assumed parameters[a]					
1. GDP growth rate (r)	.05(.042)[b]	.05(.032)	.055(.064)	.06(.07)	.05(.047)
2. Incremental capital/output ratio (K)	3.4	4.0(5.2)	3.0(2.6)	3.0(2.7)	4.0
3. Investment/GDP ratio (Kr)	.17(.143)	.20(.166)	.165(.166)	.18(.189)	.20(.188)
4. Initial savings/GDP ratio (S_0)	.10(.097)	.136	.136	.136	.164
5. Savings growth rate (s)	.073	.08	.10(.14)	.08	.06
6. Year when savings $\geq$ investment (t_1)	26	15	6	17	22
7. Initial foreign debt/GDP ratio (D_0)	.142	.096	.058	.064	.108
8. Return on existing foreign debt (i_1)	.05	.05	.04	.03	.05
II--All new resource transfer in form of loans bearing return of i					
Limiting value of i	.106	.140	.310	.226	.106
i=0					
Year of maximum debt (t_3)	27	15		16	22
Maximum debt/initial GDP ratio ($D_{t_3} \div Y_1$)	2.01	.82		.60	.89
Maximum debt/current GDP ratio ($D_{t_3} \div Y_{t_3}$)	.57	.42		.25	.21
Debt service/current GDP ratio at t_3[c]	.007	.005		.001	.005

134

i=.06

Year of maximum debt	39	20	21	34
Maximum debt/initial GDP ratio	6.47	1.44	1.13	2.38
Maximum debt/current GDP ratio	1.01	.57	.35	.48
Debt service/current GDP ratio at t_3[d]	.060	.034	.020	.028

i=.10

Year of maximum debt	86	26	28	74
Maximum debt/initial GDP ratio	280	3.01	2.63	42
Maximum debt/current GDP ratio	4.4	.89	.55	1.14
Debt service/current GDP ratio at t_3[d]	.44	.080	.052	.11

$t_3=25$

Maximum rate of return on new debt (i)	e	.0925	.0825	.0125
Year 25 debt/initial GDP ratio $(D_{25} \div Y_1)$	e	2.53	1.67	1.05
Year 25 debt/year 25 GDP ratio $(D_{25} \div Y_{25})$	e	.78	.41	.33
Debt service/GDP ratio in year 25[d]	e	.067	.033	.008

(Continued)

TABLE 9 (Continued)

III--All loans bear return of .06, debt maximized in year 25[g]

Year when first loans made (t_L)	e	1	1	11
Maximum debt/initial GDP ratio ($D_{25} \div Y_1$)	e	h	h	.47
Maximum debt/current GDP ratio ($D_{25} \div Y_{25}$)	e	h	h	.15
Grants and zero-interest loans/initial GDP ratio ($G \div Y_1$)	e	0	0	.50
Total aid/initial GDP ratio $[(G+D_{25}) \div Y_1]$	e	h	h	.97
Loans/total aid ratio $[D_{25} \div (G+D_{25})]$	e	1.0	1.0	.48
Grants and zero-interest loans/total aid ratio $[G \div (G+D_{25})]$	e	0	0	.52

Notes:

a. The actual and assumed parameters for East Asia are such as to permit that area to achieve financial independence within so short a time, assuming any reasonable rate of return on foreign debt, as to make East Asia uninteresting from the viewpoint of our analysis. Hence for East Asia no calculations are made under Parts II and III.

b. Where two figures are given, the one in parentheses represents actual data as given in or computed from indicated sources, the other is the assumed value used in computing the results in Parts II and III.

c. $i_1 D_0^a (1+i_1)^{t_3-1} \quad Y_{t_3}$

d. $\left[\dfrac{i D_{t_3} + (i_1 - i) D_0^a (1+i_1)^{t_3 - 1}}{3} \right] \div Y_{t_3}$

e. This section is not relevant to Africa, since that area's t_1 is 26, meaning that the assumptions of the model do not permit Africa to maximize its debt in year 25 under any circumstances.

f. $\left[i D_{25} + (i_1 - i) D_0^a (1+i_1)^{25} \right] \div Y_{25}$

g. In this Part, debt and loans not specifically identified as zero-interest actually exclude any zero-interest loans, which are interchangeable with grants for the purpose of this analysis.

h. Not applicable, since maximum debt is reached before year 25 even without any grants or zero-interest loans.

137

defined here as the year in which the last increase in debt occurs; the amount of debt that will be accumulated by that year, shown as a ratio to GDP of year 1 and then of year t_3, taking into account presently existing debt; and the ratio of return payments on debt in t_3 to current GDP. Part II shows this relationship in two ways: first, by assuming that resource transfer takes place on fixed weighted average terms of 0, 6, and 10 per cent, respectively, and then seeing how long it takes to attain t_3 and how much debt is accumulated in the process; second, by imposing a specific independence constraint of $t_3 = 25$ years and then seeing how high a return on debt is compatible with this condition, as well as how much debt will be accumulated given such a return. Part II also gives a limiting value for the rate of return on foreign debt, defined as the maximum rate a country can pay and still approach any of the independence criteria asymptotically (assuming, of course, that all other relevant parameters remain constant). The formula for this limiting value is given in the Mathematical Appendix at (8).

Finally, Part III of the table reintroduces the independence constraint of $t_3 = 25$ years, assumes that any nongrant or nonzero-interest resource transfer bears a fixed rate of return, and then proceeds to show (a) how much transfer on such terms can be serviced entirely out of domestic resources by t_3, (b) how much transfer must be provided in grant or zero-interest loan form to make this possible, and (c) the relative proportions of grants/zero-interest loans and other loans in the total transfer package. Also shown is t_L, the year in which our formula assumes the first loans at the indicated positive rate of return will be made, although this has little or no practical relevance.

Commenting on the specific results given in the table, we note first that East Asia is projected to raise its level of savings up to the level of investment already in the sixth year. This is a result of the extremely favorable assumption of a 10 per cent annual growth rate of savings, which nevertheless discounts fairly heavily the 14 per cent annual growth rate actually achieved, according to AID data, during 1960-65. With t_1 such a short time off, East Asia would be able to meet any conceivable independence constraint on any reasonable terms without help from grants or soft loans and is, therefore, uninteresting from the viewpoint of our present analysis. We have accordingly omitted further calculations for East Asia. This should not, however, be interpreted to mean that East Asia is in fact so well off that none of the countries in the region need resource transfer on noncommercial terms. The parameters we have used for East Asia are heavily biased by the exclusion of Indonesia and Indochina, where usable data for savings and investment are not available. Our World Bank source shows that including Indonesia and South Vietnam in the GDP growth calculations reduces the region's average annual performance during 1960-65 from .064 to .050.

Turning to Part II, we note that, even if all new resource transfer is in the form of interest-free loans, the four regions in question will carry repayable debt ranging from 21 to 57 per cent of their respective GDP's in the year of independence. If the weighted average return rises to 6 per cent, the ratio of debt to current income ranges between .35 and 1.01, with the corresponding annual return ranging between .02 and .06 of GDP. Raising the rate of return from zero to 6 per cent also has the effect of prolonging the date of independence by 12 years for both Africa and Latin America, to 39 years in the former case and 34 years in the latter. An average return of 10 per cent is close to the limit for both Africa and Latin America, delaying independence until years 86 and 74 respectively and pushing debt to extremely high levels--4.4 times GDP in the case of Africa and 114 per cent of Latin America's GDP. In both cases, the addition of another percentage point to the rate of return would make independence unattainable, even at infinity (assuming all other parameters remained constant, which, of course, they would not do).

With the final entry in Part II and all of Part III, the specific independence criterion that debt should be maximized in the 25th year is introduced. This part of the analysis is not relevant to our Africa model, where savings becomes equal to investment only in the 26th year; hence the Africa column is omitted here. One can, however, interpret the model to say that an independence constraint of 25 years would require all transfer to Africa to be in the form either of grants or zero-interest loans. In the cases of South Asia, South Europe and Middle East, and Latin America, this constraint is satisfied if new resource transfer occurs on weighted average terms of 9 1/4 per cent, 8 1/4 per cent, and 1 1/4 per cent, respectively. Thus, with respect to Part III, it is obvious that fixing the return on transfer other than grants and zero-interest loans at 6 per cent enables South Asia and South Europe and the Middle East to satisfy the constraint easily. On the other hand, under these conditions, Latin America requires an infusion of grants or zero-interest loans larger than the amount of loan money it can simultaneously accept at a 6 per cent return.

SENSITIVITY OF THE MODEL TO SMALL CHANGES IN PARAMETERS

Any model that attempts to predict events in a future as far distant as our t_3's by assuming constant rates of change is subject to the pitfall that small variations in these rates, well within the margins of error associated with measuring past and current trends, will be greatly magnified by the workings of compound interest and will lead to wide variations between predicted and actual results. To illustrate this, it is interesting to examine the partial derivatives of certain of the variables with respect to the others. An earlier study has provided the formulae for 57 such derivatives in the original Alter model (i.e., assuming a constant marginal per capita savings ratio).[16] The formulae give derivatives of:

Debt in any given year:

t_1;

t_4;

t_3 on the alternative assumptions (a) that all transfer is in loan form and (b) that it includes sufficient grants or zero-interest loans to enable interest-bearing debt to be maximized by t_3;

Debt in t_3 under the same alternative assumptions; and

Grants or zero-interest loans required under the second assumption, with respect to some or all of the following: the GDP target growth rate, the population growth rate, the marginal per capita savings ratio, the initial average savings ratio, the incremental capital/output ratio, the rate of return on debt, and t_1, t_3, and t_4. The study also computes values of these derivatives in the case of an application of the Alter model to parameters based on Tunisian data. This computation establishes the following examples of how small changes in the basic parameters affect the results of the analysis:

(1) Raising the capital/output ratio from 3.0 to 3.2 postpones the attainment of independence by at least 5 years and raises the total required inflow by an amount equal to half of initial GDP:

(2) Raising the target GDP growth rate from .045 to .05 delays independence by a year and increases the required resource inflow by roughly the same amount as under (1);

(3) A .01 error in measuring the initial average savings ratio implies an error of 4 years in predicting t_3 and over 75 per cent of initial GDP in estimating the resource transfer need;

(4) A .01 error in predicting the marginal per capita savings ratio, which is the variable we have the most doubts about to begin with, implies an error of 2 years in predicting t_3 and 25 per cent of initial GDP in projecting the transfer requirement;

(5) A .001 addition to the population growth rate, raising it from .020 to .021, delays independence by nearly 2 years and raises the transfer requirement by about 25 per cent of initial GDP; and

(6) Increasing the average rate of return on foreign debt by .01 postpones independence by at least 3 years and raises the transfer bill by more than half of initial GDP.

If an aid source wanted to apply the Alter-type analysis to a particular less-developed country, it would presumably use a range of values for each parameter and calculate corresponding ranges for the dependent variables. While these ranges would be so wide as to provide minimal help, in for example, selecting a specific interest rate on public loans, the analysis could call attention to the likelihood that the country could not meet any reasonable independence constraint unless it received, say, on the order of half its required inflow on IDA-type terms. The model could be recalculated periodically on the basis of new trends in the parameters, and the terms on new transfer could be adjusted to reflect changed probability distributions. (Or, if use was made of loan agreements with AID-type renegotiation clauses, the terms on existing agreements could be renegotiated to reflect such developments.) Fortunately, a decision made regarding the terms on a particular loan or aid package within a limited period of time is always subject, over the duration we are concerned with here, to effective reversal by future decisions on new loans and aid packages.

THE DEBT BURDEN CONSTRAINT

The rationale for the debt burden constraint is subsumed within the set of objectives introduced earlier concerning the independence constraint. Heavy indebtedness of one government to another and ownership of a major share of a country's physical capital by private foreign interests are both political issues which lend themselves to exploitation by elements that are unfriendly to the capital source countries and wish to renounce the indebtedness unilaterally as well as expropriate the private investment without compensation. However, it is even more difficult to quantify this constraint and say what levels of indebtedness and foreign investment (as ratios to national income) should not be exceeded than to set a time limit for financial independence. One way of looking at the problem, at least from an American viewpoint, is to imagine the political opposition that would be aroused in the United States if the U.S. Government were in debt to other governments or if foreigners owned physical capital in the United States to the extent of specified percentages of U.S. GNP. Assuming GNP at a 1967 level of approximately $750 billion, the ratios of existing public and publicly guaranteed debt to output in 5 less-developed regions given in Table 9 would yield a range of $43-106 billion if applied to U.S. output. This compares with 1966 totals of $12.6 billion in foreign holdings of U.S. Government obligations, $9.1 billion in direct foreign private investments in the United States, and $60.4 billion in total foreign assets and investments in the United States.[17] Table 9 shows that, with a weighted average return of 6 per cent on foreign resource transfer, the ratio of foreign liabilities to current income in 4 of the regions concerned would rise to a range of .35 to 1.01

in year t_3 (and would moderately exceed these levels for a few years between t_2 and t_3). Looked at in U.S. terms, these are very high ratios indeed--but then, one may rejoin, the United States is not dependent on foreign resource transfer in order to escape from grinding poverty, and those countries that are have to swallow their pride and beat down political opposition to high levels of foreign liabilities.

Given that a specific value can be chosen for the debt burden constraint, the most convenient means of applying it is to use it in conjunction with an Alter-type formula for debt in t_2, the year when the rate of increase of debt falls to the level of the rate of increase of GDP. Specifically, a set of i, Dt_2 pairs can be calculated such that t_2 satisfies the equation given in the Mathematical Appendix at (9); then Dt_2 can be taken as a ratio to current GDP and evaluated against the constraint. For example, if we take the Latin American model in Table 9 and set the debt burden constraint at .45--that is, debt is at no time to exceed 45 per cent of current GDP--we find that, at $t_2 = 19$, i = .035 generates a total debt, including a projection of pre-existing debt, which equals just about 45 per cent of GDP in that year. In this case, then, aid sources will want to hold the weighted average return on resource transfer to Latin America at 3 1/2 per cent.

NOTES TO CHAPTER 6

1.   Dragoslav Avramovic and Associates, Economic Growth and External Debt (Baltimore, Md.: The Johns Hopkins Press, 1964), pp. 53-55.

2.   Government of India, Planning Commission, Third Five Year Plan (New Delhi, 1961), pp. 28-29.

3.   Government of India, Planning Commission, Third Five Year Plan--Draft Outline (New Delhi, June, 1960), pp. 10-11.

4.   As reported in The New York Times, December 3, 1967, p. 11.

5.   President's Task Force on Foreign Economic Assistance, The Act for International Development--a Summary Presentation, June, 1961 (Department of State Publication 7205, General Foreign Policy Series 169, released June, 1961), p. v.

6.   U.S. Agency for International Development, Proposed Foreign Aid Program, FY 1968--Summary Presentation to the Congress, (Washington, D.C., May, 1967), p. 2.

7.   Ibid. p. 140.

8.   Avramovic et al., op. cit., p. 57.

9.   Ibid., p. 73.

10.   Ibid.

11.   Clive S. Gray, "The Spectrum of International Capital Transfer to the Underdeveloped Countries" (Unpublished Ph.D. dissertation, Department of Economics, Harvard University, 1964), pp. 407-8 and 411-12.

12.   International Bank for Reconstruction and Development, Annual Report 1966-67 (Washington, D.C.) Table 2, p. 27, and IBRD, Economics Department, External Medium- and Long-Term Public Debt--Past and Projected Amounts Outstanding, Transactions and Payments: 1956-75 (Report No. EC-149, October 14, 1966).

13.   U.S. Agency for International Development, Office of Program Coordination, "Economic Growth Trends," three separate reports for Near East and South Asia, Far East (both published in September, 1966), and Latin America, (October, 1966). Locus of savings data was in each case a table entitled "Gross National Product, Investment, and Domestic Savings."

14.   Debt data are given in IBRD, External Medium- and Long-Term Public Debt, Table 5a, pp. 15-18; GNP in U.S. Agency for International Development, Office of Program Coordination, Gross National Product--Growth Rates and Trend Data, by Region and Country (Washington, D.C., March 31, 1967; Report RC-W-138), sections of Table 3.

15.   Debt data: ibid. Debt service data from IBRD, External Medium- and Long-Term Public Debt, Table 5c, pp. 25-29.

16.   Gray, op. cit., pp. 359-66.

17.   U.S. Department of Commerce, Survey of Current Business, September, 1967, p. 40.

CHAPTER **7** THE DEBT SERVICE
RATIO CONSTRAINT

The weighted average terms, (including amortization of principal) on resource transfer to a less-
developed country should be no more severe than
will enable the benefiting country to maintain its
ratio of annual foreign investment service liabilities to current foreign-exchange earnings at or
below a specified level.

Of all constraints relevant to our study, this is the one that
has exercised the greatest influence on the policies of capital
sources and about which the most has been written. Both the theoretical and practical justifications for this constraint are discussed
thoroughly by Avramovic et al. in their 1964 study, and we will
draw extensively on their findings.

RATIONALE FOR THE DEBT SERVICE
RATIO CONSTRAINT

The basic theory behind the debt service ratio constraint is
the premise that any borrower, whether a government, corporation,
or individual, is a better credit risk if there is a reasonable probability that it can service its loans out of current income, preferably
income generated by investment of the loan proceeds, rather than
having to refinance them by fresh borrowing or drawing on liquid
reserves, which it may not have in sufficient quantity. Debt-
servicing capacity out of current income is that amount of income
which is not required to meet other obligations so pressing that
the borrower would sooner default on his debt, and face all the
disadvantageous consequences arising therefrom, than forego
meeting these obligations. In the case of an individual, his first
concern is to keep body and soul together, and he will not allocate
to servicing his debts, even at the risk of bankruptcy, more of his

144

income than will leave him enough to survive physically. A corporation, on the other hand, will allocate up to 100 per cent of its income--that is, revenues less current expenses--for debt servicing. Under law, its creditors' claims are senior obligations vis-à-vis the equity claims of stockholders.

On the other hand, even in the absence of liquid reserves, a corporation or individual normally has fixed assets which serve as security for loans and can be realized by creditors if there is no other recourse. The only comparable security the government of a less-developed country can offer its foreign creditors is its foreign reserves, which, however, are normally depleted to the minimum level required to finance current foreign trade once the development effort is undertaken in earnest. Therefore, even more than is the case with corporations and individuals, lenders to governments of less-developed countries must assess debt-servicing capacity on the basis of current income and access to fresh supplies of capital. As we saw in Chapter 5, such supplies are available by and large only from the same few sources that are appraising debt-servicing capacity for the purpose of current lending.

Leaving aside this questionable element of debt-servicing capacity for the moment, we note that the current income (more accurately, receipts) relevant here are foreign-exchange earnings, which overlap only in part with national income and are generally small--in the large majority of less-developed countries, less than 25 per cent--in comparison with it. As with an individual, a country has certain obligations other than debt service which it must meet out of its foreign-exchange earnings in order to survive or at least to prevent severe economic dislocation which would cost any government its political life, and these will enjoy first priority in any foreign-exchange squeeze. Avramovic defines a "minimum tolerable" level of imports, indicating that foodstuffs, raw materials, fuels, and capital goods, to the extent not produced locally, would normally enjoy such priority. Thus, an important factor in assessing a country's debt-servicing capacity is the amount of "compressible" items in its import bill--i.e., imported goods and services a government could afford politically to severely restrict or even eliminate in order to save foreign exchange for the purpose of meeting debt service obligations. The most obvious candidate for this category, according to Avramovic, is nonfood consumer goods.

On the other hand, creditors must anticipate occasional situations in which, far from being able or willing to "compress" the regular import bill in order to meet debt service obligations in a foreign-exchange squeeze, the government of a less-developed country will be unwilling or politically unable to prevent an extraordinary increase in that bill. Avramovic refers to these as "emergency or inflation-induced import increases." The most obvious example of such a situation is a crop failure, which

necessitates the government arranging extraordinary food imports
in order to keep the population alive. If foreign-exchange earnings could be quickly adjusted to compensate for extraordinary
rises in imports, such occurrences would not place debt service
obligations in jeopardy. But, of course, the products on which
most less-developed countries depend to earn foreign exchange
are subject, at least in the very short run, to severe inelasticities
on both the demand and supply sides.

For all these reasons, the larger the ratio of debt service
obligations to ordinary foreign-exchange earnings, the greater
the risk that short-run disturbances will prevent debtors from
meeting their obligations and the more likely it is that creditors
will be forced into explicit refinancing of existing obligations
simultaneously with maintaining the normal inflow of capital to
new projects and other end-uses. It is this type of situation the
debt service ratio constraint is designed to avoid. The objective
behind the constraint thus derives from considerations of short-
run financial strategy in contrast to the much longer-term objective underlying the independence constraint. In other words,
it is based on cash concepts rather than on the underlying
productive potential of a less-developed economy. As we noted
in Chapter 5, the division of a country's sales between external
and internal markets is irrelevant to its aggregate productive
capacity. But financial constraints need be no less compelling for
their partial divorce from long-run productive forces.

During the course of development, a number of conflicting
influences bear on a country's flexibility with regard to allocating
foreign exchange to debt service. Much depends on whether the
country's comparative advantage, not to mention its government's
policies, enable it to increase its exports more rapidly than income. This may be illustrated by considering two countries with
identical GDP's, exports, and debt service ratios at a given point
in time. We assume that the debt service ratios remain constant
and identical. Thus, that country whose exports increase more
rapidly than the other's is sustaining larger debt service obligations. However, it also has more residual foreign exchange with
which to finance imports and thus a bigger foreign-exchange
cushion to fall back on in the event of short-run disturbances that
affect both countries equally in an absolute sense. Such a country
is in a better position to maintain a given debt service ratio.

It has been suggested by Pieter H. Lieftinck, writing in the
Princeton International Finance series, that growth biases the
maturity structure of a less-developed country's international debt
toward short- and medium-term obligations, thus increasing the
need for compensating infusions of external capital on easy
terms.[1] The reason for this is the existence in such countries
of a relatively high marginal propensity to import out of private
income. The rising incomes that accompany growth thus generate
increased private imports of both consumer and capital goods that are

eligible at best for short- or medium-term export or supplier credits, rather than easy-term public loans or grants. Other writers--e.g., Avramovic--have pointed out that, insofar as the demand for manufactured consumer goods is met internally by the establishment of import-substituting industries, the composition of the import bill shifts toward raw materials and intermediate goods that are similarly not eligible for traditional project-oriented public finance.[2] Moreover, a country has less flexibility to restrict such imports in balance-of-payments crises because doing so forces domestic plants to operate below capacity and idle part of the labor force. Insofar as foreign equity capital participates in the development of import-substituting industries, a further element of rigidity arises in the balance of payments due to the fact that income remittances in such industries do not vary, as do remittances from export-oriented industries, in response to fluctuations in foreign-exchange earnings.

All these considerations have to be evaluated in the contest of the individual country's circumstances, the most that can be said in general is that, despite the less-developed countries' urgent need for external capital which cannot help but raise their debt service ratios, it is by no means clear that their capacity to maintain high ratios, without periodic recourse to debt rescheduling, is on a constant uptrend.

QUANTIFYING THE CONSTRAINT

Once the debt service ratio is accepted in principle as a valid constraint, the next problem is to quantify it, i.e., decide what level of the ratio to regard as critical. Avramovic notes that past efforts to determine this level have been largely unsuccessful, if for no other reason than the fact that "policy responses to balance of payments pressures inevitably differ from one period to another and from country to country."[3] He adds, however, that the most fundamental reason for this failure is that the debt service ratio combines only two out of nine variables relevant to measuring the impact of the debt service burden on a country's balance of payments and thus to an assessment of debt-servicing capacity based on foreign-exchange availability. The nine variables, classified as "fluctuating," "offsetting," or "rigid," are:

1. Fluctuating variables

    (a) exports

    (b) capital flows

    (c) emergency and inflation-induced imports

2. Offsetting variables

    (a) reserves

    (b) compensatory finance

    (c) compressible imports

3.   Rigid variables

(a) minimum tolerable imports

(b) debt service--interest

(c) debt service--amortization [4]

It would appear that Avramovic made a slip of the pen when saying that the debt service ratio combines only two variables, for 1 (a), 3 (b), and 3 (c) make up the ratio--on page 42, Avramovic notes specifically that amortization is included--thus leaving only six unaccounted for.

Before turning to the six residual variables, it is necessary to look more closely at the two debt service variables. Ideally, in order to assess the balance-of-payments pressure and thus what is crudely described as the "temptation to default" arising out of existing foreign debt service obligations, capital sources should take into account the charges on all fixed debt, whether public or private. It can be argued that they should also include profits, dividends, and "normal" repatriation of capital arising out of foreign equity investment. The bulk of the statistical effort in this field has gone into collecting data on official debt service, for which the World Bank now has extensive series.[5] Partial evidence as to how far inclusion of private debt service and profits, etc., would increase debt service ratios based on the official debt series is given by Avramovic in a table whose highlights we reproduce in Table 10. An indication of the statistical problems involved in computing official debt service ratios is given by comparing Avramovic's series for 1962 public debt service ratios with the revised figures for the same year given in the World Bank's 1966-67 Annual Report, reproduced in Column Ia of Table 10.

The entries for some countries (Avramovic does not say which) are not strictly comparable because in some but not all cases interest payments on private debt and private profits and dividends are counted net of similar receipts from abroad. It is for this reason that an entry in Column II or III is sometimes less than the corresponding entry in Column I or II respectively--in these cases, gross receipts from abroad exceed gross outpayments to abroad in regard to the private components. Because the denominator of the debt service ratio, exports of goods and services, is a measure of gross receipts, it is misleading to include a net element, incorporating a component of the denominator but giving it a negative sign, in the numerator. The problem is basically one of availability of statistical resources, especially when one is trying, as Avramovic does, to provide measures for a large group of countries.

Where private foreign investment is concentrated in export industries, it generates by itself the foreign exchange required to service it, and one can argue that it need not be counted in appraising the debt service ratio. The most obvious illustration of this in Table 10 is Iran, where inclusion of private profits and dividends, arising very largely from petroleum operations, gives rise to the highest value in the table. On the other hand, if such payments are to be excluded from the numerator, then the receipts that finance them should similarly be excluded from the denominator. In the case of Iran, subtraction from exports of the difference between public debt service payments and service payments on all foreign investment, public as well as private, increases the public debt service ratio by 40 per cent, from .09 to .127.

About as much as one can conclude from Table 10 is that, for most developing countries, public debt service represents a substantial share of total investment income obligations, especially when the private component of the latter is measured net. As public debt continues to accumulate, in most less-developed countries, more rapidly than private foreign investment, especially net investment, it seems likely to maintain its share in such obligations, despite the lower average return payable on public investment. Therefore, public debt service obligations are a useful indicator in appraising the burden of debt service, even though their weight in the total picture varies from one country to another and should be interpreted in the light of more complete information about each country's situation.

Turning now to Avramovic's six residual variables, a case can be made for saying that at least two of them are already taken into account--more accurately, discounted--implicitly. As far as 2 (a), reserves, is concerned, it is taken for granted that a less-developed country embarked on a serious development effort will soon run down its reserves to the minimum level required to keep foreign trade running smoothly, and, at such a level reserves cannot be regarded as being available for debt service because a foreign-exchange crisis will simultaneously impose so many other extraordinary demands on them. Moreover, 2 (b), compensatory finance, can also be ruled out on the ground that it will normally behave perversely in a foreign-exchange crisis. In other words, whenever a less-developed country faces such a crisis, the threat of devaluation far outweighs any possible gain resulting from higher interest earnings, and short-term capital moves, on net, out of rather than into the country.

Apart from the three variables representing imports of goods and services, this now leaves only 1 (b), capital flows. If capital sources took the view of creditworthiness we described in Chapter 5 as the traditional one, they would also discount capital flows in evaluating the debt service ratio because, with most less-developed countries, the same few agencies are likely to be for many years the only significant sources of capital available directly or indirectly--mostly the latter--to refinance debt.

TABLE 10

Three Measures of the Debt Service Ratio, 1961–62

Region/Country	Measure Number: [a]	1961			1962			
		I	II	III	Ia	Ib	II	III
Latin America								
Argentina		.20	.18	.22	(.27)	.22	.13	.16
Brazil		.17	.31	.36	(.31)	.20	b	
Chile		.23			(.22)	.25		
Colombia		.13	.14	.20	(.13)	.11	.14	.19
Costa Rica		.06	.06	.07	(.08)	.09		
Ecuador		.08	.09	.23	(.08)	.08	.09	.21
Honduras		.04	.01	.06	(.03)	.03		
Mexico		.11	.30	.22	(.19)	.16	.19	.28
Nicaragua		.05	.05	.06	(.04)	.05	.03	.05
Paraguay		.07	.14	.15	(.06)	.06		
Uruguay		.05	.02	.03	(.06)	.05		

Region / Country	I	Ib	Ia	II	III
South Asia					
India	.06	.13	(.11)	.09	.19
Pakistan	.05	.04	(.065)	.07	.09
East Asia					
Philippines	.07		(.04)	.03	.05
Africa					
Rhodesia & Nyasaland	.05	.15			
South Europe & Middle East					
Iran	.08	.07	(.09)	.06	.38
Israel	.27		(.19)	.29	
Spain	.03	.09	(.02)	.10	
Turkey	.20	.28	(.16)	.17	.24
Yugoslavia	.09		(.11)	.14	.19

Notes:

[a] The three measures are defined as follows:

I & Ib -- ratio of public debt service to exports of goods and services as given in Dragoslav Avramovic and Associates, Economic Growth and External Debt (Baltimore, Md.: The Johns Hopkins Press, 1964), Table 7, pp. 44–45.

Ia -- ratio of public debt service to exports of goods and services in 1962 as given in International Bank for Reconstruction and Development, Annual Report, 1966–67, (Washington, D. C.), Table 7, pp. 32–33.

[b] Empty spaces denote data not available in Avramovic table.

II -- ratio of service payments on all fixed interest debt to exports of goods and services as given in Avramovic, loc cit.

III -- ratio of service payments, including profits and dividends on all foreign capital (but excluding repatriation of capital), to exports of goods and services as given in ibid.

However, since these agencies have been forced into the position of presuming their own continued willingness and ability to lend as an element in debt-servicing capacity, Avramovic's variable 1 (b) is relevant to our present exercise. One way of taking it into account would be to set the limit on the debt service ratio so as to include an amortization factor of whatever magnitude could be safely expected to come in for refinancing each year in accordance with ongoing programs of resource transfer. Excessive accumulation of short-term debt would raise the amortization element above this allowable level and would thus increase the debt service ratio toward or above its prudent limit.

As for Avramovic's three import variables, there is no doubt that, as we have already argued, these are highly relevant to measurement of debt-servicing capacity. One could still excuse the debt service ratio for failing to include them explicitly as long as they were taken into account in setting the critical value of that ratio. In other words, it would be reasonable to say that, because of the structure of imports in a given country, the ratio of debt service to exports should not be allowed to exceed a certain level.

Nevertheless, such systematic calculations have rarely, if ever, been undertaken in regard to any particular country. Avramovic discusses in general what factors would have to be taken into account in the process and gives a table showing the percentages of nonfood consumer goods (i.e., "compressible" imports) in the merchandise imports of 19 countries in 1961. But this is only the barest beginning. Still, Avramovic says that the debt service ratio is the "most frequently used rule of thumb in appraising the creditworthiness of borrowing countries."[6] He attributes its "strange powers of survival," in spite of widespread recognition of its inadequacy, to three factors: (1) simplicity and easy understandability; (2) a firm statistical basis, in contrast to measures based on national income; and (3) the absence of any alternative.

THE 10 PER CENT RULE OF THUMB

In the absence of any quantitative basis for evaluating the debt service ratio constraint, one wonders how it can have received any practical application over all these years. I personally miss in Avramovic's discussion any examples of a capital source that, viewing a less-developed country's debt service picture in relation to its exports, has set a specific limit on the ratio and refused to lend if the ratio was projected to exceed that limit (or, more relevant to our present study, examples of a capital source adjusting its terms on new loans accordingly). On the basis of limited contact with international aid personnel in the late 1950's and early 1960's and two years of employment with U.S. AID during

1961-63, it is my understanding that there was a rule of thumb in
vogue at the time to the effect that less-developed countries should
be given aid on such terms as would not raise their public debt
service ratio above .10 in a "normal" year--i.e., with exports
near a multiyear trend line and discounting any "lumpy" amortization obligations. In late 1961, when AID headquarters was deciding which alternative sets of terms on the new dollar-repayable
loans would apply to various countries, I had the responsibility
of drafting the AID Nigeria Mission's recommendations to Washington on where Nigeria should fit in this scheme. The analysis
departed from the explicit assumption that external financing of
the pending 1962-68 Development Plan should not saddle Nigeria
with a post-1968 public debt service ratio of more than .10. It
can be said, at least, that Washington never contradicted this
point, and the terms eventually assigned to AID loans to Nigeria
closely corresponded to the Mission's recommendations. (I do
not pretend, however, that this was a case of direct cause and
effect; rather, nearly all African countries were placed in the
group eligible for loans on the most lenient terms--40-year
maturity, 10-year grace period, 3/4 per cent interest--applied by
AID, on general considerations of comparative economic backwardness.)

A further piece of evidence for the 10 per cent rule of thumb
at that time can be found in repeated implications in Chapter 4 of
the 1960 Avramovic and Gulhati work, Debt Servicing Problems
of Low Income Countries, 1956-58, to the effect that any public
debt service ratio above .10 is on the high side. At the time the
International Development Association was set up, the public debt
service ratios of a number of the World Bank's most important
borrowers were just beginning to exceed .10, and the Bank was
anxious to retard any further increase. By way of emphasizing its
desire to hold down these ratios, the Bank assigned IDA's inaugural
loan to Honduras, whose ratio at the time was only .043.

I have been unable to find any explicit rationalization of the
10 per cent rule of thumb. Probably there is little to be said for
it other than that 10 per cent is regarded in many walks of life as
a threshold beyond which a quantity becomes significant. It might
be argued that, as soon as foreign debt service payments become
a "significant" claim on foreign-exchange resources or government revenues, they pose a target for political elements within the
borrowing country who discount the disadvantages of defaulting.
Perhaps of greater significance is the leverage that short-run
disturbances such as declines in export earnings or emergency
import needs exert on a debt service ratio whose numerator is
holding to a stable growth path parallel to the long-run trend line
of exports. Avramovic et al. show that at least some less-
developed countries experienced, between 1955 and 1962, short-
run declines in their export earnings, from peak to trough, of
20 per cent or more, the highest being Uruguay's at 54 per cent.[7]

Given a debt service ratio of .10 based on long-run trends, a drop of 50 per cent in export earnings would raise the ratio to .20 at a time of generally severe pressure on the balance of payments. If 10 per cent is the threshold of significance, then 20 per cent is, very simply, double it.

Again, from the viewpoint of responsible creditors such as the World Bank, there may have been some disciplinary value in maintaining a rule of thumb which, in its brief heyday, was not so strict as to preclude any significant additional borrowing by most less-developed countries but which set a low enough limit to (hopefully) induce some less-developed countries to follow more prudent policies, with respect to national expenditures and the accumulation of short- and medium-term debt, than they might otherwise have done. At the same time, the 10 per cent rule has served as a specific peg for the Bank and some member governments, notably the United States, on which to base pressure for easing of terms by other capital-exporting nations, as well as justification for the establishment of soft-loan agencies such as IDA and the Fund for Special Operations of the Inter-American Development Bank.

By 1964, it was becoming evident to the World Bank that appropriations to the IDA by governments of advanced countries and bilateral aid by these governments on easy terms were not going to suffice to keep the weighted average terms on the amount of transfer required to meet general aid objectives at a level that would prevent public debt service ratios from rising considerably above .10 or, if already above .10, staying there, in a number of countries. Table 11 shows the development of these ratios during 1962-66 in countries where data published by the World Bank show that ratios have exceeded .10 in one of these years. Entries for a few countries in the table show no discernible trend or, in two or three cases, a downward trend. This is a result of heavy concentrations of short-term maturities in particular years (some of these cases have already led to debt-rescheduling exercises) and does not vitiate the long-term upward trend of public debt service ratios in countries that have been receiving large-scale assistance on fairly constant weighted average terms over a number of years. An example of the latter case is India, to which special attention is called in the Bank's 1966-67 Annual Report.

The Bank continues agitating for easier terms on development assistance, which it hopes to achieve partly by expanding the operations of IDA. This question was high on the agenda of the Bank/International Monetary Fund (IMF) annual meetings in September, 1967, at which Bank President George D. Woods noted that "if the volume of development finance does not grow, and if there is no improvement in the terms, development aid will simply eat itself up."[8] One manifestation of aid eating itself up is the increase in debt service ratios. Yet, in order to provide

TABLE 11

Public Debt Service/Export Ratios of Countries, 1962-66

Area and country	1962	1963	1964	1965	1966
Latin America					
Argentina	.273	.244	.307	.223	n.a.
Bolivia	.074	.059	.128	.126	.091
Brazil	.311	.259	.244	.328	.294
Chile	.224	.177	.180	.124	n.a.
Colombia	.130	.151	.128	.147	n.a.
Costa Rica	.082	.088	.076	.078	.131
Dominican Republic	.008	.003	.027	.169	.143
Guatemala	.113	.044	.061	.038	n.a.
Mexico	.188	.168	.233	.230	.214
Uruguay	.056	.061	.060	.086	.131
South Asia					
India	.108	.098	.152	.160	.220
Pakistan	.065	.116	.100	.102	n.a.
Africa					
Swaziland	.030	.026	.063	.113	n.a.
South Europe & Middle East					
Israel	.190	.181	.197	.149	n.a.
Turkey	.160	.147	.202	.137	.116
Yugoslavia	.106	.120	.117	.133	n.a.

Source: International Bank for Reconstruction and Development, Annual Report, 1966-67 (Washington, D.C.), Table 7, p. 33.

155

an essential minimum of capital aid to those countries with high
ratios, the Bank has had to continue making them loans on its
ordinary terms, which are fixed at "hard" levels (except for some
flexibility with regard to maturities) by the action of world money
markets. Thus, ten of the countries listed in Table 11, all having
public debt service ratios above .10 in the most recent year for
which data are available, received regular World Bank loans in
1965-66 or 1966-67.

In the face of the apparently irresistible trend toward higher
public debt service ratios, and the need which the Bank sees to
continue its regular lending operations notwithstanding, Avramovic
could not very well imply that the Bank is making loans to borrowers who are no longer creditworthy. His 1964 analysis thus
omits the implicit emphasis of his earlier work on .10 as the
dividing line between "low" and "high" public debt service ratios.
Instead, he notes evidence presented by Raymond Mikesell, among
others, to the effect that major borrowers in the nineteenth and
early twentieth centuries, notably Argentina, Australia, and Canada,
at various times sustained ratios of total investment service to
exports in the .30's and even .40's without defaulting. According to
Mikesell, "the breaking point in most countries during the 1930's
(was) 25 to 30 per cent."[9] These estimates are not strictly comparable with today's public debt service ratios because they, on one
hand, include investment income payments on private account, and,
on the other hand, exclude amortization payments. But comparable
ratios for the earlier periods would certainly be in the .20's at
least and possibly higher than the available estimates. Avramovic
also notes that countries such as Canada and Australia have completed their transition back to low debt service ratios, with domestic
capital playing the dominant role in further economic expansion.
A similar path is traced by the debt service ratio implied by the
parameters Avramovic uses in his growth model, to which we now
turn.

THE DEBT SERVICE RATIO DURING GROWTH-CUM-DEBT

To illustrate the behavior of the debt service ratio during the
growth-cum-debt process, Avramovic uses the Alter-type model
described in Chapter 5 to derive the cumulative resource transfer
requirement, representing foreign debt at the end of a given year,
and then grafts onto it assumptions about the rate of amortization
of foreign loans, the initial ratio of exports to GDP, and the rate of
growth of exports. The debt service ratio in any year is then
given by the sum of the assumed interest and amortization rates
times debt outstanding at the end of the preceding year, divided by
exports in the given year. For the savings, investment, and income
parameters Avramovic uses the same assumptions as for the initial

run of the model described in Chapter 6--GDP growth target of 5
per cent, initial gross domestic savings rate of .10, marginal
savings rate of .20, and capital/output ratio of 3:1. He then
assumes that foreign debt bears an interest rate of 6 per cent and
is amortized over 15 years, terms "fairly representative of conventional lending."[10] An initial export ratio of .10 and export
growth rate of 4 per cent are also assumed. Avramovic then shows
that a maximum debt service ratio of over .50, in force between
years 16 and 19 of the growth-cum-debt process, results from
these assumptions. Avramovic does not go on to conclude that this
is an intolerably high debt service ratio and that steps must be
taken to avoid such a magnitude. He does, however, suggest that,
if a country with parameters less favorable than the values chosen
for the model run receives capital predominantly on hard terms,
"the rising debt service may cause a threat to liquidity which will
be critical," and the only way to prevent such a tenuous financial
situation from lasting decades would be to ease the terms on resource transfer.[11]

    In evaluating the quantitative result of Avramovic's model--
i.e., a debt service ratio in excess of .50--it is important to note
that this ratio covers not only public debt service obligations
(unless it is assumed the country can attract no private capital at
all) but rather incorporates service payments on all resources,
public or private, that are transferred to the country in order to
fill the gap between investment and domestic savings and enable GDP
to grow at the target rate. If 6 per cent seems too low a return for
private equity investment (although it could also be regarded as a
weighted average between hard loans, private investment, and easy-
term finance), the annual amortization factor of .0667 assumed for
hard loans is probably a heavier service burden than corresponds
to "normal" repatriation of private capital--assuming the country
maintains a favorable private investment "climate."

    As was true in applying the independence constraint in Chapter
6, slight modifications in the assumed parameters affect substantially the maximum debt service ratio attained during the growth-
cum-debt process. To solve the model for that ratio, it is necessary first to determine in what year the ratio will be at a maximum.
This will be the first year after the year in which the rate of increase of debt is reduced to the same level as the rate of increase
of exports. The simplified equation whose solution gives the year
before the year in question mirrors the equation used in Chapter 6
to solve for t_2, the year in which the rate of increase of debt becomes equal to the rate of growth of GDP. The Mathematical
Appendix gives, at (10), the appropriate equation for each of three
variants of an Alter-type model, assuming a constant growth rate
of aggregate savings. These variants are: (a) the aid requirement
determined by the investment-savings gap; (b) the aid requirement
determined by the import-export gap, with imports growing at the
same rate as GDP and exports more rapidly; and (c) the aid

requirement determined by the import-export gap, with exports growing at the same rate as GDP and imports more slowly.

For his debt service ratio model, Avramovic chose values for the initial export/GDP ratio and the export growth rate which he describes as reflecting "a relatively closed economy" with a large population and low initial income (e.g., India or Pakistan), as well as "an economy where relative emphasis is on import substitution, rather than on rapid expansion of exports," a situation Avramovic considers "a reasonable approximation of reality."[12] The relative emphasis on import substitution is illustrated by the fact, not brought out by Avramovic, that the cumulative investment-savings gap implied by his model up to t_1, when savings becomes equal to investment, coupled with an export growth rate of only 4 per cent, or 1 per cent less than the GDP growth rate, equals the cumulative import-export gap that would arise if imports grew at a constant annual rate of only 1 per cent.* This contrasts with an annual import growth rate of 6 per cent during 1960-65 reported by the World Bank for 40 selected developing countries (of 5 regions, only Latin America, with 3.1 per cent, showed a rate below 6 per cent).

Export growth rates recorded during 1960-65 and given in the World Bank's 1966-67 Annual Report for 5 regions of the less-developed world are all higher than Avramovic's assumption of 4 per cent. If we recompute his maximum debt service ratio using these data as well as recent estimates of initial average export ratios for the same areas, we obtain estimates below Avramovic's .53 for every region except South Asia, where the high value of .81 results from Pakistan's and India's low average export ratios. Table 12 compares these results.

The table suggests that, with the poorest and most highly populated countries in the sample whose problems Avramovic was trying to illustrate, the debt service ratio is likely to be an even more severe constraint on aid terms than his results implied. To compare the severity of this constraint with that of the independence constraint discussed in Chapter 6, we must trace the debt service ratio in the context of aid requirements calculated with the same data as were used in that chapter's Table 9. This we do in Table 13.

Part II of Table 13 shows the maximum debt service ratios attained in 4 regions on 2 alternative assumptions about the weighted average terms on resource transfer: (1) a zero interest rate with amortization over 40 years at 2 1/2 per cent per year--similar to terms on IDA, Canadian, and (at one time) AID soft loans; and (2) interest at 6 per cent with amortization over 15 years at 6 2/3 per cent annually--the terms chosen by Avramovic as representing

---

*For method of computation, see Mathematical Appendix at (13).

TABLE 12

Maximum Debt Service Ratio Attained in Avramovic
Model on Varying Assumptions About Exports

| | | Source of Export Assumptions Data for: | | | |
	Avramovic	Africa	South Asia	South Europe & Middle East	Latin America
Initial export/GDP ratio	.10	.200	.054	.081	.117
Export growth rate	.040	.049	.052	.102	.080
Year when maximum debt service/export ratio attained	19	17	17	11	13
Maximum debt service/export ratio	.53	.23	.81	.30	.26

Sources: Values of all parameters underlying the computations
in the table, other than initial export/GDP ratio and export
growth rate (for which, see following notes), are taken from
Dragoslav Avramovic and Associates, Economic Growth and External Debt (Baltimore, Md.: The Johns Hopkins Press, 1964),
pp. 57-59, as is the model specification.

Value for Africa was computed from 1965 data for 8 countries in
the International Monetary Fund's International Financial Statistics;
for all other regions, the data were taken from AID Economic
Growth Trends booklets for the Far East, the Near East and South
Asia, and Latin America, published in 1966, the oil-producing
countries Iran, Iraq, and Venezuela being excluded.

Values for 1960-65 reported in the International Bank for Reconstruction and Development, Annual Report, 1966-67 (Washington, D.C.), p. 27.

"conventional lending." The amortization assumptions are consistent with use of the equal annual installment (of principal) or level
annual payment (of principal and interest) method, the final maturities being 40 and 15 years respectively; or with the hypothetical
"net value" (principal repayments a constant proportion of the outstanding balance) method, the proportions being .025 and .0667

TABLE 13

Effects of Debt Service Ratio Constraint

	Africa	South Asia	South Europe & Middle East	Latin America
I--Values of actual or assumed parameters				
1. GDP growth rate (r)	.05	.05	.06	.05
2. Incremental capital/output ratio (K)	3.4	4.0	3.0	4.0
3. Investment/GDP ratio (Kr)	.17	.20	.18	.20
4. Initial savings/GDP ratio (S_0)	.10	.136	.136	.164
5. Savings growth rate (s)	.073	.08	.08	.06
6. Year when savings $\geq$ investment (t_1)	26	15	17	22
7. Initial foreign debt/GDP ratio (D_0)	.142	.096	.064	.108
8. Return on existing foreign debt (i_1)	.05	.05	.03	.05
9. Annual amortization rate on existing foreign debt (a_1)	.05	.05	.05	.05
10. Initial export/GDP ratio (X_0)	.200	.054	.081	.117
11. Export growth rate (x)	.049	.052	.102	.080

II--Maximum debt service ratios attained

$i=0$, annual amortization rate = .025

	18	12	10	12
Year of maximum debt service/export ratio	18	12	10	12
Same-year debt service/initial GDP ratio	.063	.031	.016	.028
Same-year exports/initial GDP ratio	.451	.094	.194	.273
Maximum debt service/export ratio	.14	.31	.08	.10

i=.06, annual amortization rate = .06 2/3

	29	16	14	18
Year of maximum debt service/export ratio	29	16	14	18
Same-year debt service/initial GDP ratio	.596	.157	.099	.143
Same-year exports/initial GDP ratio	.763	.116	.287	.433
Maximum debt service/export ratio	.78	1.35	.34	.33

III--Operation of the constraint
Debt service ratio limited to maximum of .20 (Latin America only)

i=.02
Maximum permissible annual amortization rate (a)	.065
Corresponding weighted average maturity	15

i=.06
Maximum permissible annual amortization rate (a)	.006
Corresponding weighted average maturity	159

Sources:
   parameters 1-8: see Chapter 6, Table 9.
   parameter 9:   assumed arbitrarily to be .05 in all regions,
      implying 20-year average maturity without grace
      period. World Bank data suggest that maturity
      structure of existing debt is actually somewhat
      harder than this.

   parameters 10-11: see Table 12.

respectively. The reason for this indifference between methods of amortization is that we are only looking at the period during which debt is still growing, and principal repayments on whatever system are assumed to be offset instantaneously by new infusions.

All the ratios in the table take into account service on pre-existing debt, which is assumed, as it was in Table 9 of Chapter 6, to be continually refinanced at the presently applicable weighted average interest rate. Since the amortization rate is relevant here, as it was not in Chapter 6, we have to assume a rate applicable to pre-existing debt. For every region, we assume it equal to 5 per cent per annum. Requirements for net additional resource transfer, which make up new debt and thus determine the major component of debt service in the critical future years, are identical with those calculated in Table 9, utilizing the Alter-type model variant which assumes a constant rate of increase of aggregate savings.

Compared with the values in Table 11, Table 13 shows that debt service ratios attained in the assumption of future capital inflows at zero interest and 40-year maturities are comparable with or lower than presently existing ratios in all regions except South Asia. But, with a shift to resource transfer exclusively on hard terms, the maximum service ratio exceeds .30 in every case and in two cases, Africa and South Asia, effectively renders the growth-cum-debt process not feasible. The value of 1.35 attained in South Asia does not mean that the region would be paying out net, on account of debt service, more than its total foreign-exchange receipts, because such receipts also include fresh capital inflow, which would offset some of the debt service payments. But even if capital sources discounted the amortization component of the service ratio, as we suggested earlier in this chapter they may already be doing in the knowledge that the fundamental objectives of aid to less-developed countries will be defeated unless existing debt is "rolled over," the roughly 50 per cent of the ratio corresponding to interest payments would still disqualify the region for further transfer except on the easiest of terms.

DERIVING OPTIMUM TERMS

Part III of Table 13 is a brief illustration of how the debt service ratio constraint can be applied directly to yield limiting values for the terms on resource transfer. Because these terms consist of two different components--the rates of interest and amortization (grace periods for payment of principal and/or interest are a third component which we ignore for the moment)--the process of solving a system of equations for limiting terms involves calculating a set of value-pairs. This, in turn, is done by fixing the value of one or the other component and then solving the system for the second. The mathematics of the Alter-type model makes it far simpler computationally to fix values for the interest rate and then solve for the amortization rate, rather than vice versa, and this is the procedure followed in the two computations shown in Table 13. However, if the analyst has access to a suitably programmed computer, no time is lost in following the opposite procedure.

The Mathematical Appendix gives, at (11), the final expression for the amortization rate which was evaluated to yield the entries in Table 13. The procedure followed was to fix the interest rate at 2 per cent and 6 per cent alternately, determine the year of the maximum debt service ratio in the manner already outlined, assess the total amount of debt service in that year permitted by the constraint (here set at .20), and then solve for the amortization rate. The table shows that, with the interest rate set at 6 per cent, the solution for the amortization rate in our Latin America model is insignificantly different from zero, meaning that an interest rate of that magnitude can be tolerated only if the finance is in the form of a perpetual loan. With any higher interest rate, the solution for the amortization rate would, of course, be negative, meaning that so high a weighted average interest rate is incompatible with a debt service ratio constraint of .20.

Obviously, the foregoing procedures can be varied in a great many ways. One variant worth mentioning would correspond to a policy decision by capital sources to limit the debt service ratio attained in a given future year, such as the year of "independence" according to one of the criteria in Chapter 6, rather than over the entire growth-cum-debt process. Such a decision would allow the less-developed country to attain higher debt service ratios in the interim and thus make it "creditworthy" for a harder mix of loan terms than would be acceptable under the original conditions. This policy can be rationalized on the ground that capital sources would consider a manageable debt service ratio to be a condition of financial independence--if a country which is nominally independent of extraordinary net capital inflow has to run to its creditors for emergency debt rescheduling in the event of reasonably probable short-run disturbances, then its independence is shaky. At the same time, the creditors would not be worried if the country attained a considerably higher debt service ratio in the interim, on the ground that occasional emergency debt rescheduling is just another of the many responsibilities capital sources have to bear vis-à-vis less-developed countries during the growth-cum-debt process.

One of the chief practical advantages the debt service ratio constraint has over the independence constraint is that capital sources do not have to look so far into the future in order to apply it. To apply the independence constraint, one must decide by what year one wants a less-developed country to be more or less independent of extraordinary resource transfer, and, given the extreme relative poverty of so many countries today, this unavoidably becomes an exercise in foreseeing the distant future. The debt service ratio constraint, on the other hand, is as relevant to the near as to the more distant future. The analyst can fix a desired level of the debt service ratio five or at most ten years hence, when the effects of inevitable divergencies of real from predicted values of exports, imports, and other parameters will not yet snowball out of control, and make corresponding recommendations for aid terms within a margin of error not exceeding, let us say, 25 per cent. Within this shorter period, it will frequently be an acceptable approximation to reality to project the net resource transfer requirement as a constant annual amount. In that event, the task of deriving maximum aid terms is greatly simplified. The Mathematical Appendix gives at (12) an equation that can be solved directly for the sum of the interest and amortization rates, and iteratively, with little computational effort, for the interest rate (assuming the sum of the interest and amortization rates is known) or, assuming interest and amortization are determined, for a factor giving the proportion of aid that must be provided in the form of either grants or loans that generate no service obligations before the target date. The proof is given in my earlier study of capital transfer to the underdeveloped countries.[13] The study also shows how grace periods can be built into this analysis and derives the relevant formula for a two-year grace period.[14]

IMPLICATIONS OF HOLDING DEBT SERVICE RATIO CONSTANT

Because a number of countries already have debt service ratios (probably we should restrict this to public debt service ratios, about which most is known on an internationally comparable basis) that are regarded as too high, or in any case as high as they should prudently be allowed to go, it is relevant to consider what is required to prevent an existing debt service ratio from increasing. Very broadly, if a country can attract new loans only on the same weighted average terms as apply to its presently outstanding debt, only if the country increases its indebtedness no faster than its exports will the debt service ratio not increase. The question then arises whether an increase in debt limited to this rate will suffice to help less-developed countries achieve the income targets they and their creditors set for them.

From Table 13 we note that existing average ratios of public debt to GDP in selections of countries comprising four regions range between .06 and .14. For 12 countries identified in the World Bank's 1966-67 Annual Report as the larger debtors among less-developed countries the range is from roughly .10 to .26. This is shown in Table 14 following:

TABLE 14

Ratios of Existing Public External Debt
to GDP of Twelve Major Debtors

Israel	.26
Chile	.23
Yugoslavia	.20
Colombia	.16
Pakistan	.16
Argentina	.12
India	.11
Turkey	.10
Brazil	.10
Nigeria	.10
Mexico	.10
Iran	.09

Source: Numerator is external public debt (for Brazil, includes also private debt) at 12/31/64, including undisbursed
loans, given in International Bank for Reconstruction and Development, Annual Report, 1966-67 (Washington, D.C.), Table 6, p. 31.

Denominator is 1966 GNP in constant 1965 prices, given in
Agency for International Development, Office of Program Coordination, Gross National Product--Growth Rates and Trend Data,
by Region and Country (Washington, D.C., March 31, 1967; Report
No. RC-W-138), excepting Iran and Yugoslavia, for which are used
1965 data taken from the International Monetary Fund's International Financial Statistics. Debt data for 1964 are related to GNP
data for 1966 in order to allow debt disbursements to catch up--
World Bank data indicate this takes an average of two years.

A country with a debt/GDP ratio of .10 that increases its debt by
10 per cent per annum will be borrowing initially at the rate of about
1 per cent of GDP per annum. However, if less-developed countries are to invest at the rate required to achieve a target growth
rate of 5 per cent or more, they will require annual capital inflow
equal to several percentage points of their GDP (i.e., the difference
between the investment/GDP and initial savings/GDP ratios in
Table 13). At the same time, very few less-developed countries
have been able to increase their exports as rapidly as 10 per cent
per annum. Thus, most of these countries can prevent their debt
service ratios from rising further only if new capital inflow is
on substantially easier terms than existing debt.

To cite a more specific example, India's debt service ratio
in 1966 was .22. The World Bank 1966-67 Annual Report expresses a strong view that this rate is already excessive.[15]

If India's exports grow at 5 per cent per annum, her debt service ratio will continue to increase if she borrows more than 0.6 per cent of her GDP per annum at the terms applicable to existing debt (0.6 per cent = .05 x .12, the latter being India's debt/GDP ratio according to Table 14). In 1966, according to DAC estimates, the net official financial flow to India from DAC member countries and multilateral agencies was $1.2 billion, corresponding to roughly 2.3 per cent of India's GNP. Somewhat less than half of this flow consisted of grants and grant-like contributions (P.L. 480 sales), but this still leaves about 1.2-1.3 per cent of GDP which India borrowed on terms only slightly more favorable than the weighted average terms applicable to her present external public debt. Thus, the upward movement of India's public debt service ratio has not yet been reversed. It is in situations like India's that the debt service ratio presents an immediate, compelling constraint on aid terms.

NOTES TO CHAPTER 7

1.   Pieter H. Lieftinck, External Debt and Debt-Bearing Capacity of Developing Countries (Princeton, N.J.: Princeton University Press, 1966; Princeton Essays in International Finance, No. 51), p. 19.

2.   Dragoslav Avramovic and Associates, Economic Growth and External Debt (Baltimore, Md.: The Johns Hopkins Press, 1964), p. 68.

3.   Ibid., p. 40.

4.   Ibid., p. 13.

5.   Published in International Bank for Reconstruction and Development, Economics Department, External Medium- and Long-term Public Debt, Past and Projected Amounts Outstanding, Transactions and Payments: 1956-1975 (Washington, D.C., October 14, 1966).

6.   Avramovic et al., op. cit., p. 38.

7.   Ibid., Table 1, p. 15.

8.   George D. Woods, ''Address to the Board of Governors and Concluding Remarks,'' September 25, 1967 (Washington, D.C.: IBRD, 1967), p. 9.

9.   Raymond F. Mikesell, ''The Capacity to Service Foreign Investment,'' in U.S. Private and Government Investment Abroad (Eugene, Ore.: University of Oregon, 1962), pp. 382-83. Quoted in Avramovic et al., op. cit., p. 40.

10.   Avramovic et al., op. cit., p. 59.

11.   Ibid., p. 66.

12.   Ibid.

13.   Clive S. Gray, "The Spectrum of International Capital Transfer to the Underdeveloped Countries" (Unpublished Ph.D. dissertation, Department of Economics, Harvard University, 1964), pp. 522-26.

14.   Ibid., pp. 527-30.

15.   International Bank for Reconstruction and Development, Annual Report, 1966-67 (Washington, D.C.), p. 31.

CHAPTER **8** THE END-USE CONSTRAINT

The weighted average terms (including amortization)
on resource transfer to a less-developed country
should be no more severe than will enable the
sources of such transfer to match it with acceptable
end-uses other than refinancing of existing liabilities.

ECONOMIC EFFECT VERSUS NOMINAL PURPOSE
OF RESOURCE TRANSFER

In the export of capital, there is a distinction between the
net economic effect of a given capital transfer and the nominal
or secondary purpose of the transfer. Beginning with the net
economic effect, nearly all exports of capital have one fundamental characteristic in common: They add to the stock of real
resources available to or in a foreign economy. (An obvious
type of exception would be a case in which a particular capital
transfer was the direct cause of withdrawal of an equal or
greater amount of resources. Taking account of future events
and including their discounted cost in present calculations, one
could also attribute reduction of real resources to a particular
investment if the contractual return payable on it was above a
certain level or if it was directly responsible for setting off a
chain of events leading to net reduction of resources over the
situation that would otherwise have prevailed.)

The specific activity that takes place as a result of an infusion of foreign capital and which would not have taken place in
the absence of that infusion need not lead to an increase in
physical capital and/or current output. The resources in question
may be diverted to financing an equivalent net increase in consumption or they may end up as an indefinite net addition to
the country's foreign-exchange reserves over the level at which
they would otherwise have been maintained. An apparent instance
of the latter happened in the case of U.S. aid to Honduras in 1960.
ICA had given Honduras $1.5 million for budget support;

meanwhile, Congressman Otto Passman's researchers had informed him that Honduras bought $800,000 worth of gold from the United States in 1960. In 1961 hearings before the Passman committee, an ICA official, James P. Grant, then deputy director for program and planning, said, "I am sure they did not use our funds directly to buy gold, Mr. Chairman."[1] Passman answered: "How could you be sure? They could take dollars we gave them and use them for budgetary support, and any dollars they earned from exports would then be released to them and they could use them to buy gold." Grant had to agree: "It could be that way, yes."

On the other hand, a foreign investment may have the effect of enabling certain physical activities to take place that would otherwise at least have had to be postponed; but these activities may be totally unrelated to the nominal purposes of the invest- ment. For example, until the Chinese invasion of India in 1962, virtually all foreign aid extended to India was intended for economic rather than military use. Yet this did not prevent the Indian Government from increasing its military expenditures from Rs.1.96 billion in fiscal year 1951-52 to Rs.3.15 billion (budgeted) in 1960-61; on the contrary, without the economic aid, India could not have afforded such an increase in a totally nonproductive sector with a substantial direct foreign-exchange component. Meanwhile, Pakistan was receiving large amounts of direct military aid; however, the Kennedy Administration wanted to shift Pakistan aid onto a basis similar to India's. In 1962, the AID deputy administrator for program, Frank Coffin, expressed his Agency's "hope that adequate capital (i.e., economic assist- ance from the Aid-to-Pakistan consortium) will permit Pakistan to finance its own military expenditures without grant assistance, beginning next year."[2]

Thomas C. Schelling has provided a succinct description of the problem posed for public capital exporters by the effective transferability of aid resources:

> What matters is not whether we finance only "sound" projects, in the "right" industries. If the country is financing unsound projects in the wrong industries with its own resources, and is doing so because we have taken care of the sound projects and the right industries, the net effect of our program is to make possible the unsound projects and the wrong industries. This is the same point that was recognized in the Marshall Plan. If one buys all of a country's necessi- ties for it, its own resources are free to be spent at the country's own discretion on lesser priority goods. Only by a comprehensive review of the resources available, and some understanding of how they will be applied, is it possible to judge the net effect of an aid program. This is true whether the country's main shortage is foreign exchange or domestic saving.[3]

CAPITAL SOURCES' END-USE POLICIES

Although recognizing that the net economic impact of a capital transfer may be such that the investor has little or no direct control over it, most capital exporters prefer to match their contributions with stated end-uses defined with varying degrees of precision. Thus, a loan or grant is normally provided "for" a nominal purpose such as construction of an identifiable facility such as a dam, road, school, or factory; purchase of equipment for an enterprise in the transportation or communications fields; purchase of specific classes of imports, or any imports; providing foreign exchange to enable a country to maintain a given rate of economic activity that cannot be sustained by the country's own exports or domestic saving. In this last case, the nominal purpose of the transfer explicitly recognizes its fundamental economic effect, although it does not specify the activities which would be delayed or canceled in the absence of the capital transfer. (What these are may not be known to anyone, including the host government, as long as the issue does not have to be faced.) At the other extreme, by financing projects in some countries and not in others, even those public capital exporters who follow the specific project approach in its most restricted form show awareness that specific project aid is required because an over-all resource deficit exists. Thus, even a lending institution, whose officers derived their greatest satisfaction, and most easily impressed their responsible political authority by nominally financing highway systems in underdeveloped countries, would not make loans for this purpose to Kuwait or Saudi Arabia unless directed to do so by the political authority as a bribe to the governments of these countries.

Some capital sources that supply the bulk of their aid to narrowly defined projects have made more or less frequent exceptions to the specific project approach in response to situations which call for larger infusions of aid than can conveniently be channeled to such projects within a given period of time. In countries whose over-all development plans and policies are acceptable to the United States and whose use of total resources is defensible before Congress, AID has shown readiness to forego the burden on its administrative resources associated with project assistance and rely instead on "nonproject" aid. The World Bank has regularly made what are essentially nonproject loans to developed countries such as Australia, Italy, and Japan, but not until 1964 did it depart from a strict specific project approach in regard to less-developed countries, when it lent India $90 million to finance imports of a wide range of equipment, spare parts, and raw materials for four different industries. The purpose of the loan was to enable the companies concerned "to make fuller use of existing capacity and to produce more capital goods."[4] At the same time, the Bank reiterated its and IDA's policy of being "concerned primarily with basic projects, especially in the fields of transportation and electric power, which require large amounts of capital and have a broad impact throughout the economy."[5] The Bank has, however, made further nonproject loans to both India and Pakistan. Such loans to India during 1966-67 were described in the Bank's 1966-67 Annual Report as being "designed to support economic policy changes, including the easing of import and other controls, initiated by the Government of India."[6]

Apart from restrictions on general purposes with which capital sources agree to associate their funds, a number of standard policies in regard to lending procedure similarly affect the amount of aid that can be channeled to any country within a given period of time. Most sources limit the proportion of the cost of a given project or other activity which they will finance. Thus, the foreign contribution is frequently restricted to the foreign-exchange component of an activity; and, where the aid is provided by an institution controlled by a single country, there is normally the further restriction that only offshore purchases made in the donor country will be financed. Apart from the foreign-exchange, local-cost angle, many donors will not contribute more than a given percentage--e.g., one half--of the total cost of an activity, leaving it to the host country to finance the remainder out of its own resources.

In addition, most capital sources apply some form of what might be called "sector eligibility" criteria, according to which activities in certain economic sectors are treated as ineligible for aid usually on account of the apparently low economic priority of the sectors. Sectors generally excluded from World Bank or AID capital assistance in some or all underdeveloped areas include health, housing, government administration, and defense. (In the latter instance, political considerations would lead many less-developed countries to refuse aid from certain sources even if it were offered.) This policy is followed even though it is undeniable that every country must devote some resources to these sectors, and marginal productivity or utility calculations would award high priority to selected projects.

RATIONALE FOR THE END-USE CONSTRAINT

Following is a list of some of the principal reasons underlying constraints on the nominal purposes for which foreign capital can be provided:

(1) Some agencies are responsible, by law or custom, to legislative authorities or private bondholders for the economic and technical soundness of the particular activities with which their

capital is associated. This factor normally dictates a preference for the specific project approach. Both law, which applies here in many respects to AID, and custom, which strongly influences the World Bank, are partially rooted in the often disastrous experience gained with general-purpose lending in pre-World War II money markets.

(2) In some instances, the net economic effect of a capital transfer directed to a specific project may overlap, or even be identical with, its nominal purpose. Even though aid sources generally prefer to finance the higher-priority elements of a country's development program, it is not always true that the aided projects would be carried out in the absence of aid. The borrowing country may not entirely agree with the aid agency's priorities for the borrower's development, or it may be unable, for reasons of poverty or administrative inertia, to carry out a high-priority activity when this requires a reduction of current expenditure levels in other areas. Without the security that involvement of a foreign or international agency provides to foreign personnel who may be essential to the success of a project, a less-developed country may be unable to attract such personnel with any reasonable level of expenditure out of its own resources. Thus, use of the specific project approach may enable an aid agency to control the net economic impact of its aid.

(3) For many agencies, such as the World Bank, what Thomas Schelling calls "the educational process" associated with the specific project approach is a contribution to the growth of less-developed countries of no lesser importance than the input of physical resources financed by aid. These agencies agree with Schelling that "high standards of analysis, planning, consideration of costs and alternatives, and careful consideration of whether the technical and management skills are available to handle the project once built, can all be encouraged by a well-conducted project procedure."[7] Thus, application of the administrative procedures associated with the specific project approach may enable an aid agency to ensure much more efficient execution of a project than would occur in the absence of the agency's involvement and, in this qualitatively important way, influence the net economic effect of the aid.

(4) The specific project approach can be a useful way of rationing available capital among eligible borrowers without broadcasting in advance total allocations for individual countries and thereby stimulating insidious international comparisons. By following this approach, lenders can maintain that total allocations are an ex post facto phenomenon, determined by which borrowers put forward the best applications for aid. Since disproportionate shares of finance can still be directed toward individual countries on whatever grounds motivate the political authority, this line may be partly fictitious, or there may be a

genuine concern to stimulate competition among potential borrowers to present well-prepared projects.

(5) In the case of capital-exporting countries with balance-of-payments deficits or agencies whose legal purpose is to promote a country's exports, the restriction of finance to imports from a single source is obvious.[8]

(6) The U.S. Government has argued that, apart from the need to safeguard the U.S. balance of payments, restriction of our aid to financing U.S. exports has the effect of maximizing total free-world aid by forcing other developed countries to expand their credit facilities in order to compete in world trade.

(7) A number of agencies prefer to restrict their financing to offshore expenditures on the theory that requiring the borrower to finance local costs is a useful way of imposing the discipline of self-help.

(8) The same agencies consider that this rule, by implying a substantial investment of the borrower's own resources, ensures that he attaches some priority to the project and is more likely to operate it economically in order to preserve his own financial stake in it.

(9) Both the foregoing considerations apply when the apportionment of financial shares is based on percentages of the total cost rather than on loci of expenditures.

(10) A variety of factors lie behind the sector eligibility criteria. As with (1) above, some aid sources are under strictures of law or custom to confine themselves to areas conventionally regarded as the most productive economically. Capital sources tend to regard sectors such as health and housing as bottomless swamps in which large sums of foreign capital may be mired without producing visible results in terms of increased production. Capital aid for defense may be ruled out on political grounds. In general, the existence of excluded sectors is regarded as another incentive toward self-help.

EXPLICIT REFINANCING OF DEBT--POLICIES AND DATA

Whereas most capital sources are willing under special circumstances to relax certain of these restrictions, there is one category of end-uses which nearly all sources approach with the greatest reluctance, and usually only as a last resort to averting a borrowing country's financial collapse. This is the explicit financing of service payments on existing debt. With respect to

financing the interest component of such payments, the taboo is
virtually absolute. Such a practice leads to a compound increase
in debt with no corresponding increase in productive capacity to
enable the debt to be serviced and is universally frowned upon.
I know of only one special type of situation in international finance
where exceptions are made to this rule. This concerns the type
of project that takes so long to complete that substantial interest
must be paid on the loan draw-down before the project is completed
and able to contribute to its own financing. The World Bank allocated $10 million of its $90 million 1960 loan to Pakistan for the
Indus River project to meet interest and other loan charges during
the first eight years of construction. (The pace of activity in the
project is indicated by the fact that, by June 30, 1967, nearly seven
years after the loan agreement was signed, the Bank had disbursed
only 25 per cent of the total loan.)

With debtors who have a "reasonable" ratio of liquid assets
to current liabilities, financing of the amortization component of
debt service, i.e., refinancing existing debt, is not regarded as an
unsound practice. In many situations, it is considered excellent
business both for the borrower and investors who buy the new obligations; this is true in regard to debt of financially strong corporations, municipalities, and governments of developed countries.
But most of the world's currently underdeveloped countries belong
to the category of debtors for whom a position of economic strength
is not yet even in sight, indeed, regarding whom there is still
serious doubt as to whether they will progress rapidly enough to
avoid being drawn into the Communist orbit, an outcome that implies immediate and indefinite default on most forms of debt.

As we saw in Chapter 5, capital sources realize that the
less-developed countries cannot achieve the objectives of resource
transfer unless their debt is "rolled over" up to the time when
self-sustaining growth is under way. They also realize that they
themselves are the only significant sources of such refinance.
But they detest being reminded of this fact, and the pseudo-
banking institutions in the group especially--agencies such as the
World Bank and Export-Import Bank--will go to great lengths to
avoid letting it become explicit via consolidation credits and other
forms of debt rescheduling. Because nearly all sources prefer,
for one or more of the reasons stated earlier in this chapter, to
finance specific projects or, at most, special classes of imports,
a resort to debt refinancing suggests that the borrower has
exhausted all preferred end-uses for foreign capital, has taken
on a debt burden that is excessive in relation to his economic
prospects, and may well be forced to refinance cumulatively until
default is the only course open to him. No lending institution
interested in eventually getting its money back or even merely
leveling off its commitment in a particular country can view such
a process with equanimity.

Despite this reluctance, many of the major Western aid sources have repeatedly found it necessary to reschedule the external debt service obligations of less-developed countries, as Table 15 illustrates.

TABLE 15

Consolidation and Refinancing Credits Extended to
Less-developed Countries by Official Western
Sources and Japan, 1956-65[a]

Year	U.S. \$ million[b]
1956	134
1957	196
1958	351
1959	527
1960	113
1961	41.3[c]
1962	51.4
1963	128.8
1964	110.8
1965	288.3[d]
1966	115-120
Total (approximate)	2,060

Notes:

[a]Consolidation credits involve extention of maturities on loans originally made by governments or official agencies; refinancing loans involve extension of maturities (and sometimes adjustment of interest rates) on loans originally made by the private sector, taken over by governments or official agencies.

[b]Commitments with respect to gross principal amounts (including capitalized interest, if any) covered by the credits.

[c]Includes only credits with less than five years final maturity and is, therefore, an underestimate.

[d]Data for 1966 is given by DAC in terms of a percentage rounded to one decimal place, hence the range of absolute values.

Sources: Organization for Economic Cooperation and Development, The Flow of Financial Resources to Countries in Course of Economic Development in 1960 (Paris, February, 1962); The Flow of Financial Resources to Less-Developed Countries, 1956-1963 (Paris, 1964); The Flow of Financial Resources to Less-Developed Countries, 1961-1965 (Paris, 1967); and Development Assistance Efforts and Policies--1967 Review (Paris, 1967); The Flow of Financial Resources to Countries in the Course of Economic Development, 1956-59 (Paris, 1961).

Much of this refinance has been provided within the framework of multilateral consultations described by DAC as "an in-
formal 'club' technique";[9] such clubs have been convened since 1956
on behalf of Argentina (3 times), Brazil (twice), Chile, Ghana, and
Indonesia. Turkey and Liberia have also had their external debts
rescheduled under slightly different multilateral arrangements.
According to DAC,

> The informality of the 'club' arrangement is de-
> liberate. Creditor countries have no desire to
> make rescheduling an easy matter for recipient
> countries and have therefore sought to avoid in-
> stitutionalizing the process . . . . It goes without
> saying that all rescheduling exercises involve dis-
> cussions of the source of the difficulty and how it
> is to be avoided in the future.[10]

Even quasi-bank lenders that pride themselves on their
orthodoxy occasionally have such a stake in the continued financial
stability of a country that they have no choice but to participate
in refinancing operations. Thus, the Export-Import Bank,
sufficiently orthodox to have received words of praise from Congressman Passman,[11] and whose then President, Samuel Waugh,
told the Special Senate Committee to Study the Foreign Aid Program in 1957 that his bank never lent to a country whose capacity
to repay depended on its receiving foreign aid, has been obliged
at various times to reschedule $547 million of debt owed to it
by 6 countries, with Brazil accounting for 73 per cent of this total.
The countries and amounts involved are: Argentina, a total of
$87.4 million on 2 occasions; Brazil, $397.2 million on 3 occasions;
Chile, $40.4 million once; Costa Rica, $5.1 million twice; Liberia,
$13.2 million once; and Yugoslavia, $3.5 million once.[12] Reporting the first (and largest) Brazilian exercise, The New York
Times indicated that U.S. officials were not expecting a political
quid pro quo, such as Brazilian support in regard to Cuba, but
rather that "the reason for the aid is that the United States
cannot afford to let Brazil collapse financially."[13]

The World Bank has remained much more a citadel of
orthodoxy on the refinancing question, although I am informed
that a desire to help rescue Colombia from heavy debt service
obligations incurred by the dictator Rojas Pinilla was or came
close to being the dominant factor in the timing of several large
project loans to Colombia after the 1957 revolution there. However, in March, 1964, World Bank President George D. Woods
told the United Nations Conference on Trade and Development
that the Bank would be willing to refinance loans of "a few
countries now caught in an acute cash squeeze," if they would
agree to "appropriate disciplines."[14] A news report on Woods'

remarks noted that "one discipline the bank probably will insist
on is that nations with long-term obligations to the Bank refrain
from accumulating a load of short-term heavy debts to other
sources."[15] It added that "it was understood" that Woods was referring particularly to Brazil and Argentina as countries that
might be in line for refinancing. Four years after this statement, the Bank has still not found it necessary to redeem Woods'
pledge. Presumably, the major capital sources, which are, of
course, simultaneously members of the Bank, have chosen to continue carrying the burden of rescheduling debt rather than risk
impairing the Bank's credit in the private money markets that are
its source of funds. However, the Bank notes in its 1966-67 Annual
Report that it was represented at the 1966 meetings of Ghana's
creditors and also sent observers to 1967 meetings of Indonesia's
creditors.

Even where capital sources are agreeable under certain
circumstances to refinancing debt, they rarely, if ever, agree to
refinance explicitly any debt besides that owed to themselves or
to commercial interests in their own country. However, as we
have already seen, the question of what activities a piece of aid is
actually facilitating, and specifically whether it is effectively refinancing debt owed to the source concerned or to third parties,
becomes rather arbitrary. Only if a country's annual debt service exceeds the sum of its exports and reserve draw-down can
one say unequivocally that at least part of the debt service is
being financed by capital inflow, and this situation does not yet
apply anywhere in the less-developed world. At most, where
foreign capital is provided for local costs of projects or for
general purposes involving some local costs such as defense or
budget support, one might argue that effective shares in meeting
debt service obligations should be attributed on a pro rata basis
to foreign aid, exports, and reserve draw-down. (If one believed
that the only significant net economic effect of project aid lay in
its contribution to total resource availability, such aid might also
be accorded a pro rata share in meeting debt service obligations.)

The distinction between the nominal purposes of foreign aid
and borrowing countries' debt service payments does not impress
all the ultimate sources of such aid. In the 1961 hearings of his
subcommittee on Foreign Operations Appropriations, Congressman Passman listened to Eximbank president Harold Linder's
explanation of how, after lengthy negotiations, the Chinese (Taiwan)
Government had agreed to start repayments on some early postwar loans to the mainland and then declared impatiently, "We
could have saved a lot of time by just getting them to repay it out
of one of those grants!"[16]

QUANTIFYING THE END-USE CONSTRAINT

We saw already in Chapter 5 that the heavier the service requirements on foreign resource transfer, the larger the balance-of-payments gap that must be financed to enable a less-developed country to follow a given growth path. The larger the balance-of-payments gap to be financed, the more gross resource transfer is required. If capital sources wish to avoid explicit refinancing of debt, the more gross transfer they want to finance, the more acceptable vehicles for transfer they must find. Thus, any limit on the amount of acceptable vehicles for resource transfer ultimately manifests itself as a constraint on the terms of such transfer. This is the "end-use constraint" that forms the subject of this chapter.

Although I am not familiar with any writings that treat this constraint on a par with others such as the debt service ratio, it has been recognized by Dragoslav Avramovic et al. in their 1964 study, by Göran Ohlin in his OECD study published in 1966, and by the World Bank itself in its 1966-67 Annual Report. According to the Bank, "Even when growing amortization and interest payments are offset in the aggregate by an increase in the gross flow of aid, debt service becomes more and more difficult to manage because of the large proportion of aid which is country-tied and commodity-restricted. Debt-service payments must be financed from free exchange, leaving inadequate amounts available to finance imports and other payments to non aid-giving countries or to purchase commodities not eligible for aid-financing."[17] The inevitable result, as Ohlin points out, is that a "pressure to borrow to pay interest and to support the balance of payments arises. Consolidation credits and general balance of payments support already figure in many aid programmes and may be expected to become more frequent in the future, but this development will lend new content to the issue of project vs. programme aid."[18] Avramovic points equally to the terms on aid and restrictions on aid vehicles as variables in the situation: "The practical implication is that in many countries the mechanism of 'hard' lending could not work properly unless at some point a substantial part of capital exports were put on a non-project basis."[19]

The algebra of applying the end-use constraint involves three principal steps: (1) projecting a country's gross annual external resource requirement on varying assumptions as to the terms on resource transfer; (2) projecting those expenditures eligible to be matched with external resources on whatever criteria are being applied; and (3) selecting those terms which make (1) no greater than (2). We will now proceed to illustrate the application of the constraint to less-developed areas represented by the same data as featured in the analogous exercises in Chapters 6 and 7. The constraint will be interpreted as limiting resource inflows to two alternative broad categories of end-uses, namely, gross investment and imports of goods and services.

As we have already indicated, there are many other possible specifications of the constraint, reflecting a variety of aid policies in current use. However, the overwhelming proportion of resource transfer to less-developed countries today is matched with either (1) investments, (2) imports, or (3) both. This is clear from DAC data on the percentage allocations among various program categories of gross aid to less-developed countries in 1965-66. In these two years, total direct bilateral commitments of $6.76 and $7.83 billion respectively were divided as shown in Table 16.

TABLE 16

Bilateral Commitments of DAC Members by Major
Program Categories, 1965-66

	1965	1966
Technical assistance	17.7%	18.1%
Nonproject assistance	41.8	49.7
Capital project assistance	21.3	16.8
Official export credits	10.8	11.0
Consolidation and refinancing loans	4.3	1.5
Other	4.1	2.9
	100.0	100.0

Source: The above reproduces Table VIII.2 in Organization for Economic Cooperation and Development, Development Assistance Efforts and Policies--1967 Review (Paris, 1967), p. 127.

To these figures must be added commitments of multilateral agencies,totaling $1.88 and $1.95 billion in 1965 and 1966 respectively, over 80 per cent of which was directed into capital projects and all or nearly all of the remainder into import financing. Unfortunately, no breakdown of the category "nonproject assistance" in Table 16 is available. This includes budgetary support and other forms of aid not matched with investments or imports; however, the DAC tells us that the major part of nonproject aid "was in the form of food and other commodity assistance"[20]--viz., P.L. 480-- which is, of course, a form of import financing. The DAC goes on to note that "the provision of assistance for budget support, which was more typical of earlier colonial relations, has become relatively insignificant."[21]

Investment projects and imports are not, of course, mutually exclusive vehicles for external resource inflow. In fact, the form of aid nearly all capital sources most prefer is to finance the import component--specifically, that portion of it which originates from the capital source's country--of specific investment projects. In practice, therefore, the two measures of eligible expenditures overlap considerably. Which is the larger in any given situation depends on the values of an individual country's parameters and on the specific procedures followed by its capital sources. Ordinarily, nonproject import financing is a capital source's second line of defense once the desired resource inflow can no longer be effected exclusively via specific projects. Thus, where imports are viewed as a separate measure of eligible expenditures, the effect is normally to broaden the scope for resource transfer. In principle, however, by going in for local cost financing and relaxing a few of the supervisory procedures associated with aid-financed investment projects, a capital source can just as easily increase the vehicles for its aid without abandoning the specific project approach.

To illustrate the end-use constraint, we make use of the same Alter-type model variant that underlay the quantitative analysis in Chapters 6 and 7--i.e., involving a constant annual rate of increase of aggregate savings. The gross inflow of resources in any year has three analytically distinct components: (1) the difference between investment and savings in that year; (2) interest and amortization on new debt outstanding at the end of the preceding year; and (3) interest and amortization on the debt that has grown out of pre-existing debt at the start of the period under review. As in the previous chapters, we assume that pre-existing debt is refinanced at the same weighted average interest rate it bore at the start of the period, all interest payments being capitalized from one year to the next.

What we now want to do is compare the gross inflow corresponding to alternative weighted average terms on new debt with alternative measures of annual eligible expenditures. The two measures to be used are, very simply, annual gross investment and annual imports of goods and services. Gross investment in any year can be derived immediately from the assumptions of the Alter-type model. It is given by the constant investment/GDP ratio times one plus the GDP growth rate to the power n-1--(i.e., $Kr(1+r)^{n-1}$ in the notation used in our tables and the Mathematical Appendix). In the case of imports, some new assumptions have to be grafted onto the model. To obtain an estimate of the initial import/GDP ratios, we take the initial export/GDP ratios, computed in Chapter 7 as sources of data for illustrating the debt service ratio constraint, and we add to these the 1960-65 current account deficit/GNP ratios estimated by the World Bank for five regions, comprising 40 selected countries, in its 1966-67 Annual Report.[22] We further assume that imports increase at a constant annual rate, such that their growth path from the aforementioned initial import/GDP ratio, in juxtaposition to the growth path of exports defined as in Chapter 7, yields a cumulative import-export deficit, up to year t_1 (the year when savings first equals or exceeds investment), equal to the cumulative investment-savings deficit up to the same year.*

These attempts to handle import behavior in a manner consistent with other assumptions in the model introduce inconsistensies of their own, and we do not suggest that such procedures should be followed by an aid agency interested in deriving appropriate terms in a real-world situation. For example, the foregoing assumption about the rate of increase of imports, while yielding the same cumulative net resource deficit in year t_1 as the savings and investment parameters used in the model, will not ordinarily make imports equal to exports in that year, as they must be if savings and investment are equal ex post. Depending on the algebra of a given situation, imports may be either greater or less than exports in t_1. I believe, however, that the procedures used are defensible at the level of abstraction characterizing this study.

As in illustrating the debt service ratio constraint, we want to find the year in which the ratio of gross resource inflow to investment or imports is maximized. The ratio of inflow to investment is maximized in year t_2 plus one, i.e., the year after the year in which debt increases no faster than GDP, whose rate of increase applies also to investment. As already noted, the formula for t_2 is given in the Mathematical Appendix at (9). The ratio of gross inflow to imports is maximized in the year after the year in which the rate of increase of debt becomes equal to that of imports; the equation for determining this year is identical in form to that in the Mathematical Appendix at (10), with the rate of increase of imports being substituted for that of exports. Again as in the case of the debt service ratio, the inclusion of service on pre-existing debt, which is projected to grow at constant annual rates of 5 per cent in three of our regions and 3 per cent in the fourth, affects the timing of the maximum ratios only marginally and can therefore be ignored in calculating the year in question.

The results of these computations are given in Table 17, which shows maximum ratios of gross resource inflow to investment (Part II) and imports (Part III) on the two alternative assumptions about the terms on inflow used in Chapter 7. These are (1) interest rate of zero and amortization rate of .025,

---

*The formula for deriving the rate of increase of imports in this way is given in the Mathematical Appendix at (13).

TABLE 17

Effects of End-Use Constraint

I--Values of actual or assumed parameters	Africa	South Asia	South Europe & Middle East	Latin America
1. GDP growth rate (r)	.05	.05	.06	.05
2. Incremental capita/output ratio (K)	3.4	4.0	3.0	4.0
3. Investment/GDP ratio (Kr)	.17	.20	.18	.20
4. Initial savings/GDP ratio (S_0)	.10	.136	.136	.164
5. Savings growth rate (s)	.073	.08	.08	.06
6. Year when savings = investment (t_1)	26	15	17	22
7. Initial foreign debt/GDP ratio (D_0)	.142	.096	.064	.108
8. Return on existing foreign debt (i_1)	.05	.05	.03	.05
9. Annual amortization rate on existing foreign debt (a_1)	.05	.05	.05	.05
10. Initial export/GDP ratio (X_0)	.200	.054	.081	.117
11. Export growth rate (x)	.049	.052	.102	.080
12. Initial import/GDP ratio (M_0)	.245	.085	.132	.139
13. Import growth rate (m)	.045	.0525	.0625	.0733
14. Initial resource inflow/GDP ratio	.052	.030	.048	.024
15. Initial resource inflow/investment ratio	.365	.181	.254	.130
16. Initial resource inflow/import ratio	.214	.354	.362	.176

II--Maximum gross resource inflow/investment ratios attained

i=O, annual amortization rate = .025

Year of maximum resource inflow/investment ratio	18	12	12	16
Same-year resource inflow/GDP ratio	.053	.033	.022	.028
Same-year investment/GDP ratio	.170	.200	.180	.200
Maximum resource inflow/investment ratio	.31	.16	.12	.14

i=.06 2/3, annual amortization rate = .06 2/3

Year of maximum resource inflow/investment ratio	29	16	16	26
Same-year resource inflow/GDP ratio	.138	.068	.047	.059
Same-year investment/GDP ratio	.170	.200	.180	.200
Maximum resource inflow/investment ratio	.81	.34	.26	.30

III--Maximum gross resource inflow/import ratios attained

i=O, annual amortization rate = .025

Year of maximum resource inflow/import ratio	19	12	12	13
Same-year resource inflow/GDP ratio	.050	.033	.022	.033
Same-year import/GDP ratio	.225	.087	.135	.181
Maximum resource inflow/import ratio	.22	.37	.17	.18

i=.06 2/3, annual amortization rate = .06 2/3

Year of maximum resource inflow/import ratio	30	16	16	20
Same-year resource inflow/GDP ratio	.134	.068	.047	.069
Same-year import/GDP ratio	.213	.088	.137	.211
Maximum resource inflow/import ratio	.63	.77	.34	.32

(Continued)

TABLE 17 (Continued)

Notes:

The procedure used to derive parameters 14-16 was as follows:

From OECD/DAC publications--notably Development Assistance Efforts and Policies--1967 Review (Paris, 1967) and Geographical Distribution of Financial Flows to Less Developed Countries, 1960-64 (Paris, 1966) and 1965 (Paris, 1967)--we computed total official financial flows to the countries covered in the World Bank sample of 40 countries to which other data in the table relate, with a few adjustments as indicated below. These flows were computed gross of amortization on bilateral loans, but net of amortization on multilateral loans, for which the DAC reports do not give separate data. In an effort to increase the "grossness" of the estimates, negative entries were ignored wherever they appeared; however, this adjustment has only a marginal effect, and the estimates understate gross flows, which are the relevant quantity here, by an unknown amount. This is particularly true in regard to private capital inflows, for which the available data are fragmentary.

By the foregoing procedures, we obtained the following series on official inflows into the countries of our sample: Africa--$474 million; South Asia--$1,808 million; South Europe & Middle East--$502 million; Latin America--$1,074 million. Before these data can be used to compute meaningful ratios of current inflows to investment and imports, they must be adjusted to exclude expenditures on technical assistance, nearly all of which relate to activities that do not figure in estimating investment or imports in less-developed countries (although a good case can be made for saying that they should be included). DAC data indicate that its about one sixth of total net official disbursements in 1965 was in the form of technical assistance. The proportion varies from one region to another, with Africa receiving probably closer to 30 per cent of its official inflow in that form and Latin America and South Europe and Middle East probably less than 10 per cent. A country breakdown of technical assistance data, required in order to make a precise adjustment for our sample, is not available, but the figures below represent a crude attempt to make the necessary adjustment.

For private inflows, we used DAC data for Latin America, because it was available in summary form, and balance-of-payments (private capital, not included elsewhere) data from country pages of the International Monetary Fund's International Financial Statistics for the other three regions.

This exercise yielded the following series for average annual inflows during 1963–65:

($ millions)

Type of inflow	Africa	South Asia	South Europe & Middle East	Latin America
Official (adjusted)	330	1,500	450	970
Private	446	67	366	699
Total	776	1,567	816	1,670

It should be stressed that the data for Africa and South Asia refer only to samples of countries in those regions. Moreover, we excluded Iran from the latter sample because of the absence of a GNP estimate for that country in our source of GNP data; however, in the case of Latin America, we included three small republics not in the World Bank sample.

We then took GNP estimates for the same group of countries during 1963–65 from U.S. AID, Office of Program Coordination, Gross National Product—Growth Rates and Trend Data, by Region and Country (Washington, D.C., March 31, 1967; Report No. RC–W–138), and calculated ratios of total inflow to GNP. These ratios were then divided by (1) the average 1960–65 ratios of investment to GDP given in the World Bank's 1966–67 Annual Report (Washington, D.C., 1967) and (2) the initial average ratios of imports to GDP whose source is described in the accompanying text. Apart from the obvious discrepancies in time periods covered, it should also be noted that the GDP series used implicitly in the Bank report undoubtedly diverges somewhat from the explicit AID/GNP series we have used. All these statistical shortcomings can be excused only on grounds related to the general level of abstraction of this study.

Sources:
Parameters 1–8:   see Chapter 6, Table 9.
Parameters 9–11: see Chapter 7, Table 12.
Parameters 12–13: see text above.
Parameters 14–16: see note above

corresponding to 40-year maturities; and (2) interest rate of .06 and amortization rate of .06 2/3, corresponding to 15-year maturities. For purposes of comparison, ratios of actual capital inflows during 1963-65 to current measures of investment.and imports, respectively, are also shown (as parameters 15 and 16 in the table).

The table shows that provision of future resource transfer on zero-interest, 40-year terms would eventually reduce the present ratio of gross annual inflow to investment in Africa and South Europe and Middle East. In Latin America, such terms would keep the ratio roughly constant (.130→.14), whereas in South Asia it would decline insignificantly (.181→.16). Thus, insofar as capital is now moving in accordance with a strict project approach, these very easy terms would not require that approach to be relaxed. On the other hand, use of hard terms on aid would raise the ratio in question substantially above current levels in every region except South Europe and Middle East. In the case of Africa, the ratio rises from .365 at present to .81 at a maximum in year 29. This means that provision of resources only for specific investment activities would necessitate finding enough acceptable end-uses of this type to match external resources with 80 per cent of total investment. In the cases of South Asia and Latin America, at least a third of total investment would have to be molded to fit the procedures of external capital sources. We say "at least" because that portion of the investment in externally aided projects which must still be financed locally--and this is customarily a significant share--is usually subject to numerous conditions laid down by the external sources. Turning to the inflow/import ratio, we find a roughly similar picture, except that use of the very easy terms keeps the ratio more or less at its current levels in Africa and South Asia (.214→.22 and .354→.37 respectively).

As in the case of the debt service ratio constraint, given a level for either the inflow/investment or inflow/import ratio that capital sources desire not to exceed, it is a simple matter to solve for maximum terms. Because the procedure is very similar to that introduced in the preceding chapter, we content ourselves here with giving, in the Mathematical Appendix at (14), the appropriate formula for the amortization rate.

EVALUATING THE CONSTRAINT

The next problem is how to evaluate the end-use constraint-- in other words, what levels of the inflow/investment and inflow/ import ratios are attainable. As with the previous constraints, this one can only be evaluated in the light of conditions peculiar to each individual country situation. The end-use constraint is also intimately wound up with circumstances internal to the capital

sources--such as the availability in the United States of agricultural surpluses with strong domestic political pressures behind
unloading them overseas for whatever quid pro quo less-developed
countries can offer. And the constraint is actually defined in
terms of the institutional policies and practices to fit different
country situations. Were the end-use constraint ever to be taken
explicitly into account in the determination of aid terms, the
sources concerned would undoubtedly make trade-off calculations
as between varying the terms and modifying their aid procedures.
The weight of adjustment would fall on the terms insofar as capital
sources desired to retain a strict approach in order to maximize
their influence over the execution of development activities, and/or
insofar as their own balance-of-payments difficulties caused them
to restrict financing to their own exports, perhaps subject to an
"additionality" requirement such as is practiced by U.S. AID. On
the other hand, a source with little or no flexibility in its terms
would have to relax its procedures if it wanted to ensure continued
resource inflow in the face of a scarcity of end-uses acceptable
under standing procedures. Such a trade-off calculation would be
limited to the medium or long run, since the terms on loans in a
given year would not perceptibly affect the ratio of required gross
inflow to acceptable end-uses until full service charges were being
incurred on such loans.

ASSESSING THE AID-ELIGIBILITY OF NIGERIA'S 1962-68 INVESTMENT PROGRAM

To illustrate how the end-use constraint might be applied, I
will describe an exercise which I carried out as a member of the
U.S. AID mission to Nigeria in 1963 when the mission was attempting
to estimate the proportion of public development expenditures during Nigeria's 1962-68 Plan period that might be financed in the
light of existing and projected commitments from external aid
sources and the procedures followed by these sources. The main
potential public sources for Nigeria's Plan were the World Bank-
IDA-IFC complex; U.S. AID and the U.S. Export-Import Bank;
the U.K. Government and its Commonwealth Development Corporation (CDC); the West German Government; other West
European governments; technical agencies of the United Nations;
and U.S. foundations, notably Ford and Rockefeller. All the
major sources were following a strict project approach, and most
official bilateral sources were tying their aid to purchases of
their own exports, either openly or, in the case of the West Germans, "off the record." There were, however, differing nuances
of policy on financing local costs, imported goods as opposed to
services such as engineering, etc.

In its 1962-68 Plan document, the Nigerian Government stated an explicit hope that public foreign aid would be forthcoming at the rate of approximately 50 per cent of the federal and regional governments' capital budgets, or £327 million out of budgets totaling £654 million (net of officially estimated underspending), as compared with projected total gross fixed capital formation of about £1.2 billion.[23] In addition, a substantial contribution toward meeting the over-all target was expected from private foreign capital-- the same official source projects private foreign investment at £200 million out of projected total private capital formation of around £400 million. (Projected private investment of £400 million and public capital budgets of £654 million do not add up to gross fixed capital formation of £1.2 billion since the latter includes investment items in government operating budgets, virtually none of which are eligible for foreign capital aid, less capital expenditures on defense and private inventory investment.)

By 1963, all sources were finding that it took much more time than originally anticipated to locate eligible projects to absorb their aid and then bring these projects to the stage of execution in a manner that satisfied the procedural conditions attached to the aid. In view of the actual inflow of public foreign capital and the rate of conclusion of specific aid agreements, it was not at all clear when my exercise was carried out that the funds already committed, which amounted to considerably less than the 50 per cent of public capital expenditure the Nigerians were hoping for, could actually be disbursed on specific projects by the end of the Plan period, even though the sources were anxious to disburse as much of the commitments as possible within this time.

Alone of the governmental sources listed above, AID was discussing projects with the Nigerian authorities in terms that indicated a willingness to finance some local costs (of projects where its main contribution would be in the form of U.S. goods and services) on a regular basis. In addition, it was trying with very limited results to persuade other agencies to do likewise. While the United Kingdon was planning to provide most of its aid in Commonwealth Assistance Loans under the Export Credit Guarantees Act, which meant that the aid would be tied to purchases of U.K. goods and services, it had committed a £5 million untied grant for construction of educational facilities. Of the other agencies, CDC and the U.S. foundations provided untied aid, part of which would be expended on local costs; but, apart from the World Bank complex, the rest intended to restrict their contributions as far as possible to direct offshore costs.

With this picture in mind of the policies of Nigeria's major foreign capital sources, I undertook to break down the public capital expenditure program according to eligibility for foreign aid. The first step in this procedure was to rule out projects, or activities not identifiable as separate projects, that appeared unlikely to

receive any foreign aid. A large share of the disqualified activities
consisted of what might be described as "bits and pieces" of investment, i.e., construction of new small facilities or minor extension and improvement of existing ones. Some typical examples
were: upgrading existing dirt roads to grade "B" status through
minor grading and application of a cheap surface treatment; erection
of single classroom or dormitory buildings in existing "bush"
schools; dredging of minor inland waterways, construction of simple
docks, and purchase of locally made ferryboats; and construction of
buildings and purchase of equipment for agricultural extension
stations and demonstration farms. One of the principal reasons for
ruling out such activities was the substantial administrative effort
required on the part of donor agencies to establish capital aid
projects--in the case of AID, this usually involved initial feasibility
studies, often requiring a contract with a U.S. engineering firm, then
economic and engineering review in Washington, processing through
several stages of committees, followed by negotiation of loan agreements, approval of contract documents and selection of contractors,
detailed supervision during construction, and eventual audits.

Some of the "bits and pieces" of investment could be financed
under foreign technical assistance programs, notably that of AID,
which was allocating a larger proportion of its grant funds for
equipment and minor construction than any of the other aid sources,
the bulk of whose technical assistance contributions represented
costs of foreign personnel, an item not generally included in Nigerian capital budgets. In such activities, the administrative procedures were simpler, partly because the sums being invested were
smaller and partly because foreign personnel would be involved in
the supervision and use of these funds. But, in the majority of
small activities where technical assistance-type aid was not needed,
wanted, or available, to institute capital aid would have required a
disproportionate investment of administrative resources.

Moreover, the Nigerians were rapidly learning that application of AID standards to a project often raised its cost far above
their initial estimates and, in some cases, even called for a host
country contribution, as a proportion of the total cost, that was
little less than the originally budgeted total cost. In consequence
of the serious difficulties caused for the U.S. foreign aid program
by Congressional "exposés" of allegedly shoddy construction on
aid projects in certain countries, the Agency sometimes insisted,
in areas such as road construction, on standards that most economists, evaluating opportunity costs in the context of a particular
underdeveloped country, would have considered uneconomic. Thus,
the Nigerians became wary of asking for AID assistance in minor
activities where they were concerned to hold total expenditures at
a minimum.

In some cases, what the Nigerians regarded as the necessary
timing of certain small investments was itself an obstacle to their

receiving aid. For example, aid agencies were discussing with the Nigerian authorities a broad program of telecommunications development which several of the agencies were willing to consider underwriting, at least to the extent of purchases of equipment from their own suppliers. Equipment for relatively minor aspects of the program, such as telephone exchanges in and connections between branch towns, was potentially eligible for coverage under this financing. But the process of drawing up plans and specifications for the entire program required a minimum of two years between agreement on the scope of work for the initial feasibility survey and the awarding of contracts, only after which foreign loans could be finalized. Meanwhile, political and economic pressures required that some investment be carried out, and this the Nigerians had to finance themselves.*

Other projects treated as probably disqualified for aid were those in which the direct offshore cost component was only a small fraction of the total cost--for example, less than 25 per cent. In such cases, it appeared that agencies would not consider it worth the necessary expenditure of administrative resources to make an aid project out of an activity to which their own contribution would be so small. This type of situation was illustrated by the AID mission's own experience in attempting to interest Washington in supporting at least two soundly conceived projects with high local cost components. These were (1) an oil-palm rehabilitation scheme, whose main cost element consisted of small acreage payments and subsidies in kind, i.e., fertilizer and seedlings, to induce peasants to cut down semiwild oil-palm trees and replace them with higher-yielding varieties; and (2) a scheme for paving the main streets and constructing a storm drainage system in a growing provincial capital. Although agreeing with the Nigerians' (and the mission's) assessment of the economic priority of these projects, AID headquarters felt that extending U.S. aid to them would not be consistent with Congress' intent, expressed in the Foreign Assistance Act, to restrict foreign aid financing as far as possible to the purchase of U.S. goods and services.** It appeared in 1963 that this restriction would be interpreted, at least in Africa, to prohibit U.S. loans for most conceivable schemes of agricultural credit aimed at peasant producers. For it was generally recognized that requiring the peasants to spend their credit on U.S. goods and services would be uneconomic at

---

*However, the U.K. agreed to finance some urgently required expansion of trunk facilities between the two largest cities, Lagos and Ibadan, out of a 1962 Commonwealth Assistance Loan.

**However, the mission was eventually permitted to make a small contribution of U.S.-made fertilizer and equipment to the oil-palm scheme as part of a technical assistance project.

best and virtually impossible in fact, considering the nonsuitability of U.S. mechanized equipment for peasant agriculture in its current stage of evolution.

Finally, a number of projects were regarded as ruled out under the sector eligibility criteria mentioned earlier in this chapter. Although the United Kingdom and Canada were already providing or had offered technical assistance to Nigeria's defense organization and medium-term commercial financing was arranged on a naval frigate purchased in Holland, Nigeria could expect little foreign aid in connection with her £27 million six-year capital budget for defense.* Other sectors in the 1962-68 Plan for which overseas capital was not likely to be available included social welfare, police, general government (e.g., construction of executive offices or legislative assembly buildings), and public housing. (With respect to AID, the treatment of public housing as an ineligible sector was an explicit policy of the African regional office in AID headquarters; the Latin American arm of AID has made numerous loans in this area, as well as for agricultural credit.) The West German Government had allocated about £0.5 million as a loan for rural clinics in Northern Nigeria, but the remaining £16.5 million of budgeted capital expenditures in the health sector appeared to be considered ineligible by the other capital sources.

An analysis of the Nigerian public capital budgets based on the foregoing considerations yielded a rough estimate that no more than 60 per cent of budgeted expenditures related to projects that were likely to qualify for foreign capital aid. The next stage in the analysis was to estimate what proportion of the costs of these projects would be met by foreign donors and lenders. The first step in this process was to estimate the direct foreign-exchange component of the budgeted expenditures. For some projects in the Plan, including the largest single item, a £70 million multipurpose hydroelectric power scheme on the Niger River, results of official cost analyses were available. For most projects, however, sufficiently detailed plans were not available to do more than "guesstimate" the foreign-exchange component. In conducting a similar exercise earlier, the Federal Ministry of Economic Development had developed certain rules of thumb, such as the principle that reinforced concrete buildings and major paved roads involved a direct foreign-exchange component of 50 or 60 per cent, whereas for lesser structures and grade "B" roads this component went as low as 25 per cent. Applying these rules, and using whatever information on specific projects was available to it, the AID mission estimated the offshore component of eligible projects to be between 55 and 60 per cent of their total cost.

---

*Capital expenditures for defense do not, of course, comprise investment in the national income accounting sense, but, to the extent foreign aid is provided for such expenditures, local resources are freed for investment in other sectors.

It could not be assumed, however, that this entire offshore cost element was itself eligible for foreign aid. In the first place, not all of the goods and services comprising the foreign-exchange component of a project can always be conveniently supplied from one country. In the case of Nigeria, since British suppliers had long enjoyed the inside track in selling to that country, most of the myriad of small intermediate products used in construction, which were available in Nigeria and which no contractor would want to bother having imported specially for one project, had originally been imported from the United Kingdom. A non-U.K. source of tied aid would not want to finance such items, yet it would not always be practicable to obtain finance from the United Kingdom or any other country for a minor project element of which it happened at the time to be the least-cost source.

Secondly, foreign aid sources differ both in their definitions of foreign-exchange costs and in the types of such costs they will finance, even where suppliers of their own nationality are the source. The AID mission to Nigeria quickly found that, in order to obtain cost breakdowns meaningful in AID's terms of reference, engineers responsible for preparing these breakdowns had to be given detailed lists of which items were to be counted in U.S. costs, which in non-U.S. offshore costs, and which in local costs. AID headquarters ultimately came out with its own instructions on the subject. According to these instructions, the following items were to be considered U.S. costs: materials and equipment of U.S. origin or manufacture incorporated into the project; transport costs and depreciation of equipment owned by a U.S. contractor and used in the project; home office overhead and profits of U.S. engineering firms and contractors; and salaries, per diems, and transport costs of U.S. personnel employed in the project. Non-U.S. offshore costs were defined in a manner parallel to the foregoing, and local costs were defined as: purchase for incorporation into the project of materials and equipment more than half of whose wholesale value is derived from processing within the host country; depreciation or rental of equipment obtained locally (and not imported specifically for the purpose); total costs of any subcontracts with local engineering and construction firms, less any direct foreign purchases made by them; and wages and other expenses for locally hired labor.

It is clear that some of the expenditures allocated to U.S. costs in the above list would probably not take place within the United States Transportation of contractor-owned equipment could occur on non-U.S. vessels; so could transportation of overseas personnel, and per diem payments are specifically intended to compensate for local living expenses. However, these items would ordinarily form a very small proportion of the total cost of a project, and their blanket attribution to U.S. costs was presumably made in order to simplify cost breakdowns made for planning purposes, as well as subsequent bookkeeping.

With regard to Britain, local U.K. representatives indicated that their government's policy was to limit financing under the Export Credit Guarantees Act as closely as possible to loans for goods, on a c.i.f. basis, as opposed to services. Thus, while the United Kingdom had agreed to finance, out of its 1962 Commonwealth Assistance Loan, the offshore element of the civil engineer-- ing as well as equipment costs of a new waterworks in one Nigerian city, it hoped to confine its lending to offshore equipment costs of such projects in the future. Because of the relatively high civil engineering component in road-building, the United Kingdom was reluctant to accede to Nigerian requests that part of its loan funds be allocated to roads. This policy reflected pressure from manufacturing interests in the United Kingdom, which were naturally anxious to use aid funds to stimulate a maximum volume of business for themselves. It meant that the Nigerians would have to meet a portion of even the foreign-exchange costs of some eligible projects out of their own resources, since no other source was likely to agree to picking up civil engineering costs while the British sold all the equipment.

A final step in estimating the ratio of eligible to total budgeted public capital expenditures was to estimate how much local costs in eligible projects might be covered by foreign aid. This procedure was unnecessary in regard to projects where the total amount of aid a particular source intended to give the project was already known. However, for the majority of projects, such a decision had not yet been made, or its results were not generally known.

This exercise involved some speculation as to World Bank-IDA intentions in regard to two or three projects in which the Bank was already involved at the planning level despite fairly high local cost components (probably well over half) associated with the projects. In regard to at least one of these projects, Bank officials had hinted that they would at least follow a very liberal definition of foreign-exchange costs in determining their contribution and might finance enough local costs to raise their total contribution to 50 per cent or even more of the project's total cost.

The key question in projecting the amount of local cost financing by foreign sources was how much AID itself would do over the Plan period. AID's then official policy on financing local costs was given in Manual Order No. 1011.6, which stated: "AID will consider requests to finance up to 50 per cent of the local costs of a project or group of projects." If an AID mission recommended that more than 50 per cent of the local costs of a capital project be financed by AID, it was called upon to provide a "thorough rationale" based on criteria set forth in the manual order. The AID mission to Nigeria prepared such a rationale, based mainly on the argument that, unless we were allowed maximum flexibility in financing local costs of those capital projects that met AID criteria, it was going to be very difficult to find sufficient vehicles to transfer to Nigeria, during the Plan period, the full amount of $225 million publicly committed in late 1961 to support of the Plan. (My earlier study analyzes the criteria in the AID manual order and describes the mission's rationale in some detail.)[24]

However, as of late 1963, all we had to go on was the fact that AID headquarters had agreed to finance 50 per cent of local costs in two major loan projects. In both projects, it so happened that the consulting engineer's breakdown of 60-40 per cent between U.S. and local costs, respectively, meant that AID financing of half the estimated local costs would raise AID's total share to 80 per cent, and the African regional office at AID headquarters had previously instituted a rule that AID would finance no more than 80 per cent of the cost of a project regardless of the offshore-local cost breakdown. Thus, it was yet to be determined whether AID would accept the mission's arguments and finance more than 50 per cent of local costs in a project with an estimated local cost component greater than 40 per cent.

Using all available information and expectations of what the policies of AID and the other aid sources would be, I finally estimated that between 60 and 65 per cent of the total costs of eligible public sector projects could be met by foreign aid sources in accordance with current interpretations of the specific project approach and its variations. Whereas eligible projects had been estimated at 60 per cent of the total public capital budget, this calculation implied that between 36 and 39 per cent of the total public capital budget, or £235-255 million out of a budget of £654 million, could potentially be covered by foreign aid. However, not all the budgeted amount was likely to be spent over the Plan period--indications in 1963 were that the shortfall in the public sector program would probably amount to not less than 25 per cent. Assuming that private investment, which had been budgeted in the Plan at an unrealistically low level in relation to current levels of private capital spending, would take up much of the slack and accepting at face value the Plan's projection that private foreign investment during the Plan period would be around £200 million, I concluded that total inflow of external resources would equal roughly 33 per cent of gross capital formation during 1962-68.

Even this appears in retrospect to have been an overestimate. According to AID, as of mid-1967, Nigeria was "financing nearly three-quarters of its own development."[25] If a range of 25-33 per cent represents the maximum proportion of gross investment that can be financed from abroad on the specific project approach and other, narrower criteria in an African country where public capital sources take a virtual saturation approach and are ready to provide, in principle, larger amounts of long-term finance (albeit largely for their own exports) than can be matched with

eligible projects, then Africa's present inflow/investment ratio of
.365 in Table 17 is already higher than can be sustained on the
basis of a strict project approach. Use of very easy terms on resource transfer to Africa would appear to ease the situation, but
the harder terms are incompatible with sole reliance on the project
approach. Actual inflow/investment ratios for the other regions
and ratios projected for them on the easy-term assumption fall
substantially below the above range (with one exception--in South
Europe and Middle East, the current ratio is within the range); the
hard-term assumption brings all of them within the range. However, the results of our Nigerian exercise say little or nothing
about circumstances in other regions. At most, I would venture
the unsubstantiated opinion that, in a region with as sophisticated
and active a private sector as Latin America's, the proportion of
total investment in the money economy that could be fitted into
standard molds of eligibility for external financing would be considerably less than in Africa.

ASSESSING THE ELIGIBILITY OF IMPORTS
FOR NONPROJECT AID

To establish a limiting value of the inflow/import ratio in any
less-developed country requires no less detailed an exercise than
that described above in regard to Nigeria's inflow/investment ratio.
Not having engaged in such an exercise, I can only refer in general
to some of the limitations that apply to the proportion of a less-
developed country's imports that can be financed externally on
normal criteria of nonproject financing. Such limitations arise from
restrictions capital sources impose on (1) the classes of goods
whose export they will finance, and (2) the countries whose purchases of eligible goods they will finance.

Under category (1), the sources prefer to finance the export
of capital goods because of their obvious connection with development and in the expectation that productive investment will generate
the resources required to service its finance. In addition, raw
materials and intermediate goods destined for further processing
in a less-developed country are now regarded by many sources as
eligible for nonproject financing on the ground that enabling the
country to operate its productive plant at a higher proportion of
capacity than would otherwise be possible is conducive to growth
and, ultimately, the earning of foreign exchange with which to
service debt.

AID nonproject loans show how broad a definition can be
given this category of goods in order to widen the channels for
infusion of resources. A typical list is the following, announced
as being eligible for financing under a 1962 AID loan to Taiwan for

"essential industrial imports": Eligible goods "include [but are not restricted to] artificial graphite electrodes, hides and leather, zinc and lead, sulphur, pharmaceuticals, rubber, pulp, vehicles and spare parts, iron and steel, chemicals and machinery."26

On the other hand, with one major exception--surplus food-stuffs the United States finances under P.L. 480--capital sources are unwilling as a matter of standard procedure to match their funds with consumer goods. Financing imports of consumer goods is, of course, a perfectly feasible means of resource transfer--the United States in particular has used it with a number of its military allies and still does in South Viet Nam, where the objective of effecting a certain transfer within a limited period of time has priority over the considerations underlying normal aid procedures. Of course, any resort by an aid source to nonproject financing is generally tantamount to accepting a need for more rapid transfer than can be effected via the specific project approach. (In some exceptional cases, it may also involve a greater or lesser degree of reliance on the benefiting country's management of its affairs, coupled with a readiness to forego the administrative burdens the project approach imposes on the source. The World Bank has indicated that its cautious shift to nonproject financing in the cases of India and Pakistan reflects a growing confidence in their respective policies.) But the banker's objections to medium- or long-term financing of commodities that are consumed within a few months, together with the resistance of public opinion in source countries against using taxpayers' money to (as it appears superficially) subsidize the consumption of those classes of society that can afford imported consumer goods, constitute powerful institutional obstacles to covering such transactions under aid programs.

A feeble attempt to measure the ultimate constraint implied by the foregoing restrictions on end-uses of nonproject aid is made in Table 18, which gives a proportional breakdown of less-developed countries' 1964 imports by sources and major commodity groups: Nonproject financing is generally limited to portions (very rarely 100 per cent) of the food, raw materials, base metals, and capital goods categories. Imports of these items from Western Europe, North America, Japan, and the Sino-Soviet bloc, which between them contain virtually all the significant sources of capital for the less-developed countries, amounted to 46.5 per cent of less-developed countries' total imports in 1964. This may be regarded as an upper limit on the proportion of these countries' present imports that could potentially be financed directly out of nonproject aid, other than in special situations involving, for example, an aid source's military security interests.

Over several years, a less-developed country may, of course, be able to increase the proportion of its total imports eligible for aid by altering the structure of domestic production, building up inventories, etc. Thus, it is clear that most recipients of P.L. 480 aid have allowed factors to transfer out of domestic production of

TABLE 18

Less-developed Countries' Imports, 1964,
by Sources and Commodity Groups

(All figures represent proportions of total
imports by less-developed countries from
all sources.)

Sources of supply

Commodity group	(I) Western Europe, North America, Japan	(II) Sino-Soviet bloc	(III) (I)+(II)	(IV) Less-developed countries	(V) World[a]
Primary products					
Food	.101	.015	.117	.061	.187
Raw materials	.024	.003	.028	.024	.054
Fuels	.011	.005	.016	.077	.094
Subtotal	.137	.024	.161	.161	.336
Manufactures					
Base metals	.055	.004	.059	.005	.066
Capital goods	.236	.025	.261	.007	.271
Passenger cars	.018	.001	.019	--	.019
Textiles & clothing	.052	.006	.058	.014	.073
Other manufactures	.176	.016	.192	.021	.217
Subtotal	.537	.053	.590	.047	.646
Residue	.015	.001	.017	.001	.019
Grand total	.690	.078	.768	.209	1.000

Note:

[a]Including South Africa, Australia, and New Zealand, which
are not included elsewhere.

Source: Percentages in the table were calculated from absolute
data in General Agreement on Tariffs and Trade, International
Trade--1965 (Geneva, 1966), Table 8, pp. 36-37.

197

such commodities and/or invested less new resources in such production than they could have afforded to in the absence of this form of assistance. Furthermore, to the extent that a country develops by substituting domestic production of consumer manufactures for importation of such goods, it may increase the relative shares of raw materials, base metals, and capital goods in its import basket, thereby enhacing its eligibility for nonproject finance--India and Pakistan are cases in point. These are trends that can only be studied in the context of an individual country.

As for the geographical distribution of aid, most bilateral capital resources prefer to restrict their aid to a limited group of countries, in many cases comprising nations with which the source has a special historical and political relationship. As a general rule, of course, in countries with which a capital source enjoys such a relationship, its share in the import market is also likely to be substantial. However, many sources have acquired over time a sizable share of the market in countries where they had no such relationship and where noncommercial motives for extending aid are of minor importance. For example, this is the situation in which Japan now finds herself throughout the less-developed world, excepting only those Asian countries to which historical circumstances have obliged her to pay reparations. As a low-cost supplier of consumer manufactures Japan has built up substantial favorable trade balances in a number of African countries, among them Nigeria, where Japan's 1965 exports to and imports from were $59.0 and $9.3 million, respectively; Kenya--$25.7 vs. $5.6 million; Ghana--$23.6 vs. $7.9 million; Sudan--$19.6 vs. $8.9 million; and Malawi--$3.4 vs. $0.3 million.[27] Her over-all 1965 balance in Africa was $310 million of exports to vs. $180 million of imports from.[28] Several African countries are pressing Japan very hard to provide long-term finance to cover all or part of these deficits. As an adviser in Kenya's Ministry of Economic Planning and Development during 1964-67, when Kenya imposed quantitative restrictions on imports of Japanese goods in an effort to rectify the imbalance, I was able to watch the process at close range. The Japanese Government's answer was to offer a multiyear credit which was only a fraction of the trade deficit and was, moreover, tied to additional purchases in Japan for development projects. Clearly the Japanese were trying to get away with the minimum amount of aid necessary to protect their commercial interests. But the approach of not allowing new loans to be used to finance any part of an existing level of commercially financed imports from the source country, with the occasional exception of equipment for major capital projects, is typical of most sources. It is obvious that this approach severely limits less-developed countries' ability to approach their maximum inflow/import ratios as defined by the commodity distribution of imports.

Some comparative light is shed on the readiness of capital sources to finance their commodity exports to less-developed countries by comparing trade and aid figures. Table 19 gives

TABLE 19

The Flow of Financial Resources to Less-developed
Countries in Relation to Capital Sources' Exports
to Such Countries, 1965

(All figures except column V are in $ millions.)

Source	(I) Exports to less-developed countries	(II) Gross official financial flows, less technical assistance[b]	(III) Net private flows[c]	(IV) Total relevant flows-- (II)+ (III)	(V) Ratio (IV) ÷ (I)
United States	8,920	3,334	1,873	5,207	.584
Canada	600	95	45	140	.233
EEC	7,460	1,217	1,289	2,506	.336
United Kingdom	3,500	407	517	924	.264
Other European Free Trade Area	1,510	82	86	168	.111
Soviet Union	1,210	500	--	500	.239
Other East Europe	880				
Japan	3,640	245	242	487	.134
Australia	560	102	23	125	.223
Total, capital sources	28,280	5,982	4,075	10,057	.356
All other countries	9,200	70[a]	n.a.[b]	n.a.	..[c]
Total, world	37,480	5,982	4,075	10,057	.268

(Continued)

199

TABLE 19 (Continued)

Notes:

[a]The only significant source of official capital not in-
cluded under capital source countries as defined in the table is
Kuwait. According to the World Bank's 1966-67 Annual Report
(Washington, D.C., 1967), Table 10, p. 36 the net outflow from
Kuwait to less-developed countries in 1965 was $62 million.
This is rounded upward to $70 million to allow for amortization
of Kuwaiti funds and minor contributions by other sources.

[b]"N.a." denotes not available.

[c]". ." denotes negligible.

Sources:

Column I data are from United Nations Department of
Economic and Social Affairs and Statistical Office, Yearbook of
International Trade Statistics, 1965 (New York, 1967), Table B,
pp. 20-31. Data are f.o.b., supplier's port, and include goods
subsequently re-exported from their original destinations. It
would be preferable to use c.i.f. data net of re-exports; however,
for this I have been able to find no comparable breakdown by
source. The same U.N. publication gives less developed countries' total imports, c.i.f., net of re-exports, as $37,600 million,
which is virtually the same as the world total in the table.

From Organization for Economic Cooperation and Development, Geographical Distribution of Financial Flows to Less-
Developed Countries, 1965 (Paris, 1967), pp. 1-5. Official amortization flows given by the same source are added to net bilateral
aid figures in order to give the gross measure relevant to our
discussion. Technical assistance figures from OECD, Development Assistance Efforts and Policies, 1967 Review (Paris, 1967),
Table 4, pp. 188-89, are deducted inasmuch as very little of this
form of assistance finances commodities. (This also applies to
part of the DAC's category "other grants," but no breakdown is
available.)

From OECD, Development Assistance Efforts and Policies,
1967 Review, Table IV.1., p. 57. These figures are net of repatriation of private investment funds of residents of the source countries
but gross of any capital transfers out of less-developed countries
by residents of such countries.

(1) total 1965 exports of major individual capital sources or groups
of sources to the less-developed world as a whole; (2) a measure
of the relevant flow of financial resources; and (3) the ratio of (2)
to (1). To some extent, multilateral finance is available to take up
the slack between the level of imports from developed countries
required to attain desired growth rates and bilateral finance available from these sources. In 1965, gross disbursements from
multilateral sources amounted to 4.4 per cent of total exports from
capital sources listed in the table. A less-developed country also
has some leeway to adjust its import purchasing pattern according
to which sources provide finance on the most favorable terms.
However, since large-scale foreign aid disbursements had already
been going on for nearly a decade by 1965, it is likely that the
trade-aid pattern in Table 19 reflects the situation after a large
share of whatever adjustments are feasible had been made. African
countries may continue to try to pressure the Japanese to finance
a larger share of their bilateral trade balances, but it is most unlikely that they could find any other source to finance importation
of the largely consumer goods involved, and diversion of trade to
other suppliers would merely raise import prices.

NOTES TO CHAPTER 8

1. U.S. House of Representatives, Subcommittee of the Committee on Appropriations, Hearings on Foreign Operations Appropriations for 1962 (87th Cong. 1st Sess.), June 27-August 18, 1961,
Part 2, p. 1112.

2. Frank M. Coffin, "Some Thoughts on Policy-Making in
A.I.D.," Speech before the Conference on Foreign Aid, Trade, and
Investment, Washington, D.C., May 4, 1962 (AID, mimeographed
release).

3. Thomas C. Schelling, "American Aid and Economic De-
velopment: Some Critical Issues," International Stability and
Progress: United States Interests and Instruments (New York:
The American Assembly, 1957), p. 160-61.

4. International Bank for Reconstruction and Development,
Annual Report, 1963-64 (Washington, D.C.), p. 30.

5. Ibid., p. 8.

6. International Bank for Reconstruction and Development,
Annual Report, 1966-67 (Washington, D.C.), p. 12.

7. Schelling, op. cit., p. 161.

8.   How much protection this constraint actually provides for a capital source's balance of payments is another matter, which depends on the normal trade relations between the source and benefiting countries, the competitiveness and state of capacity utilization of the industries supplying the commodities to which aid is tied, the aid policies of other capital sources, etc. See Walter S. Salant and Associates, The United States Balance of Payments in 1968 (Washington, D.C.: Brookings Institution, 1963).

9.   Organization for Economic Cooperation and Development, Development Assistance Efforts and Policies, 1967 Review (Paris, 1967), p. 84.

10.   Ibid., p. 85.

11.   See U.S. House of Representatives, Committee on Foreign Affairs, Hearings on the Foreign Assistance Act of 1962 (87th Cong., 1st Sess.), testimony of Eximbank president Harold F. Linder.

12.   Data from U.S. Agency for International Development, U.S. Overseas Loans and Grants and Assistance from International Organizations: Obligations and Loan Authorizations, July 1, 1945–June 30, 1966, March 17, 1967.

13.   The New York Times, May 18, 1961.

14.   Ibid., March 26, 1964.

15.   Ibid.

16.   U.S. House of Representatives, Committee on Foreign Affairs, op. cit., p. 32.

17.   IBRD, Annual Report, 1966-67, p. 31.

18.   Göran Ohlin, Foreign Aid Policies Reconsidered (Paris: Development Centre of the Organization for Economic Cooperation and Development, 1966), p. 92.

19.   Dragoslav Avramovic and Associates, Economic Growth and External Debt (Baltimore, Md: The Johns Hopkins Press, 1964), p. 90.

20.   Organization for Economic Cooperation and Development, op. cit., p. 127.

21.   Ibid.

22.   IBRD, Annual Report, 1966-67, p. 27.

23.   Government of the Federation of Nigeria, Ministry of Economic Development, National Development Plan, 1962-68 (Lagos, 1962, p. 33.

24.   Clive S. Gray, "The Spectrum of International Capital Transfer to the Underdeveloped Countries" (Unpublished Ph.D. dissertation, Department of Economics, Harvard University, 1964), p. 607–13.

25.   U.S. Agency for International Development, Proposed Foreign Aid Program, FY 1968: Summary Presentation to the Congress (Washington, D.C., April, 1965; reprinted March, 1966), p. 223.

26.   U.S. A.I.D. press release of June 16, 1962.

27.   Data from United Nations Department of Economics and Social Affairs and Statistical Office, Yearbook of International Trade Statistics, 1965 (New York, 1967), p. 423. Exports f.o.b., imports c.i.f., Japanese ports.

28.   General Agreement on Tariffs and Trade, International Trade 1965 (Geneva, 1966), Appendix, Table D. Both figures are f.o.b. supplier's port.

9

THE GROSS OUTFLOW CONSTRAINT: CONCLUSIONS OF THE CONSTRAINT ANALYSIS

The weighted average terms on resource transfer to a less-developed country, or to the less-developed countries as a whole, should be no more severe than will enable sources of capital to maintain the required net outflow to such country or countries, subject to institutional and other limitations on gross outflow.

Whether this constraint has practical significance depends on the extent to which limitations on gross, as opposed to net, outflow of resources to less-developed countries actually exist. In the case of private foreign investment, economic limitations are likely to predominate, the rate of gross new investment being determined by the profitability of investment opportunities in the less-developed country. On the other hand, in the case of public foreign aid, where the policy objectives are political rather than commercial, any such limitations are inherently institutional, since the true economic cost of foreign aid to the donor nation and its government is measured by net rather than gross outflow. Still, institutional limitations on resource outflow can be as effective as any other kind, and post-war experience indicates that they are highly significant. The practical importance of the gross outflow constraint in present-day resource transfer is aptly described in the following excerpt from the DAC's most recent report, Development Assistance Efforts and Policies--1967 Review:

> Gross disbursements . . . should probably be given more attention than they usually receive. Very few countries operate their foreign lending on a revolving fund basis, and amortization and interest revert in large part to general treasury funds. Gross amounts must be appropriated and they compete in that form with the other demands upon the Treasury. There is little doubt but that the gross amount represents the amount of contributed "assistance" in the minds of Finance Ministers and legislators. Even if an equal amount were being paid back as the result of previous

loans, the gross out-payments would still be regarded as indicating the size of the national effort,
measured as a budgetary burden. In a sense, whatever receipts there are must be appropriated again.
Furthermore, even if one were operating a revolving fund with no net increase, and thus providing no
aid according to the UNCTAD and DAC definitions,
there would still be the problems of operating the
fund, with all the policy issues associated with the
direction and form of providing assistance efficiently
and effectively. While the net figure is obviously a
better measure of burden on the budget associated
with assistance programs, the gross figure may
better indicate the attitude and intention of the
country concerned.[1]

DOMAR'S FOREIGN INVESTMENT MODEL

The fundamental contribution of Evsey Domar in the paper
that introduced this constraint[2] was to establish some simple
formulae interrelating four variables--(1) the rate of growth
of gross foreign lending; (2) the rate of interest and (3) the
final maturity or amortization rate on foreign loans; and (4)
the ratio of service payments to gross loans--and then evaluate
the implications from the viewpoint of terms on postwar U.S.
lending. Essentially, Domar showed that whether and when the
annual return flow of service payments on foreign loans will exceed gross new loans depends on (1) the relative levels of the
interest rate and the rate of growth of gross lending, and (2) the
final maturity or amortization rate. On the simplifying assumption
that all loans are made on identical terms and ignoring any debt
contracted before the first loans in the period under consideration,
the ratio of service payments to gross lending reaches a constant
level one year after the first loans are fully repaid. If the interest
rate is greater than the rate of growth of gross lending, the foregoing ratio is greater than unity (i.e., service payments exceed
gross lending from the year in question); if the two rates are equal,
the ratio is unity; and, if the interest rate is less than the rate of
growth of gross lending, the ratio is less than unity, so that a continuing (and increasing) net outflow of resources is maintained.
(It should be noted that the foregoing is true on two alternative
assumptions about the method of repayment--equal annual installments of principal and level annual payments of principal and
interest, sometimes referred to as the "equated annuity" method.)
Domar also constructs formulae for the "net value" method,
where amortization payments form a constant percentage of the declining loan balance, and full repayment occurs only at infinity.
In this case, a limiting value of the above ratio is attained only at

infinity; however, the ratio becomes insignificantly different from
that value very soon after a period of years equal to the reciprocal
of the assumed annual amortization rate. Although this method is
not used in international lending, it offers the advantage of a limiting ratio of service payments to gross loans that is much simpler
mathematically than the analogous formulae ... once the constant
level is reached ... in the other two cases.*

Domar's application of this model starts from the premise
that "a wise foreign economic policy" for the United States in the
post-Marshall Plan era would involve a continuing program of
foreign investment, "probably (the) most important" objective being
to "assist in the development of less advanced countries." However, he notes that the inflow of service--amortization and interest--
payments on the investment "is expected after a relatively short
interval to exceed the outflow--a phenomenon which seems to be
embarrassing to both the borrower and the lender." In order to
achieve its ends, gross lending should be maintained at a level no
lower than the return flow of service payments from borrowing nations as a whole. Domar expresses the belief that it would be
feasible for the United States to invest in foreign countries over
the long run at a rate equal to a constant 1 or 2 per cent of U.S.
national income.   In this event, gross foreign lending would increase at the same rate as national income, for which Domar thinks
that a rate of more than 3 per cent "may be too much to hope for."
If that is so, Domar continues, a weighted average interest rate of
more than 3 per cent would raise the ratio of service inflow to gross
loan outflow above unity before very long. He adds that "a yield
below 3 per cent on all foreign investment in our institutional conditions"--especially on private investment--"is not easily
achieved, . . . but there is really no compelling reason why our
government should charge as much as 3 or 4 per cent on its foreign
loans. A reduction of this rate to 2 per cent or less would offset

---

*Thus, with a defined as the annual percentage of amortization
by the net value method, i the rate of interest, r the rate of growth
of gross outflow, and k the length of the amortization period in the
level payment case, the formula for the limiting value of the net
value ratio is:

$$\frac{a+i}{a+r}$$

The analogous formula for the final value of the ratio corresponding to the level payment method is:

$$\frac{i[1 - (1+r)^{-k}]}{r[1 - (1+i)^{-k}]}$$

and the formula for the equal principal installment method is
still longer.

the higher yields on private investment and perhaps bring about a
rough equality between the rates of growth and interest.'' Domar
goes on to develop the idea of a revolving fund from which public
"loans can be made at an increasing (absolute) rate, and yet
without any additional Congressional appropriations! Now assisting in the development of one project and now of another, these
loans could become a major instrument of a wise foreign economic
policy.''[3]

Although Domar does not make it explicit, in order for an
interest rate of 2 per cent on public loans to offset yields on private
foreign investment and make the average return come out at 3 per
cent, the volume of public capital outflow would have to be several
times greater than that of private outflow. If the return on private
investment were as low as 6 per cent, the volume of public capital
outflow would have to equal 3 times that of private capital; if the
return were no less than 10 per cent, as we have suggested may be
the minimum required to attract private direct foreign investment into
most of today's less-developed countries, annual public capital outflow would have to be 7 times as great as private foreign investment.

MODIFICATIONS OF THE DOMAR MODEL

In the light of seventeen years of experience since Domar
wrote, it is appropriate to modify his analysis in certain respects.
First, there is now good reason to believe that the United States
(and major capital sources as a whole) does not have to content itself with a growth rate of national income not exceeding 3 per cent.
According to the AID report on global trends and growth rates in
GNP used in preceding chapters, the following average annual percentage real growth rates were achieved in Europe and North
America during the three 5-year periods 1950-55, 1955-60, and
1960-66: European developed countries--5.0, 4.5, and 4.5; United
States--4.3, 2.2, and 4.8; Canada--4.6, 3.4, and 5.6. Second, as
is shown in Table 21, over the 10-year period 1956-66 as well
as the 6-year period 1960-66, the United States and other OECD
member countries have maintained growth rates in excess of 5 per
cent in most measures of resource outflow to less-developed countries, net as well as gross.[4] However, at the present time, there is
widespread concern that gross resource outflow to less-developed
countries, and to an even greater extent net outflow, are beginning
to level off. Most measures of U.S. official aid grew more slowly
during the shorter, recent period than over the past decade. Congressional appropriations under the Mutual Security and, from
fiscal 1962, Foreign Assistance acts for 11 fiscal years from 1958
to 1968 show a declining trend of 2 per cent per annum.[5] Although
these appropriations are not a definitive measure--they include
certain types of military assistance and exclude aid programs

such as P.L. 480 and the Eximbank—a continuation of this trend
will almost certainly reduce the rate of growth of total U.S. aid disbursements below the rate of growth of GNP by 1970.

As we saw in Chapter 2, the bulk of foreign private investment in less-developed countries today is in the form of equity,
which is not subject to regular amortization schedules. The Department of Commerce data reviewed in Chapter 2 show that net
capital repatriation is a phenomenon more closely associated with
the petroleum industry, in countries where petroleum development
has reached a peak for one reason or another, than with other
industries. There are, of course, instances where the initiative
toward repatriation is taken by local authorities in accordance with
policies of localization or nationalization. However, such policies
are exogenous to our present treatment, whose primary concern is
the aid policies that should be followed in transferring the necessary
residual resources once endogenous private investment has done all
that can be expected of it. We noted already in examining the independence constraint in Chapter 6 that a continuing absolute increase
in private foreign investors' equity in a developing economy (though
not necessarily an indefinite increase in its ratio to total output of
the economy), far from being inconsistent with financial independence, is a healthy sign of financial maturity. Financial independence
is rather defined as independence from extraordinary resource
transfer by foreign governments, and it is here that the concept of
amortization is relevant. In general, it would seem appropriate to
treat private foreign investment within the framework of a modified
(and, as it happens, simplified) Domar model, where amortization
is assumed to be zero and the growth rate applies to net rather than
gross data. The advantages of this procedure are considerably en-
hanced by the fact that the DAC reports only net data for private
outflows to less-developed countries.

It is self-evident that, as long as the rate of growth of annual
net private investment is greater than the rate of return on such
investment, the absolute net inflow of resources will increase con-
tinuously from the first year. As long as the two rates are equal,
such absolute net inflow will not fall below the first year's level
(if each year's net inflow starts earning the given return one year
later, the absolute net inflow will remain constant at the initial
level). And, if the rate of return is greater than the rate of growth
of annual net investment, the two payment streams will cross at
some future year and return payments will thereafter exceed net
new investment. Again, assuming the full return is earned one year
after inflow, the absolute net inflow will constantly decline from its
initial level. In practice, because there is normally a longer gestation period before private investment earns its target return (in the
petroleum industry, this may last decades while exploration is
carried out), net inflow may increase for a few years even though
its rate of growth is lower than the eventual rate of return.

We have already suggested that 10 per cent is the minimum rate of return required to attract private foreign investment into less-developed countries. On the other hand, none of today's major bilateral capital sources can expect its GNP to grow at such a rate for a protracted period, nor can this be expected of the collective GNP of countries supplying funds to multilateral sources. Hence, the third case outlined above--rate of return greater than rate of increase of net investment--is the typical one and merits closer study. Because we share Domar's concern to forestall an excess of return payments from less-developed countries over net capital flows into such countries, at least in the foreseeable future, we are interested in seeing how long it takes for the two payment streams to become equal (after which point such an excess arises). Table 20 gives values for the year in which return payments become equal to net new private foreign investment for various pairs of values of the rate of return and rate of growth of net investment. Thus, for example, if net investment runs at a constant rate (i.e. rate of growth equals zero), and the rate of return is .10, the payment streams cross in the 11th year. If the growth rate is zero, the year in question is given by the reciprocal of the rate of return plus the gestation period. The table assumes a gestation period of one year; a gestation period of n years adds n-1 to each value in the table.

TABLE 20

Year in Which Annual Net Inflow of Private Resources
Becomes Negative

Rate of growth of annual net investment	Rate of Return on Private Investment											
	.01	.02	.03	.04	.05	.06	.07	.08	.09	.10	.15	.20
Zero	101	51	35	26	21	18	16	14	13	11	8	6
.01		70	42	30	23	20	17	15	13	12	8	7
.02			57	37	27	22	18	16	14	13	9	7
.03				48	32	25	20	17	15	14	9	7
.04					43	30	23	19	16	15	9	7
.05						38	27	22	18	16	10	7
.06							35	25	20	17	10	8
.07								32	24	19	11	8
.08									30	22	11	8
.09										28	12	8

Source: Computed from equation in Mathematical Appendix at (15).

One further modification to be made in the Domar analysis before applying it to current data relates to the specific level Domar assigns to his central constraint. As we have seen, he argues in favor of an interest rate on public loans that will prevent the ratio of service payments to gross new loans from falling below unity. However, in the light of intervening experience with the inertia of poverty in the less-developed world, the race between burgeoning population and sluggish food supplies, and other current manifestations of the resource gap, it is now generally recognized that the advanced countries must maintain a net outflow of resources to the developing countries for many years to come. Thus, the requirement for easy-term lending to which Domar directed attention is even greater than he foresaw at the time. To a large extent, net transfer of resources has been maintained by means of grants and what the DAC refers to as "grant-like contributions," which generate little or no flow of return payments. Domar thought that a long-run grant program "might offend international dignity and be so upsetting to the 'sound business' sense of our Congress that the payment of amortization and interest may be the lesser of the two evils."[6] In the event, overwhelming economic difficulties have forced the benefiting nations to swallow their pride, and the Communist threat and pressure from domestic agricultural interests have induced Congress to appropriate a steady flow of unrequited aid. Although Table 21 shows that bilateral and multilateral grants, etc., have grown more slowly than any other component of official aid (in the United States, they showed a declining trend during 1960-66), such contributions from all DAC countries and multilateral agencies have averaged $4.2 billion per annum in the last seven years. In 1965 and 1966, grants formed 60 per cent of total governmental commitments by DAC countries as a whole, and 61-62 per cent of total U.S. Government commitments. Obviously, a long period of lending at very stiff terms would be required to offset the net transfer effect of such a grant program and thus reduce the overall net transfer to zero.

QUANTIFYING THE CONSTRAINT

To evaluate the implications of the Domar analysis for on-going resource transfer to the less-developed countries, we use data presented by the DAC in regard to trends in resource flows and terms on official aid from its member countries, including the United States in particular, together with data presented by the U.S. Department of Commerce in regard to U.S. direct business investments in less-developed countries. The latter data we have already summarized in Table 2 of Chapter 2. Table 21 shows annual percentage rates of growth in selected components and measures of the flow of resources from all DAC countries and

TABLE 21

Resource Transfer from United States and All DAC Countries--
Growth Rates of Selected Components and Measures

(All figures are percentages.)

Component/measure[b]	Compound annual rate of change[a]	
	1956-60	1960-66

All DAC Countries

NET

Loans, grants and private capital

1. Total net outflow, all resources, bilateral and multilateral, official and private	[c] . .	6. 0

Loans and grants

2. Bilateral government and multilateral (4+14)	. .	5. 5
3. Bilateral government (5+15)	6. 0	4. 0

Loans

4. Bilateral government and multilateral (5+6)	17	18
5. Bilateral government	16	16
6. Multilateral	18	23

Private capital

7. All private loans and investment, net	1. 25	5. 5

GROSS

Loans and grants

8. Bilateral government, publicly guaranteed and multilateral (10 +14)	. .	7. 5
9. Bilateral government (11 +15)	7. 5	7. 0

Loans

10. Bilateral government, publicly guaranteed and multilateral (11 +13)	15	18
11. Bilateral government and publicly guaranteed (includes 12)	14	18
12. Bilateral government	15	17
13. Multilateral	18	23

Grants

14. Bilateral government and multilateral (includes 15)	. .	0. 5
15. Bilateral government grants and grant-like contributions	3. 25	0. 25

(Continued)

TABLE 21 (Continued)

United States

NET

1.	Total official, net	6.5	3.0
2.	Official loans, net	24	23
3.	Total private, net	-1.5	6.0

GROSS

4.	Total Official, gross (5+6)	6.5	3.5
5.	Bilateral government grants and grant-like contributions	2.5	-2.0
6.	Official loans, gross	25+	25+

GROSS/NET

7.	Total official, gross and total private, net (3+4)	4.25	4.0

Notes:

[a]All rates computed from Pesek formula in Mathematical Appendix at (7). Rates from 10 to 25 per cent computed to nearest percentage point, from 5 to 10 per cent to nearest half point, and from -2 to 5 per cent to nearest quarter point.

[b]Some of the components or measures we have chosen to portray here overlap to a minor extent with each other. For example, publicly guaranteed export credits, lumped with bilateral government loans in 8, 10, and 11, are also included in private capital movements.

[c]". ." refers to series encompassing multilateral grants, for which DAC sources do not give estimates for 1956–59. Although data on this component could have been secured elsewhere, the resulting series would probably not have been consistent with DAC's 1960–66 series.

Sources: Principal sources are the latest relevant publications of the Organization for Economic Cooperation and Development, Development Assistance Committee, notably Development Assistance Efforts and Policies, 1967 Review (Paris, 1967), referred to below as DAEP-67; The Flow of Financial Resources to Less-Developed Countries, 1961–65 (Paris, 1967); The Flow of Financial Resources to Less-Developed Countries, 1956–63 (Paris, 1964); and The Flow of Financial Resources to Countries in Course of Economic Development, 1956–59 (Paris, 1961). The latter three are referred to below as Flow, 1961–65, 1956–63, and 1956–59, respectively. Following are specific sources for the individual series in the table other than those identified as the sum of two or more other series:

All DAC

1. DAEP-67, Table I.1, p. 13. Equals total receipts of less-developed countries less estimated flow from non-DAC members.
5. DAEP-67, Statistical Annex, Table 2, p. 184; and Flow, 1956-63, Table A.1, p. 201.
6. DAEP-67, p. 90; Flow, 1961-65, p. 227; Flow, 1956-63, p. 159; Flow, 1956-59, p. 147.
7. DAEP-67, Table IV.1, p. 57.
11. Guaranteed private export credits obtained from DAEP-67, Table V.1, p. 72.
12. DAEP-67, Statistical Annex, Table 2, p. 184; and Flow, 1956-63, Table A.1, p. 201.
13. DAEP-67, Table VI.1, p. 91, for 1960-66 data. For 1956-59, we took data on World Bank disbursements from the International Monetary Fund's International Financial Statistics. The Bank and its affiliate, the IFC, which disbursed less than $20 million during 1956-59, were the only relevant institutions functioning during this period.
14. Multilateral grants obtained from DAEP-67, Table VI.1, p. 91.
15. DAEP-67, Statistical Annex, Table 2, p. 184; and Flow, 1956-63, Table A.1, p. 201.

United States

1. DAEP-67, Table III.1, p. 34.
2, 5, 6. DAEP-67, Statistical Annex, Tables 3, 4, & 5, pp. 186-91; Flow, 1956-63, Table A.4 (p), p. 224; Flow, 1956-63, Table IV.4 (p), p. 149.
3. DAEP-67, Table IV.1, p. 57.

multilateral institutions financed largely by those countries, and from the United States specifically. These rates of growth have not been calculated by taking the average annual geometric difference between the initial- and final-year values, although, in several cases, the values obtained are insignificantly different from that measure. Rather, we have used a technique, devised by Boris P. Pesek, which accords no special weight to any observation by reason of its position in time but instead generates a value for the growth rate corresponding to a straight-line set of dummy observations which minimize the squares of the differences between themselves and the actual observations on the condition that the dummy observations sum to the total value of the actuals. The relevant formula and references are given in the Mathematical Appendix at (7).

Table 22 relates gross official bilateral disbursements on loans and grants for all DAC countries and the United States

TABLE 22

Relationship Between Gross New Resource Transfers and Return Payments, 1963-66

(All entries other than ratios are $ millions.)

	1963	1964	1965	1966
All DAC Countries				
Official bilateral disbursements				
1. Loans, gross	2,161	2,304	2,746	2,986
2. Grants, etc.	4,047	3,882	3,780	3,761
3. Total	6,207	6,185	6,527	6,747
Service payments on official bilateral loans				
4. Amortization	489	700	765	828
5. Interest	307	411	450	494
6. Total	796	1,111	1,215	1,323
Ratios				
7. Total service payments/ loans, gross	.368	.482	.442	.443
8. Total service payments/ total official bilateral disbursements	.128	.180	.186	.196
United States				
Official bilateral disbursements				
9. Loans gross	1,142	1,117	1,458	1,641
10. Grants, etc.	2,668	2,485	2,300	2,258
11. Total	3,810	3,602	3,758	3,899
Service payments on official bilateral loans				
12. Amortization	253	361	295	351
13. Interest	172	239	236	247
14. Total	425	600	531	598
Ratios				
15. Total service payments/ loans, gross	.372	.537	.364	.364
16. Total service payments/ total official bilateral disbursements	.112	.167	.141	.153

Private investment	1963	1964	1965	1966
Petroleum industry[a]				
17. Net new private direct investment	52	70	192	92
18. Total U.S. earnings	1,458	1,411	1,336	1,374
19. Ratio, earnings/net new investment	28.0	20.1	7.0	14.9
All other industries[a]				
20. Net new private direct investment[b]	424	526	752	658
21. Total U.S. earnings	602	718	821	948
22. Ratio, earnings/ net new investment	1.42	1.37	1.09	1.44
All industries[a]				
23. Net new private direct investment[b]	706	829	1,206	948
24. Total U.S. earnings	2,277	2,469	2,603	2,770
25. Ratio, earnings/net new investment	3.23	2.98	2.16	2.92

Notes:

[a]Petroleum and "all other" industries relate only to Latin America, other Western Hemisphere, and Middle East; petroleum data for Africa excluding South Africa and Far East excluding Japan are not available. However, "all industries" encompasses all five regions.

[b]Sum of net capital outflow (from United States) and reinvested earnings.

Sources: Organization for Economic Cooperation and Development, Development Assistance Efforts and Policies, 1967 Review (Paris, 1967), Statistical Annex, Tables 2-5, pp. 184-91, and Table III.2, pp. 36-37; OECD, The Flow of Financial Resources to Less-Developed Countries, 1956-63 (Paris, 1964), p. 224; Survey of Current Business, issues for August, 1964, and September, 1965, 1966, 1967, articles on U.S. foreign investment.

specifically to service payments on official bilateral loans. For the United States only, because we have comprehensive data on earnings of United States, but no other, private foreign investment in less-developed countries, the table also compares net new private direct investment, including reinvested earnings, with total earnings.

The Development Assistance Committee staff, writing in the 1967 edition of Development Assistance Efforts and Policies, computed the annual levels of gross official bilateral disbursements that would be needed at successive five-yearly intervals from 1970 to 1995 in order to maintain a constant net transfer of resources at the 1965 level of $5.3 billion, assuming continuation of the same terms that applied to 1965 gross commitments.[7] (These terms were: 60 per cent of commitments in the form of grants or grant-like contributions; the loan component at 3.6 per cent interest and 22.3 years final maturity.) Taking account of existing debt and its gradual retirement, DAC found that gross annual disbursements of $10.8 billion would be required by 1995 in order to satisfy the above conditions. According to the report, this figure implies a "dramatic increase in gross disbursements."[8] However, the implied compound annual increase over actual gross official bilateral disbursements in 1966 is only 1.7 per cent, which is considerably below the rates of increase achieved in nearly all components and measures of aid in Table 21 during 1956-66 and 1960-66. It is also well below rates of increase that the principal source countries have recently achieved, and hope to continue achieving, in their GNP's. It would appear that the writers of the report have allowed themselves to be frightened by some absolute magnitudes projected for 30 years hence, which superficially appear enormous in relation to current levels. On the other hand, rates of growth of several measures of net resource transfer calculated from a base of 1963, rather than 1956 or 1960, the two base years employed in Table 21, are much lower than the rates shown in that table. Using the 1963 base, which can be questioned on the ground that that year stands considerably above the then current trend line, the DAC's 1967 report states that "the level of net official assistance has remained almost constant in recent years."[9] Undoubtedly, action such as that taken by the U.S. Congress in progressively reducing AID's appropriations does give grounds for concern over whether even a modest rate of increase of 2 per cent in gross bilateral aid disbursements can be achieved once the ratio of disbursements out of the aid pipeline to new aid commitments attains a stable level.

IMPLICATIONS OF INCREASING NET RESOURCE TRANSFER

The DAC staff exercise focuses merely on the steps required to maintain a constant net transfer of resources. Many authorities argue that it is desirable, from the viewpoint of the principal objectives of resource transfer to less-developed areas assumed in this book, to increase the rate of net transfer over the present level and to continue doing so over the foreseeable future. It is not within the scope of this study to review recent attempts made to estimate the net resource requirements of the less-developed world now and at various points in the future.[10] Personally, having

acquired from experience considerable confidence in the World
Bank's assessment of the less-developed world's real requirements in the light of its absorptive capacity, I would take my cue
from the following statement in the Bank's 1964-65 Annual Report:

> A preliminary Bank inquiry, carried out country
> by country and based on the judgment and experience
> of the Bank's country specialists and area economists,
> suggests that the developing countries could effec-
> tively use, on the average over the next five years,
> some $3 billion to $4 billion more of external capital
> per year than has been provided in the recent past.[11]

If capital sources behave according to the simplifying assumptions of the Domar model--i.e., provide their capital on constant
terms with a constant rate of growth of gross outflow--there are,
broadly speaking, three ways in which they can ensure an annual
increase in the net outflow of resources to the less-developed
world, now or after any given interval of time. First, they can increase the amount of outright grants provided by whatever rate is
required to offset the growing return flow of service payments on
loans. Second, as long as the rate of growth of gross outflow exceeds the weighted average rate of interest, the absolute net outflow of resources will increase annually beginning no later than
the year after the first loans in the process under consideration
have been fully amortized. However, unless the rate of growth of
gross outflow equals or exceeds the full service rate--i.e., including both interest and amortization--there will be some years
during this first full amortization period when the net outflow to the
less-developed world will decline (due to the fact that the ratio
of service payments to gross outflow builds up to a maximum at
the end of that period).

This case differs slightly in the two common methods of
amortization. With the equal annual principal installment method,
where the ratio of service payments to the face value of the loan
being serviced declines each year with declining interest payments on the unpaid balance, the net outflow increases after the
second year if the rate of growth of gross outflow equals the sum
of the interest rate and the reciprocal of the amortization period.
If this growth rate is less than the sum in question (but still
larger than the weighted average interest rate, as it must be if
there is ever to be an increase in net outflow), the net outflow will
decline for some time after the first year, then reach a minimum
some time during the first full amortization period and increase
indefinitely thereafter. With the level payment or equated annuity
method, where the full service ratio is constant, unless the growth
rate of gross outflow exceeds the full service ratio, net outflow
declines after the first year, which decline reverses itself only in
the year after the first full amortization period is completed.

As the third way of ensuring an increase in net outflow, we find it convenient to distinguish a special case of the second foregoing case, i.e., where the rate of growth of gross outflow exceeds the full service rate and thus ensures that net outflow increases in every year during the first full amortization period as well as thereafter. It is also possible to distinguish a fourth case which falls outside the framework of the Domar model. This case involves the use of grace periods in the repayment of principal and of interest, which Domar did not take into account but which have seen increasing use in recent years as an element of flexibility in aid policy. In general, grace periods allow net capital outflow to increase correspondingly in the short run even if the growth rate of gross outflow is less than the full service rate or the rate of interest alone.

To illustrate the foregoing discussion more concretely and to see how the principles we have considered could be applied to derive specific maximum aid terms, we construct a model on the following assumptions:

(1) Capital sources anticipate being able to increase their gross outflows of repayable loans at rates equivalent to long-term GNP growth rates, which we assume to span a range of 4 to 7 per cent.

(2) Grants can be increased at a rate sufficient only to cover any increase in service charges arising from previously existing debt, over and above the present level (which Table 22 shows to have averaged around 45 per cent of gross loan disbursements in recent years). This assumption offers the convenience of permitting us to disregard pre-existing debt. It also implies a very small (if any) increase in grants, since the weight of short- and medium-term credits in the present external/public debt structure of less-developed countries as a whole exceeds the weight of long-term debt still in the grace-period stage. The virtual stagnation in grants observed in Table 21 suggests that such an assumption is realistic.

(3) In addition, we assume that the capital sources adopt a conscious policy of extending loans on terms that will not lead to any reduction in the net outflow of resources to the less-developed world as a whole.

(4) And, finally, all debt is serviced on the level payment system (this is an assumption of convenience that represents a quantitatively insignificant departure from reality).

Table 23 gives the interest rate/final maturity pairs that represent the hardest terms consistent with the foregoing assumptions. By way of interpreting the table, let us assume that capital sources expect their GNP's to grow at a weighted average rate of

5 per cent in the future and that they wish to charge a weighted average interest rate of 3.0 per cent (corresponding closely to the rate of 3.1 per cent the DAC 1967 Review estimates was applied to gross loan commitments in 1966).[12] According to the table, the weighted average maturity in the future would have to be 31 years, compared with the 23.5 years estimated by the DAC for actual 1966 commitments. If the long-term future growth rate of gross outflow equals 3.0 per cent, the only way capital sources can fulfill the policy underlying the third assumption above is to provide all their loans with indefinite grace periods for repayment of principal.

TABLE 23

Final Loan Maturities Consistent with Constant Net
Resource Outflow

(All data in the table represent years.)

Interest Rate	Growth rate of gross resource outflow			
	4%	5%	6%	7%
0	25	20	17	14
1%	29	22	18	16
2%	35	26	20	17
3%	47	31	23	19
3.5%	60	35	25	20
4%	00	41	28	22
5%	*	00	37	26
6%	*	*	00	33
7%	*	*	*	00

Note:

    *Net resource outflow would decline even if loan maturities were infinite.

Source: Interest tables giving values for an annuity whose present value is 1; the appropriate value for a year is that corresponding to an annuity of present value equal to the assumed growth rate of gross resource outflow.

Another way in which capital sources might approach this problem, rather than designing aid terms so as to prevent any decrease in net outflow, is to design them so that the net outflow will not fall below a certain absolute amount at any time in the foreseeable future. As we have already seen, assuming that the level payment method of amortization is used, the time in question will be the final year of the first complete amortization period. The Mathematical Appendix gives, at (16), a formula for the maximum interest rate corresponding to any given final maturity, such that the net outflow in the year of that maturity will equal a given sum, which in this case will be less than the net outflow in the first year of the aid process under consideration, although still positive.

CONCLUSIONS OF THE CONSTRAINT ANALYSIS

This and the preceding three chapters have tried to meet three broad objectives: (1) to show that the financial terms on resource flows to less-developed countries are subject to real constraints, failure to observe which reduces the probability that the resource flows will serve their sources' objectives; (2) to put forward techniques for quantitative derivation of maximum terms implied by assumed values of the constraint parameters and illustrate the use of these techniques with actual data from the less-developed areas; and (3) by means of the aforementioned illustrations, to show very roughly where the weighted average of current resource flows should fit along the spectrum defined in Part I of the book in order to satisfy the constraints.

In introducing each constraint, we have had something to say about its relevance to the real world, with particular reference to the questions that arise in trying to quantify it. To conclude the quantative section of our analysis, we will compare the constraints from various points of view and then summarize the principal underlying factors that explain why the analysis in these chapters has militated in favor of a sizable grant element in resource transfer to less-developed countries as contrasted with the requirements of earlier epochs in the history of resource transfer.

In comparing the constraints outlined in Chapters 5-9, it is appropriate first of all to note a fundamental distinction between the first four and the fifth. This is that the former are defined in terms of parameters characterizing the country or countries benefiting from the resource outflow, whereas the relevant parameter in the fifth case, i.e., ability to generate a particular level of gross as opposed to net outflow, applies to the source(s) of the outflow. Moreover, this last constraint is more relevant to the total gross outflow from a single source or group of sources to the less-developed world as a whole than to the outflow to an individual country. The reason for this is that, in respect of an individual developing country, it would always be possible to counter the effects of the gross outflow constraint by reallocation within the total outflow to all countries. The first four constraints, on the other hand, are particularly relevant to assessing the needs of a particular benefiting country, although they can also be evaluated in the light of data applying to a group of such countries, as we have attempted to do above.

Given the distinction within the set of constraints, it is clear that any inconsistency of policy conclusions resulting from the application of constraint No. 5 and any of the others would be visible only in the context of a comprehensive, pseudo-general equilibrium analysis where maximum aid terms on the total resource outflow were derived by applying constraints Nos. 1-4 to each recipient country and synthesizing the results of all countries taken together. On the other hand, application of any of the first four constraints to a particular country may lead to widely varying policy conclusions, depending partly on the country's economic parameters and partly on the values chosen for the constraints, which, as emerges clearly from earlier discussions of each constraint, contain a large arbitrary element.

The variations in question may be illustrated by observing the different implications, for terms on resource transfer to South Asia and Latin America, of the 25-year independence constraint as opposed to a fairly liberal debt service ratio constraint. In Table 9, we saw that requiring t_3, the year of the last net addition to debt, to be attained in 25 years implies that the weighted average interest rate on resource transfer to Latin America should not exceed 1 1/4 per cent, whereas, in the case of South Asia, it can be as high as 9 1/4 per cent. On the other hand, Table 13 shows that applying a weighted average rate of 6 per cent and assuming amortization of the transfer over 15 years brings about an (intolerably high) maximum debt service/export ratio of 1.35 in the case of South Asia, whereas the maximum ratio implied for Latin America is only .33, probably a tolerable level when one considers that it includes service payments on future private capital inflow, which are not included in present measures of the debt service ratio.

The principal reasons for this contrast are (1) the higher savings growth rate--8 as against 6 per cent--assumed for South Asia, which permits t_3 to be attained sooner; and (2) the higher initial export GDP ratio--.117 as against .054--and export growth rate--8 as against 5.2 per cent--which are assumed for Latin America, resulting in a lower debt service/export ratio throughout the growth-cum-debt process. Assuming that these values, or at least the ratios between them, approximately reflect comparative future growth trends in the two regions, which is a strong assumption, an independence constraint of $t_3 = 25$ years has much more stringent implications for the terms on resource transfer to Latin America than the constraint of a debt service ratio not exceeding .30, and vice versa for the case of South Asia.

Table 9 also shows that an independence constraint of $t_3 = 22$ in the Latin American case and a debt service ratio constraint of .31 in the South Asian case imply a zero interest rate on resource transfer to Latin America and a similar rate, if coupled with an amortization period of 40 years, on transfer to South Asia. If the amortization period for South Asia is longer, then a low positive interest rate can be tolerated; as we have already seen, the particular amortization rate used is irrelevant in the case of the independence constraint, which assumes that any amortization prior to t_3 is offset by new gross inflow.

As for the end-use constraint, we saw in Chapter 8 that its applicability depends on the extent to which aid sources want to exercise control over the allocation of the aid proceeds, whether in order to ensure efficient project execution and/or otherwise influence the recipient country's investment or to ensure purchase of goods and services produced by the source. The degree of control desired in order to influence investment depends largely on the sources' confidence in the competence of the recipient country authorities to use external resources wisely, which confidence appears currently to be least in respect of non-French speaking African countries, whose capital sources insist on following a stricter project approach than applies in any other area. Looking at Table 17, it appears that such an approach to the use of foreign resources imposes an effective constraint on the terms of aid to Africa, in particular by putting the 6 per cent, 15-year terms out of the question, while the zero-interest, 40-year terms appear to be feasible. At the same time, Table 9 shows that a 25-year independence constraint would similarly require zero-interest resource transfer to Africa. Table 13 shows that 6 per cent, 15-year terms would lead to an intolerable maximum debt service/export ratio (.78), whereas zero-interest, 40-year terms would keep the ratio lower (maximum, .14) than is probably necessary. Thus, a continuation of the present project approach to aid to Africa has a constraining effect on aid terms similar to that of a 25-year independence criterion, and both of these are more severe than the debt service constraint. Given the arbitrariness of the independence criterion, there are good grounds for saying that the end-use constraint should, for the time being, serve as the ruling one in respect of the section of Africa to which most of our African data relate.

To summarize, speaking in very broad terms, the independence constraint is likely to be the limiting one in a less-developed country that is comparatively international trade-oriented, already exporting, say, 10 per cent or more of its GDP, and expecting its exports to grow faster than its GDP, whereas the debt service ratio constraint will be limiting in a country where exports are of lesser importance and have less favorable prospects for expansion. The end-use constraint will be limiting in a country that enjoys the relatively favorable trade position of the former case but where aid sources do not have sufficient confidence in the over-all management of resources by the local authorities to furnish aid apart from specific investment projects.

In theory, the optimal procedure in applying the constraints would be for all aid sources to agree on a set of specific values for constraints Nos. 1-4 in the case of each less-developed country and furnish aid to that country on a weighted average set of terms consistent with the constraint having the most restrictive effects in that particular case. A very modest degree of coordination along these lines is achieved through aid consortia and consultative groups (for further details on these, see Chapter 11). Thus far, the constraint that has received the most attention in this context is that of the debt service ratio. As we noted in Chapter 7, this is because the debt service ratio is measurable in the short run, whereas assessing the future date of attainment of financial independence is an extremely speculative exercise.

The value of a particular constraint aid sources will want to satisfy will vary from one country to another and also over time in respect of an individual country. Thus, for example, assuming that aid sources are able to quantify the independence constraint, they will recognize some less-developed countries as being inherently closer to financial independence than others, and they will consider that the political risks entailed in prolonging the growth-cum-debt process differ considerably among countries. The "safe" limit for the debt service/export ratio will be lower in a country whose export product mix and/or import requirements involve relatively greater inherent instability, or whose exports are growing relatively more slowly. As for the end-use constraint, one would expect that, over time, aid sources' confidence in the wise use of untied resources by authorities in African countries would increase with the growing sophistication of the governments concerned, although clearly this process is subject to occasional setbacks. The degree to which bilateral aid is tied to source exports is affected by the balance-of-payments position of each source, which is, of course, variable. The United States, for example, has repeatedly promised to relax its restrictions on third-country purchases out of aid proceeds once its payments position becomes favorable again.

The illustrative computations carried out in Chapters 5-8 in respect of each of the constraints yielded the conclusion that, if all the constraints are to be satisfied, resource transfer to three of the main less-developed regions--Africa, South Asia, and Latin America--must be carried out on terms whose weighted average is highly concessionary. In fact, the computations showed that, for each of the three regions, one or more constraints apply which dictate providing future resource transfer at weighted average terms equivalent to those on a zero-interest, 40-year loan. This is equivalent to an annual service payment of 2.5 per cent of original face value on either an equal annual principal installment or a level payment system of amortization. It so happens that this rate is insignificantly different from the weighted average service rate that applied to 1966 gross bilateral aid commitments of DAC member countries. Counting only loans repayable in foreign exchange, the loan component of these commitments, which was subject to an average interest rate of 3.1 per cent and final maturity of 23.5 years, will generate a weighted average annual service ratio of .061, using the level payment amortization system. Since these loans comprised 40 per cent of total commitments, the annual service payments in question form 2.44 per cent of total aid commitments.

On the other hand, the annual service payments generated by private foreign investment are relatively much higher, so that, insofar as private capital is expected to carry the burden of future resource transfer to less-developed countries, our computations suggest that the weighted average terms on bilateral official flows should be correspondingly lower than the 1966 level. Thus, the current tendency for grants and grant-like transfers to form a diminishing proportion of total aid commitments and the consistent pressure in the U.S. Congress to raise interest rates on long-term AID loans (see Chapter 4) raise the danger that our constraints will be violated.

The need for easy-term resource transfer is fundamentally a function of the ratio between the magnitude of the net resource inflow required by the less-developed countries in order to achieve an acceptable rate of economic growth and such basic economic parameters as the national income, savings, and exports of these countries. An acceptable rate of growth is generally considered to be one that allows for an annual increase of between 2 and 3 per cent in per capita income. As far as the major Western sources of external capital for the less-developed countries are concerned, the hypothesis that underlies the acceptability of such a growth rate is that, given reasonable equity in distribution, the rate in question will give enough people prospects of satisfactorily improving living conditions under a non-Communist regime to give them both a stake in resisting a Communist takeover and the physical means to make their resistance effective (ignoring the possibility of Communist military pressure from outside). This statement must be described as a hypothesis, because it is much too early to say whether it has been borne out in the majority of less-developed countries and it is disputed by competent social scientists.[13] We accept the hypothesis implicitly here, but it falls outside this book's scope to analyze it more systematically.

Given a growth target of 2 or 3 per cent in terms of per capita income, a specific over-all income target of at least 5 per cent is implied by the fact that a population growth rate of close to or above 3 per cent must, in the short run at least, be taken as a given in most less-developed countries. Via the capital/output ratio, which is likewise a given in the short run, the over-all growth rate target in turn defines a required rate of investment. The World Bank data used in the preceding chapters suggest that the "required" rate of investment, derived as above, is anywhere from 3.6 to 7 percentage points (of GDP) above the present average savings rate in four major less-developed regions of the world. When a resource inflow of this magnitude, juxtaposed with the values obtained earlier for current debt GDP ratios, import and export rates, and growth rates of the various parameters, is plugged into the formulae given in the Mathematical Appendix, the result is that any average terms stiffer than the zero-interest, 40-year package run afoul of at least one of our constraints in regard to three of the four regions in question. In a word, of course, it is the poverty of these less-developed areas that makes our constraints operative and requires that capital inflow be provided to such areas on terms even more concessionary than the averages now prevailing.

NOTES TO CHAPTER 9

1. Organization for Economic Cooperation and Development, Development Assistance Efforts and Policies--1967 Review (Paris, 1967), p. 35.

2. Evsey D. Domar, ''The Effect of Foreign Investment on the Balance of Payments,'' in Domar (ed.), Essays in the Theory of Economic Growth (New York: Oxford University Press, 1957).

3. Ibid., pp. 129-34.

4. GNP is given in U.S. Agency for International Development, Office of Program Coordinator, Gross National Product--Growth Rates and Trend Data, by Region and Country (Washington, D.C., March 31, 1967, Report RC-W-138), sections of Table 3.

5. Source of appropriations data is The New York Times, ''News of the Week in Review,'' November 12, 1967. The method used to compute the rate of growth is that described in the Mathematical Appendix at (6).

6. OECD, op. cit., p. 129.

7. Ibid., p. 79.

8. Ibid., p. 80.

9. Ibid., p. 37.

10.   Göran Ohlin provides detailed references to and concise summaries of the better known published efforts in his Foreign Aid Policies Reconsidered, (Paris: Development Centre of the Organization for Economic Cooperation and Development, 1966), pp. 76-80.

11.   International Bank for Reconstruction and Development, Annual Report, 1964-65 (Washington, D.C., 1965) p. 62.

12.   OECD, op. cit., p. 76.

13.   See, for example, Hans Morgenthau's article, "A Political Theory of Foreign Aid," American Political Science Review, June, 1962, pp. 301-10, reviewed critically in Clive S. Gray, "The Spectrum of International Capital Transfer to the Underdeveloped Countries" (Unpublished Ph.D. dissertation, Department of Economics, Harvard University, 1964), pp. 662-64.

PART III

THE MIXTURE OF TRANSFER TECHNIQUES

CHAPTER **10** ALLOCATING RESOURCE
TRANSFER AMONG END-USES

The quantitative exercise conducted in the four preceding chapters has given us a framework within which to estimate (1) a developing country's total net foreign capital requirement over a future period, (2) the maximum amount of service payments the country can afford during the period or any individual year in it, and (3) from (1) and (2) the maximum (i.e., most severe possible) weighted average terms on gross new foreign capital inflow. However, this framework alone does not provide us with the means to assign definite shares in the capital flow to specific techniques of capital transfer--viz., private investment, hard loans, soft loans, and grants--on precisely defined terms. The reason for this is that an infinite variety of mixes of different techniques on varying terms is compatible with any weighted average service burden computed from our models.

To design an optimum mix of techniques and terms for a given country, we first require two further types of information. To begin with, we must know which capital sources are willing to invest in the country, the terms they will apply to their investment (assuming the terms to be institutionally or otherwise predetermined), and the maximum amounts they would be willing to invest assuming an indefinite number of attractive end-uses could be found for their investment. Second, we must have data on the composition of the country's development program and other potentially eligible expenditures so that we can draw a picture of the mix of investment opportunities the foreign capital sources face. Given this information, one thing more is required in order to design an optimum aid program: some criteria for allocating the different projects and other end-uses among various techniques of capital transfer.

To be sure, from an economic point of view, there is merit in Robert E. Asher's argument:

So long as total project and nonproject aid for a
country add up to the requirements of its economy
as a whole, it will not matter greatly which projects

are financed by hard loans, which by soft loans, and
which by grants from abroad. The decision can be
based on convenience--on the commodities the aid-
giver can most readily supply, on the skills of the
people it can make available for participation in the
program, and (politically significant) on the character
of the undertakings with which it wishes to identify
itself.[1]

There is no doubt that much of the allocation of end-uses among
different transfer techniques is made on a basis of convenience;
even some of the theoretical arguments used to support certain
allocation procedures have the mark of rationalizations of en-
trenched institutional practices or rules of thumb established
merely for the sake of giving bureaucrats explicit guidelines to
follow. However, such criteria are nonetheless effective in governing the policies and actions of many aid sources, and any country
that wants to maximize its receipts of foreign resources, as well
as any aid source that accepts a general responsibility to help less-
developed countries reach certain growth targets, must take these
criteria into account in matching aggregate resource flows with
end-uses.

DEFERRING TO PRIVATE FOREIGN INVESTMENT

The first and most sacred principle of allocation is that private foreign investors have first pick of all specific investment
projects, as long as the host government is willing to accept them.
(And, even if it is not, public capital sources often refuse to move
in where private capital is known to be willing to do the job.)
Nearly all free-world public capital sources see their role as
stand-ins for private investors deterred by political risks and/or
relatively unpromising short-run profit opportunities from investing at a sufficient rate to meet the entire "resource gap" of the
underdeveloped world. Most sources are required by their con-
stitutions or enabling legislation to promote and assist private
foreign investment and to defer to private capital whenever it is
available. Thus, the second of the World Bank's five purposes is:

To promote private foreign investment by means of
guarantees or participations in loans and other
investments made by private investors; and when
private capital is not available on reasonable terms,
to supplement private investment by providing, on
suitable conditions, finance for productive purposes
out of its own capital, funds raised by it and its other
resources.[2]

The International Development Association's Articles of Agreement
state: "The Association shall not provide financing if in its opinion
such financing is available from private sources on terms which are
reasonable for the recipient or could be provided by a loan of the
type made by the Bank."[3] According to the Export-Import Bank,
"Its statutory authority requires the Bank to complement and
supplement private capital, not to compete with it. Accordingly, the
Bank does not lend where funds are readily available from private
sources."[4] Finally, AID's enabling legislation lists as the first of
six factors to be taken into account in making development loans
"whether financing could be obtained in whole or in part from other
free-world sources on reasonable terms."[5]

It will be noted that all these expressions of policy contain a
hedge, to the effect that alternative capital transfers must be
"readily available" or "on reasonable terms." In Chapter 11, we
will discuss the significance and extent of use of this hedge. For
the present, it is sufficient to note that it is used most often in
cases where the alternative transfer consists of private loan capital at higher interest rates and shorter maturities than public
sources are willing to provide. Where private equity capital is
willing to move into a country and the host government cannot provide strong reasons for rejecting it, free-world public capital
sources rarely agree to provide substitute capital in loan form.
This is not to say that good reasons for rejection are never forthcoming. A potential foreign investor may require such a high degree of protection for his operation, via high tariffs or exchange
controls against competing imports, that the host country is able to
convince foreign public investors that the private operation would
unreasonably disrupt free trade and be uneconomic for the country
to boot. I am not familiar with instances of this, but my experience
in Africa with some foreign investors' requests for government
concessions indicates that it is not unlikely.

Public lending institutions may also provide capital for certain economic sectors from which foreign governments exclude
private equity capital as a matter of policy, even though foreign
private capital may have applied for entry or is known to be willing to invest. This would probably be true of public utilities such
as power, water supply, and telecommunications, which are
traditionally reserved for public control in most countries outside the United States. Several underdeveloped countries have
excluded foreign private capital from participation in some or all
aspects of their petroleum industries, and most free-world public
capital sources have refused to substitute for the private money
that is willing, even eager, to develop any reasonably economic
situation in petroleum. But, in March, 1961, the Export-Import
Bank announced publicly that it would henceforth finance exports
of U.S. petroleum equipment to publicly owned oil companies. The
administration told Congress that the long-standing policy was being

abandoned because it "has materially held back the growth of certain nations whose advance is of critical importance to the U.S."[6] According to The New York Times, an additional reason for the change in policy was the "economic ground of assisting exports of U.S. oil equipment."[7] The implication of the change was that, if an underdeveloped country held out long enough on strongly felt grounds, whether ideological, political, and/or economic, against private development of a sector, the United States might eventually relent and furnish public capital for it.

Table 24 shows the distribution of U.S. direct private investment in the underdeveloped areas, by regions and industries, as of the end of 1966. We note that less than 5 per cent of this investment was in public utilities, with over 80 per cent of the investment in public utilities being in Latin America. Thus, the bulk of U.S. private capital in the underdeveloped areas is invested in what Professor Albert O. Hirschmann calls "directly productive activities" as opposed to "social overhead capital."[8] The trend of new U.S. private investment is also in this direction, the proportion in public utilities having fallen from 17.5 per cent in 1950.[9] The relative shift of private capital out of social overhead-type activities has occurred in response to factors on both the demand and the supply sides. On the demand side, apart from several instances of outright expropriation, there has been increasing opposition in many countries to foreign ownership of industries so basic to the national welfare and vulnerable to sabotage as electric power and telecommunications. On the supply side, public utility companies have reason to expect that such opposition will grow in the future, with an increasingly nationalistic atmosphere taking hold in countries where the companies have hitherto had a relatively free hand. Moreover, the policy in many less-developed countries is to apply stricter controls to those industries where government regulation is logically called for, and the tendency in some to treat charges for public utility services as a political football have cast a pall on the future profitability of public utility investment by foreign private interests.

With private capital concentrating by choice and necessity on directly productive activities, two broad areas are wide open for public loans and grants. These are (1) the public utilities and (2) areas that are traditionally government responsibilities, such as roads and waterways, irrigation and flood control, health, education, research, and training in its many forms, including agricultural extension. In addition, there are many types of directly productive activities in which private foreign capital would be very unlikely to develop interest. Agriculture contains a number of such activities; private capital can be obtained for plantations raising certain cash crops demanded on world markets, but it would be hard to interest it in any scheme to develop small farm enterprises scattered over a wide area.

TABLE 24

Distribution of U.S. Private Equity in Underdeveloped Areas, End of 1966, by Regions and Industries

	Latin American Republics		Other Western Hemisphere		Africa excluding South Africa		Middle East		Far East excluding Japan		Total, five regions	
	$millions	%	$millions	%	$millions	%	$millions	%	$millions	%	$millions	%
Petroleum	2,959	30.0	579	35.8	968	65.5	1,560	93.4	600[a]	41.0[a]	6,666[a]	(41.4)[b]
Mining & smelting	1,117	11.3	364	22.5	296	20.0	3	0.2	37	2.5	1,817	(11.3)
Manufacturing	3,077	31.2	235	14.5	60	4.1	51	3.1	410	28.0	3,833	(23.8)
Public Utilities	626	6.4	48	3.0	1	0.1	4	0.2	71	4.9	750	(4.7)
Trade	1,158	11.8	87	5.4	60	4.1	16	1.0	196	13.4	1,517[a]	(9.4)
Other	917	9.3	306	18.9	92	6.2	38	2.3	140[a]	9.6	1,500[a]	(9.3)
All non-petroleum	6,895	70.0	1,040	64.2	509	34.5	111	6.6	863[a]	59.0	9,418[a]	(58.6)
All industries	9,854	(61.3)[c]	1,619	(10.1)	1,477	(9.2)	1,671	(10.4)	1,463	(9.1)	16,085	100.0

Notes: [a] Figures obtained indirectly and partly through "guesstimating" due to source report's failure to provide specific values for Japan or South Africa, as well to totals based partly on such figures.

[b] Percentages in parentheses in last column represent shares of indicated industries in total value for all industries (and regions).

[c] Percentages in parentheses in bottom row represent shares of indicated regions in total value for all industries (and regions).

Source: All dollar amounts obtained from U.S. Department of Commerce, Survey of Current Business, September, 1967, Table 3, p. 42.

233

It is in industry, other than public utilities and excluding agriculture, that private foreign capital is ready to make its greatest contribution and the most serious possibilities exist for competition between public and private capital. Yet, even in this area, there are sectors in which private foreign capital is not "readily" available. For example, U.S. iron and steel companies generally shy away from foreign ventures. When U.S. Government agencies are considering loan applications for iron and steel facilities in less-developed countries, American steel industry representatives often lobby against these on the ground that it is inappropriate for the United States to finance the creation of additional steel capacity abroad when steel mills at home are working below capacity. Consortia of U.S. firms promoting iron and steel mills in underdeveloped countries usually consist of no more than would-be suppliers and engineering contractors, sometimes accompanied by financial institutions willing to consider a small medium-term loan investment. The total amount of equity and loan capital assembled by these interests rarely amounts to more than a small fraction of the total cost. (It is quite possible that this situation reflects the doubtful economics of iron and steel mills desired on prestige grounds by small countries with indifferent raw materials. The question raised here is not whether public capital should support a project for which private funds could conceivably be obtained, but rather whether anyone at all should support the project.)

Apart from particular industries in which domestic interests are reluctant to commit themselves abroad, there are a number of other situations where public capital sources consider it appropriate to lend for industrial development. Thus:

(1) Many loans are made for projects in which private foreign capital is participating and has taken the initiative in requesting public loan assistance to supplement its and other contributions.

(2) A favorite vehicle for public foreign aid to industry is the local development bank, preferably under private control, which on-lends foreign loans to local firms, many of which are too small and have insufficient needs for general finance or foreign exchange to negotiate directly with foreign lending institutions. Many of these firms see no need for foreign equity participation and/or because of their size and mode of operations would have great difficulty securing it if they tried. Through fiscal 1967, the World Bank had lent $551 million to development financial intermediaries, corresponding to 8 per cent of its total lending in less-developed countries.[10]

(3) In some countries, political and economic conditions are so precarious, not necessarily through any fault of the current government leaders that can be remedied by outside action, that private foreign investors are not interested in any significant degree of participation in the country's industrial development.

(4) As we saw above in the case of state-owned oil companies, the United States does not always rule out public aid to industries that are publicly owned as a matter of host government policy or to state-owned enterprises in industries where the government permits privately owned firms to coexist. The administration has noted:

> We know that a government which avowedly aims to centralize all initiative and the ownership of all major productive activities can become prey to approaches inconsistent with free and open societies. However, this does not mean that the U.S. must or should discourage all governmental production in countries receiving our assistance, even in fields where in our own country it is agreed that private initiative works well. The question which must be asked is whether, across the whole range of conditions present in a given country, the measures taken are sensible from the viewpoint of economic growth and are consistent with, and an expression of, efforts to create a viable free political and social system. There is no "right" body of doctrine applicable to all countries.[11]

The World Bank has long shied away from assisting government-owned industrial enterprise, but, in 1966-67, it lent $30 million to a potash facility in the Congo (Brazzaville) that is jointly owned by the Congolese and French governments. In its recent annual report, the Bank noted: "This was the Bank's first loan to a government-owned manufacturing agency. The Bank is willing to consider financing ventures of this kind provided it is satisfied that they have experienced, efficient management."[12] The implication here is that the Bank's past hesitancy about such projects has been based not on ideological considerations but on the ground that governments of less-developed countries generally lack the capability to manage industrial projects efficiently and that proper management is the central contribution of foreign private investment.

(5) Loans are often made directly to larger-size local private firms that do not want foreign equity participation and/or could not get it if they did. (With export-financing institutions such as the Export-Import Bank, the firms do not have to be very large to obtain medium-term credits.)

CRITERIA FOR ALLOCATING HARD AND SOFT LOANS AND GRANTS

In Chapter 11, we return to the question of how far the availability of public foreign aid for industrial development results in a net displacement of private foreign capital in this area. Having gotten a general idea of the division of labor between private and public techniques of capital transfer to the underdeveloped areas, we now turn to the division of labor among the different mechanisms of public capital transfer, i.e., hard loans, soft loans, and grants.

If a developing country is in a relatively strong economic position, though still unable to meet all its requirements through imports of private capital, it may be creditworthy to receive the required additional capital entirely via hard loans. A corollary of Robert Asher's statement quoted at the beginning of this chapter is the contention that, so long as total hard loans for the country add up to the requirements of its economy as a whole and repayment of foreign loans is an obligation of the economy as a whole, it does not matter greatly which projects the hard loan sources pick up. As a general rule, lending agencies like to match their contributions with those projects that offer the best ostensible prospects for contributing to the borrower's economic growth, preferably by generating large revenue surpluses for reinvestment, and/or with those projects involving the greatest amount of eligible imports from the country providing the finance. But, if a developing country does not require any such distinctive schemes or imports or needs public capital in excess of the amounts that can be allocated to them, it will be necessary to find additional end-uses for the hard finance. These end-uses may involve projects with no revenue-earning capacity at all, such as are conventionally regarded as logical candidates for soft loans and grants in a country whose economy requires these.

Following this principle, the World Bank has lent out of its ordinary resources for education, a nonrevenue-producing sector. Four countries, the Philippines, Chile, Jamaica, and Thailand, have received Bank loans totaling $24.25 million for education, although IDA has handled the bulk of the Bank complex's activity in this field, with 12 loans totaling $113.6 million. The four countries have in common the fact that the Bank has adjudged them sufficiently creditworthy to provide nearly all its assistance to them out of its ordinary resources--of 46 Bank/IDA loans extended to the four by August 31, 1967, only one, to Chile, was from IDA.

The problem of allocation of end-uses among the three major vehicles of public foreign aid thus arises only in a country whose debt-servicing capacity dictates providing it with some soft loans and/or grants as well as hard loans. To a large extent, allocation between hard and soft loans is decided on the basis of considerations having no evident relationship to the contrast in repayment terms between the two techniques. This is, in fact, the general rule regarding transfers from different capital-exporting countries. National lending agencies frequently have idiosyncratic preferences with respect to the types of expenditures, even within the offshore cost category, they like to finance. For example, we saw in Chapter 8 that the U.K. Government's preference for financing exports of British goods rather than engineering services caused it to turn down requests in 1963 to finance Nigerian roads out of its (hard) Commonwealth Assistance Loans, while the United States and World Bank were actively negotiating road projects for which the U.S. finance was to be on soft terms and the World Bank aid on either soft or hard terms or both. (Eventually, three Bank/IDA loans for Nigerian roads were signed in 1965, with two loans totaling $32 million coming from the Bank and a third, of $15.5 million, from IDA.) If a developing country has a preference for one exporting source over another with respect to a particular type of equipment, whether for reasons of price, quality, or a desire to standardize on one line of equipment in order to minimize maintenance costs and delays, the country will similarly prefer to secure the necessary finance from that source, whether it is available on hard or soft terms (unless acceptance of hard finance meant that less soft loan aid would be forthcoming over-all). Another Nigerian illustration may be offered here: Whereas nearly all water supply equipment hitherto installed in Nigeria was of British manufacture, the Eastern Nigeria Government chose in 1963 to request the United Kingdom to cover three years of its equipment needs out of a hard loan even though it knew soft loan money would probably be available for the purchase of U.S. equipment if the British funds were allocated to other uses.

Many allocation decisions are made on the basis of more haphazard considerations, such as which lending agency got into the picture first and started negotiations over a particular project. While I was in Nigeria, yet another type of consideration, arising from the bargaining positions of different agencies with respect to their total aid levels, succeeded in overriding the factor of who was the first to enter into negotiations. The AID mission to Nigeria had been engaged for several months in negotiations with the Nigerian Government regarding a (soft) loan, similar to one made in 1961 by the Development Loan Fund, for the purchase of U.S. railway track to be used for re-laying a portion of the Nigerian railway system. As the stage of approval by Washington neared, the United Kingdom suddenly offered to finance a supply of British track for the project out of funds set aside to finance purchases from depressed British industries. The United Kingdom assured the Nigerians that this loan, to be made on the usual "hard" terms (with a 20-year maturity), would be a net addition to its aid commitment to Nigeria's 6-year Plan. The Nigerians decided that they stood to gain by the additional aid, although this was not entirely clear to me, inasmuch as the difficult process of finding acceptable projects to match with the $225 million U.S. aid commitment made it uncertain that U.S. funds released from the railway scheme would represent a net additional contribution to any other project. In any case, the British offer was accepted, and AID accepted the outcome with good grace, as it was obliged to do in view of its Congressional mandate to defer before other free-world financing on reasonable terms.

Lest we appear always to be casting the British in the role of hard lender in such comparisons, a reverse example is presented by the U.K.'s 1961 £5 million Exchequer grant for capital costs of constructing new educational institutions in Nigeria. The United Kingdom had agreed to allocate out of this grant sums ranging between $1.5 and $7 million for individual institutions, whereas AID was inaugurating a policy that any U.S. contribution to capital costs of a single educational institution in excess of $500,000 should be in the form of loans (on the then current 3/4 per cent, 40-year terms) rather than grants. Similarly, the World Bank had recently started discussions about a possible credit for Nigerian educational facilities on IDA terms. The decision to make the grant, which the Chancellor of the Exchequer is reported to have agreed to reluctantly under the forceful persuasion of the Nigerian Finance Minister, Chief Festus Okotie-Eboh, reflected the then British policy of staying clear of soft loans.

In cases in which there is close coordination among different agencies interested in aiding a particular developing country, it is logical to expect that systematic considerations determine the allocation of elements in a development plan among the different public transfer techniques. In the case of Nigeria, the World Bank had organized a "consultative group" or capital-exporting countries and international agencies; in addition, there was some bilateral coordination between national agencies in their respective capitals and among their representatives in Nigeria. But, despite such coordination, the allocation of projects among hard and soft lenders rarely seemed to follow any pattern related to the contrast in servicing terms. A pattern of allocation related to servicing terms is most likely to be found with a single organization or government operating both a hard and a soft loan program and willing to provide both kinds of finance to a single country. Here, possibilities for coordination among different transfer techniques are clearly at a maximum. Agencies that fit the foregoing description are the World Bank, with its IDA and IFC; the Inter-American Development Bank, with its Fund for Special Operations and Social Progress Trust Fund; and the U.S. Government, with its Export-Import Bank, AID, and P.L. 480. It is with these agencies that rules of thumb based on the contrasting service requirements of hard and soft loans have been developed for allocating these techniques of capital transfer to different end-uses. We will now proceed to discuss these rules of thumb in the light of information on the above agencies' practices.

CRITERIA FOR HARD OR SOFT LOAN DETERMINATION

(1) Profitable and not-so-profitable projects. The division of labor between hard and soft loans in an individual country is sometimes achieved by allocating hard loans for revenue-earning

activities that are able to pay their own way or for nonrevenue-
earning activities that are so closely related and essential to
profitable activity that they are clearly seen to pay their way indirectly (e.g., roads), whereas soft loans are made for projects
that are further removed from direct profitability, even though they
may (and should) contribute no less to economic growth. Projects
in the field of education and health clearly belong in this latter
category. The theory behind this division is that a successful
revenue-earning project will more easily be able to generate the
resources required for servicing the harder loan.

Economically speaking, if the debt is an obligation of the public purse and the foreign-exchange assets of the entire economy
may be tapped to finance the corresponding service flows, the earning status of the individual project receiving a hard loan is irrelevant
to the prospects for its repayment. However, strategic considerations of development lending may give indirect validity to the theory
behind this division of labor. The propaganda impact of making hard
loans for nonrevenue-earning projects is likely to be unfavorable,
possibly leading to internal political pressure for renegotiation of
the terms on the threat of default. Moreover, it could be argued that
receipt of a soft loan for a potentially profitable activity, even though
the enterprise in question was required to service it on hard terms
to the local government, would reduce the pressure on management,
especially of a government enterprise, to charge profitable rates
and run the enterprise with maximum efficiency. Although the requirement for hard service payments to the local government is
always part of the loan agreement, which specifies that failure to
live up to it is cause for the lender to cancel the loan and declare
it immediately refundable, it may be a moot point whether such
failure is willful or caused by economic factors outside the control
of both the enterprise's management and the local government.
In the latter case, the lender might be reluctant to proceed with
cancellation. And, in any case, the host government might not feel
that refusal to meet a refund demand would be tantamount to default,
as long as the government was continuing to make service payments
on the specified soft terms. The entire arrangement contains an
element of interference by the foreign lender in the internal affairs
of the borrowing country, i.e., the financial relations between the
host government and the local enterprise in question. (To get
around this problem, AID prefers to make a loan directly to the
benefiting enterprise, with the loan agreement specifying just one
set of terms vis-à-vis the enterprise, which has the option of repaying AID in dollars or the host government in local currency.
However, it is not clear that this arrangement fully vitiates the
foregoing considerations.)

Most of the soft loan agencies have made explicit in one way
or another their willingness to finance projects of a not directly
profitable social overhead type. The Report of the Executive Directors on the Articles of Agreement of IDA states:

The Association is authorized to finance any project
which is of high developmental priority, that is, which
will make an important contribution to the development of the area or areas concerned, whether or not
the project is revenue-producing or directly productive. Thus projects such as water supply, sanitation,
pilot housing and the like are eligible for financing,
although it is expected that a major part of the
Association's financing is likely to be for projects
of the type financed by the Bank.[13]

The extent to which this expectation has been borne out in
practice is indicated by Table 25, which compares the proportional
allocations to different sectors among all IDA loans and all World
Bank loans to less-developed countries (defined to include Cyprus,
Spain, and Yugoslavia as the only European representatives).

TABLE 25

Allocation by Sectors of World Bank and IDA
Loans to Less-developed Countries

Sector	Percentage of total loans authorized through June 30, 1967	
	World Bank	IDA
Electric power	37.6	6.4
Transportation	35.7	33.5
Telecommunications	1.8	4.4
Agriculture, forestry, & fishing	8.6	16.7
Industry	13.5	29.6
Water supply	0.7	2.6
Education	0.3	6.7
General Development	1.6	--

Source: Computed from data in International Bank for Reconstruction and Development, Annual Report, 1966-67 (Washington, D.C.,
1967), pp. 66-67, supplemented by country data relating to Japan,
South Africa, Cyprus, Spain, and Yugoslavia (for purposes of subtraction in the first two cases and addition in the latter three) in
IBRD, Statement of Loans--June 30, 1967 (Washington, D.C., 1967),
available from the World Bank. The latter source gives no individual
sectoral breakdown for $58 million worth of loans to Yugoslavia,
which are, therefore, excluded from both the numerators and the
denominator in the above computations.

It is noteworthy that the only sector in which IDA's proportional activity has been significantly less than the Bank's is electric power, which is perhaps the prime revenue-producing sector--certainly the one offering the best returns relative to risk--in economic development. On the other hand, industry, which the Bank defines to comprise principally mining and manufacturing, is also entirely a revenue-producing sector, and it has seen more than twice as much IDA activity, proportionally, as Bank lending. However, the bulk of this IDA activity represents the nonproject loans to India and Pakistan described in Chapter 8. As we have already seen, the object of these loans was solely to infuse large quantities of resources into the two economies as rapidly as possible with the least resulting debt burden, and the fact that the loans financed industrial rather than, say, agricultural imports was a matter of convenience reflecting the comparatively much larger import component of industrial output. If these loans are taken out of consideration, with a resulting increase of 25-30 per cent in the other proportions in the IDA column, there is some positive correlation between the relative Bank and IDA allocations and the direct revenue-producing qualities of the different sectors. Thus, power and industry now weigh more heavily in the Bank's activity, whereas education and agriculture-- which features a number of credit, irrigation, and land resettlement schemes that are not expected to be directly profitable--figure more prominently in the IDA list. On the other hand, the IDA leads in telecommunications activity, which is revenue-earning, and transport, where railways and harbors are directly revenue earning and roads are usually not (roads have received slightly over half of IDA's transport credits, railways slightly below half). So the picture is by no means consistent.

The Inter-American Development Bank has stated that "loans from [its] ordinary capital resources [i.e., on hard terms] should be either self-liquidating or supported by other resources" (the latter phrase presumably refers to projects such as roads that generate tax revenues out of which the loans can be serviced), whereas loans from the Fund for Special Operations may be made "for a highly productive project" in a country with balance-of-payments difficulties, or "for a project which only indirectly or gradually contributes to the productive capacity of the country."[14]

Under the agreement establishing the Social Progress Trust Fund, its loans have been restricted to projects in four specific areas: (1) agricultural credit, land use improvement, rural access roads, and other programs directly benefiting small farmers; (2) low-income housing; (3) drinking water and sewerage in small communities; and (4) "supplementary financing for advanced education and training." It is clear that, among the direct beneficiaries of the three different forms of IDB assistance, those eligible to receive SPTF funds have the least capacity to service the aid. The then U.S. Executive Director of the IDB, Gen. Robert Cutler, told the Passman Committee in 1961:

None of the kinds of projects contemplated for the
social progress trust fund are suitable for the Bank
to lend, either from its ordinary resources, or from
its fund for special operations, because the Bank is
primarily devoted to accelerating economic development in Latin America, whereas the true purpose
of the social progress trust fund is to make loans
for social development projects, projects which may
not bring in earnings for some time.[15]

Making a direct comparison among the three "windows" of the IDB,
Gen. Cutler noted typical situations in which each window might
make a loan for potable water supply and sewerage: (1) ordinary
resources--a large city with well-organized public utility companies that could service the loan out of user charges; (2) FSO--
a smaller community with a comparatively strong economic base;
and (3) SPTF--poor communities with infant mortality rates of
50 per cent due to water-borne diseases, e.g., in Northeast Brazil.

AID has made the following statement of its lending policy:

Development Loans are intended for high-priority capital projects which either directly produce revenue or
are important to the economic infrastructure of a
country. These include, for example, establishing or
expanding manufacturing facilities, development banks,
irrigation, power, multi-purpose water resource development, mining, ports, transportation and commu-
nication facilities, fisheries and grain storage facilities. Loan funds are also available for programs and
projects designed to promote social development, including schools, hospitals, housing, and similar capital projects, as well as for social programs in areas
such as adult education, public health, or community
development. . . . Loans may [also] be made to finance engineering and feasibility studies and other
project surveys.[16]

As shown in Chapter 4, AID loans are available both on hard and
soft terms; however, the majority of loans by AID and its predecessor, DLF, have been of the soft variety. The hard-lending
Export-Import Bank has first refusal on all loan applications submitted to AID, except in circumstances where higher authority
in the Department of State, to which both agencies report, decides that aid for a particular project must be on soft terms regardless of Eximbank's potential or expressed willingness to
handle it. Eximbank President Harold Linder told the Passman
Committee in 1961, "The understanding is [that] the Export-
Import Bank in effect has an option on those loans which we believe
can stand proper commercial terms."[17] He went on to note that a
loan for a school would obviously not fall into this category.

Among European capital sources, the West German Government is the only one that systematically relates terms on its development loans to the purpose of the loans. Table 26 gives the terms Germany applied to different categories of projects in 1965, according to DAC.

TABLE 26

Terms on German Development Loans for Different
Categories of End-Uses, 1965

Category of End-Use	Interest rate	Maturity (years)	Grace period (years)
Nonproject financing	3 3/4%	22	5 1/2
Social infrastructure	2 3/4	18-19	4
Economic infrastructure	3 1/4	20	5
Other economic projects	4 1/2	18	4

Source: Organization for Economic Cooperation and Development, The Flow of Financial Resources to Less-Developed Countries, 1961-65 (Paris, 1967), p. 80.

The concessionary effect implied by Germany's minimum terms, applied to social infrastructure projects, is rather limited-- assuming repayment on the level payment system, the comparison of annual service payments on a $1,000 loan, after expiration of the grace period, between the maximum and minimum terms, is $82:$71. A similar comparison between World Bank terms of 6 per cent at 25 years with a 5-year grace period and standard IDA terms is $87:$29, and the IDA grace period, when payments are only $7.50, last 5 years longer. The corresponding comparison of Export-Import Bank (assuming 5 1/2 per cent, 15-year maturity, 3-year grace period) and current AID (2 1/2 per cent, 40-year maturity, 10-year grace period, 1 per cent interest during grace period) terms is $116:$48, and the AID grace period, when payments are only $10, is 7 years longer.

(2) Foreign-exchange earning and other projects. In a small number of cases, the allocation of projects among hard and soft lenders has been decided on the basis of whether or not the projects would earn foreign exchange directly, with the foreign-exchange earners being assigned to hard loans and others to soft loans. Then Under Secretary of State Douglas Dillon told the Senate Foreign Relations Committee in 1959 that the division of

responsibility between the Inter-American Development Bank's regular resources and its Fund for Special Operations would be based partly on this consideration.[18] The principle here is essentially a variant of that under (1) above, with the allocation of finance being based on a project's capacity to generate directly the funds required to service a foreign loan.

(3) Infrastructure elements of profitable projects. Frequently a soft loan agency joins with a hard loan agency in financing a single project. The principle of allocation has generally been to allocate the most compact, "glamorous" element of a project to the hard-lending agency, and the soft loan agency picks up elements that are more dispersed and/or less easily identified as part of a specific project. The reason for this is nowhere stated explicitly, but it is likely that hard loan agencies feel themselves under greater pressure to run a hard-nosed, bank-like operation whose soundness can be easily demonstrated by pointing to photogenic structures erected with their aid. A case that appears to fit into this category is a program of electric power development under the Yanhee Electricity Authority in Thailand, where a World Bank loan was made in 1957 for a hydroelectric plant, an Eximbank loan authorized 14 months later for a thermal power plant, and a DLF local currency repayable loan agreed to 4 months after that for facilities to transmit the power from both plants to Bangkok.

(4) Offshore vs. local costs. In the days before the U.S. aid program came under severe pressure to protect the balance of payments by financing only U.S. exports, the division of responsibility between DLF and the World Bank or Eximbank in a project was often based on local costs versus offshore costs with DLF picking up the former. This pattern was put into effect with roads, water supply and sewerage projects, airports, the Indus River diversion and irrigation scheme, public housing and land settlement programs, etc. In 1960, the Senate Foreign Relations Committee called upon DLF to make greater use of its authority "to make loans to meet the local currency costs of projects the dollar costs of which are financed by [hard-loan agencies]."[19] The Committee noted that "the considerations which motivate the IBRD and Export-Import Bank in this connection do not apply to DLF, which has always been conceived as a supplementary source of capital. The covering of local currency costs is a proper exercise of this supplementary role." The consideration motivating Eximbank is, of course, the requirement that it finance only U.S. exports; the consideration usually cited by the World Bank is a desire to stimulate self-help efforts on the part of the benefiting country. However, this has always been no less a concern of the U.S. aid program. In theory, the United States agrees to finance local costs only when it is satisfied that its refusal to do so will not occasion a corresponding net increase in domestic resources available for development and that the transaction is necessary in order to ensure infusion of the required amount of U.S. resources into the economy. In case of more developed economies

(e.g., Italy and Japan), where the World Bank has allowed its funds to be used to finance local costs, the aim is the very similar one of ensuring the infusion of a given amount of Bank resources. There is no less need for this approach in the underdeveloped areas where the Bank lends; consequently, it would appear that the Bank has other reasons for preferring to leave the required local cost financing to agencies such as AID.

One such reason may be the Bank's reluctance to overwork the clause in its Articles of Agreement that permits it to finance local currency costs only "in exceptional circumstances when local currency costs required for the purposes of the loan cannot be raised by the borrower on reasonable terms" (Article IV, Sec. 3b). Another reason may simply be the fact that restricting one's financing by and large to the visible imported component of a project looks somewhat "cleaner" to outside observers in the international financial community and enables the Bank to maintain its reputation as the queen of development financing agencies.

In October, 1959, the Eisenhower Administration announced a new tied procurement policy for DLF. Under this policy, in all but exceptional circumstances, the financing of offshore costs by DLF was to be restricted to purchase of U.S. goods and services. However, DLF's ability to finance local costs was not affected by the policy, and it subsequently made a number of loans, both alone and in conjunction with hard loan agencies, where it was covering as much as 70–80 per cent of the local costs of projects. But, under pressure from the continuing gold loss, Congress put increasing emphasis on expenditure of aid funds in the United States, specifying in the Act for International Development passed in the first year of the Kennedy Administration that funds could be used for procurement outside the United States only upon Presidential determination that such procurement would not result in "adverse effects" on the U.S. economy or its balance of payments such as to "outweigh the economic or other advantages to the United States of less costly procurement outside the United States."[20]   President Kennedy promised in 1961 to ensure that 80 per cent of AID funds would be spent on U.S. goods and services.

Since that time, AID has followed an increasingly reticent policy with respect to financing local costs. The result has been that, according to AID's Summary Presentation to the Congress for fiscal 1968, AID's overseas expenditures less loan repayments fell from $934 million in fiscal 1961 to $238 million in fiscal 1966.[21] The same document projects this figure at only $107 million in fiscal 1968 adding:

> Today all but three elements in the AID program are
> rigidly tied to spending in the United States. These
> are the salaries paid AID employees and contractor
> personnel overseas, only part of which is spent there;

minimal overseas purchases for AID's administrative purposes; and contributions to the United
Nations and other international organizations, although in practice two-thirds thereof, about $100
million a year, is spent in this country.

The World Bank has never intended for IDA to assume a position analogous to that once occupied by DLF and AID with respect
to financing local costs. The Association's Articles of Agreement
permit it to finance local costs with foreign exchange "in special
cases," but Bank officials make no secret of the Bank's policy to
hold IDA local cost financing to a minimum. None of the descriptions
of IDA credits contained in its or the Bank's annual reports refer to
IDA's financing local costs, although many of them do not state
specifically that IDA is financing the foreign-exchange costs of a
project. In cases where an IDA credit has been extended simultaneously with a World Bank loan, the IDA finance has either been
associated with foreign-exchange costs or its purpose has not been
indicated separately. On the other hand, it is quite possible that in a
number of projects which are normally local-cost intensive--e.g.,
construction of secondary schools, irrigation programs, building
secondary roads--an IDA contribution of the indicated magnitude implies at the very least a liberal definition of foreign-exchange costs.

(5) Purchase of surplus agricultural commodities. Two programs under P.L. 480 (Title I, "sales" of commodities for inconvertible local currency; and Title IV, dollar-repayable loans at low
interest rates and long maturities), may be regarded as forms of
capital transfer where easy service terms are closely related to
the end-use of the capital--here, simply the purchase of U.S. agricultural commodities. As we saw in Chapter 4, the Title I program
was born out of pressures in the United States to find additional
markets for growing agricultural surpluses. Because the prospective customers could not pay hard (dollar) cash for the amounts the
United States was anxious to sell (and which the customers could
absorb on easier terms), Congress agreed to accept inconvertible
local currency as the next best thing, which would still give the
transaction the appearance of a sale. Two other factors in the
formulation and continued toleration of Title I by both the executive
and legislative branches, albeit ones that influenced fewer votes in
Congress, were (1) the fact that the program could and did become
a vehicle of substantial easy-term foreign aid not subject to sabotage
by the Passman Subcommittee of the House Appropriations Committee and (2) the charity angle, viz., the principle that the United
States could afford to accept less than full value for commodities
that would eventually find their way into stomachs of undernourished
people in the underdeveloped areas. (This aspect was more explicit
in Title III, one of the outright grant sections of the program.)
Title IV was enacted after several years of mounting frustration
in attempting to deal with local currency accumulations.

However, the soft terms under Title IV, while implying a substantially smaller outright grant element, were designed no less than the local currency repayment provision of Title I to promote foreign consumption of U.S. agricultural surpluses.

It would, of course, be conceivable to finance underdeveloped countries' purchases of U.S. agricultural commodities by means of hard loans, presumably from the Export-Import Bank. (Eximbank regularly finances sales of U.S. cotton to several countries, with Japan usually the largest customer, but this is strictly short-term finance on terms of no more than one year.) However, even if the customers were interested in U.S. commodities on this basis, Eximbank would not want to engage in transactions involving no ostensible connection between the end-uses of its money and the creation of productive capacity out of which the loans could be serviced. Direct long-term financing of consumption is never regarded as compatible with the image of a bank.

GRANTS VERSUS LOANS

Having looked at some considerations extraneous to a less-developed country's debt service capacity that determine the allocation of various end-uses among the general categories of hard and soft loans, we now want to see what analogous considerations figure in allocating end-uses among grants as opposed to repayable capital transfers.

(1) Charitable activities. Among the activities generally financed via outright grants are those traditionally regarded as proper objects for charity. Included here are various aspects of medicine and public health, disaster relief, nourishment of the indigent, and remedial education and training. U.S. contributions in this area are made through foundations, Title III of P.L. 480, part of the AID technical assistance program, the President's contingency fund, special appropriations by Congress, U.N. specialized agencies, religions missions and churches, and other voluntary agencies. These programs are relevant here insofar as they contribute to economic development, which they do in two ways--by direct improvement of productive human resources and by release for productive purposes of domestic resources that would otherwise be devoted to carrying on some of the charitable activities, though, in most cases, at a reduced rate.

(2) Technical assistance. Grants are regarded as the appropriate means of financing most activities grouped under the heading of "technical assistance." Such assistance is primarily designed to develop local human resources for specialized service in government and other public functions, notably local institutions such as

schools, which are themselves concerned with human resource development, or for the exercise of specialized functions in the economy at large. As a rule, unrequited technical assistance normally comprises the services of foreign personnel with skills and experience in a particular field which they seek to impart to local counterparts and/or which they apply in carrying out operating responsibilities for which the underdeveloped country does not yet have enough trained manpower of its own. A "purist" school of thought in the field says that technical assistance is not realizing its full potential unless the "counterparts" are prepared within a few years to take over for the foreign experts, who then become superfluous. Another school of thought says that programs wherein foreign experts perform specialized operating functions in a governmental or private nonprofit institution, even where local personnel cannot yet be spared from other operating responsibilities to function as counterparts to the foreigners, are also a valid and useful form of technical assistance. In any case, most technical assistance programs involve an element of both demonstration and operating responsibilities, with sometimes one, sometimes the other, being predominant.

As in the case of loan projects, the host country is normally expected to finance part of the costs of technical assistance programs. In the first place, covering those aspects of the operating expenses of an activity which would arise even in the absence of foreign technicians is normally a responsibility of the host government or institution. (It is often difficult to draw the dividing line between those expenses which are part of the project being aided by technical assistance and those which are not.) Moreover, the host organization is usually required to provide or finance any or all of the housing, office space and supplies, clerical help, and local transport required by foreign technicians. The contributing foreign agency, on the other hand, normally finances at least the salaries, overseas allowances and international transport costs of foreign personnel. In addition, some aid sources, of which the successive U.S. technical assistance agencies have always been a prime example, finance the cost of specialized equipment needed by the foreign experts to carry out their responsibilities efficiently and in the use of which local personnel are to be trained. Regarding this aspect of technical assistance, the "purists" say that only equipment peculiar to a given profession and which serves a demonstration function vis-à-vis local practitioners of the profession should be supplied under technical assistance, whereas the more flexible school says that other items may also be supplied if they will enable the foreign expert to perform more efficiently. For example, if the foreign aid agency does not furnish its expert with a suitable vehicle for official transportation, the host institution may not be able to afford one out of its own resources, with the result that the expert will be forced to rely on less efficient means of local transport. If the foreign agency does finance the vehicle, it is in a sense making a capital grant in recognition of the recipient's lack of means to purchase the vehicle or service a loan for it; however, where it is subsumed in a technical assistance project, the transaction is not regarded as of a capital nature.

There are several justifications for the fact that technical assistance is usually conducted on a grant basis, apart from the debt-servicing capacity of benefiting countries. The first is akin to the charity consideration mentioned under (1) above. The argument here is that the skills of citizens are a human resource which developed countries should be proud to share in a limited amount on an unrequited basis with countries that have not yet had a chance to develop their own human resources. This is especially true where the required skills are to be applied in the very task of developing such resources, as in the educational and training institutions and programs where the bulk of technical assistance is provided. A further justification for grants here is that most of the activities that receive technical assistance are nonrevenue-earning and have to scrape along on subventions from public and voluntary bodies that are inadequate to enable them to service more than a fraction of the local citizens who are in need of and eager to receive the training provided by such activities. Any loans made for technical assistance purposes would probably have to be serviced by the host governments; but many governments are reluctant to mortgage their credit for the sake of expenditures that do not result in visible structures. Thus, the effective alternative to financing technical assistance via grants would probably be to ask the recipient to pay for it in cash, which would mean a corresponding reduction in resources available for aspects of the same program or for other human investment activities.

Another key reason for the grant aspect of technical assistance, although not often publicly acknowledged, is the fact that the recipients could not or would not pay the cost of the most important element in such assistance, namely, expenses of foreign personnel, if it had to be financed in any other way, whether from domestic or foreign resources. This is because the salaries, allowances, and fringe benefits that the United States, the United Nations, and, to a lesser extent, Western European governments have found they must pay their foreign aid personnel in order to attract reasonably qualified individuals are so far out of line with the salary structure in any less-developed country that a local government or public institution would be extremely reluctant to pay them. To do so might create a serious morale problem among local citizen employees; moreover, local government leaders might qeustion whether the foreign personnel were worth such high costs.

AID has found that it has to budget an average of $25,000 of personnel costs per man-year of services by a direct-hire technician. This figure includes the base salary, which ranges between $8,000 and nearly $20,000; overseas differential allowance equal to 15-20 per cent of base salary, depending on locus of assignment;

post (i.e., cost of living) allowance, based on number of dependents; "R & R" (rest and recuperation) leave benefits once during a tour for personnel operating in supposedly uncomfortable climates; round-trip transportation of employee and family once per tour between the United States and the foreign post; 100 lbs. of air freight per family member, plus surface freight for household effects and automobile on initial assignment and on transfer; storage of household effects left in the United States; education allowances for dependents, with over $1,000 allowance per high school or college student in Europe or the United States and one round trip per year between place of study and foreign post; and insurance and retirement benefits. The base salary for most United Nations technical assistance personnel is in the neighborhood of $12,000; on top of this come many of the same additional costs and allowances as with AID. As against these figures, the upper limit on salary for a top civil servant in those African countries I am familiar with is $8-9,000; in addition, he would receive free housing and some lesser fringe benefits.

These comparisons do not mean that foreign experts are rarely worth the money spent on them. It has been my observation in two African countries that the large majority of foreign personnel supplied under technical assistance there were filling significant gaps in the local manpower picture and that their marginal contributions to the local economy were generally in excess of their costs.* Even so, I am sure that most citizens of the benefiting countries would not agree with this if they knew the true sums involved. However, under the normal technical assistance scheme, the foreign aid source pays virtually all emoluments and allowances directly to the technicians, so that the relevant amounts do not enter into any local budget documents, and most local personnel, although aware that the foreign "experts" earn considerably more and enjoy a higher standard of living than locals with nominally higher rank and authority, ** are not aware of the actual amounts involved. Aid agencies are perfectly willing to release this information to authorized quarters in the host government, but, in most countries, only a few officials in the ministry responsible for coordinating foreign technical assistance activities, often the ministry for economic development or planning, even ask for the detailed figures.

---

*If the value of a 175-lb. man's contribution just equals his annual cost of $25,000, then over two 2-year tours he will be worth slightly more than his weight in gold!

**The standard of living of foreign experts, although sometimes offering enough of a discrepancy vis-à-vis local standards to give rise to invidious comparisons, in most cases does not reflect their full earnings. My impression is that most AID employees in the field save a higher proportion of their emoluments than they would in the United States, partly because there is usually less available locally to spend it on.

Only a slightly larger number of officials are ordinarily aware of the total costs, to the donors, of individual technical assistance projects or groups of them.

(3) Combined technical and capital assistance for human resource development. The United States has sometimes considered grants a suitable vehicle for financing more than just the technical assistance costs, as defined above, of human resource development projects where U.S. technical assistance is being provided. This type of financing has been carried out for a number of years in Asian countries where, in fulfillment of strategic commitments, the United States has invested large amounts of defense support and other types of grant aid. Of more interest to us from an economic point of view, however, is the International Cooperation Administration's (ICA) Special Program for Tropical Africa inaugurated in 1960 with a special $20 million appropriation, wherein technical assistance was combined with grants of up to $1 million for construction of a few educational institutions to which ICA also planned to supply personnel and demonstration equipment. The concept of the Special Program was taken over into the new category of "development grants" proposed by President Kennedy's Foreign Assistance Task Force and enacted into law by the Foreign Assistance Act of 1961. The primary justification for making capital items eligible for grants as opposed to loans was the weak financial condition of the intended recipients, notably the newly independent nations of Africa (as well as some not so newly independent, such as Ethiopia and Liberia). However, a secondary consideration, that institutions for the development of human resources are more deserving of grant aid than other types of projects, on grounds mentioned under (1) and (2) above, also figured in the minds of administration officials and, perhaps by implication, in the following quotation from the Foreign Assistance Act under Title II, "Development Grants and Technical Cooperation":

> In countries and areas which are in the earlier
> stages of economic development, programs of de-
> velopment of education and human resources
> through such means as technical cooperation shall
> be emphasized, and the furnishing of capital facili-
> ties for purposes other than the development of
> education and human resources shall be given a
> lower priority until the requisite knowledge and
> skills have been developed.[22]

Another secondary consideration was that the administration wanted to contribute to the capital costs of several projects in amounts smaller than any loan DLF had made or was interested in making, due to the expenditure of administrative resources involved. It was felt that the United States could exercise considerable leverage, both politically and in terms of providing the necessary margin of resources to launch a project, by making contributions below $500,000, the informal minimum set by DLF

and eventually taken over by the development lending arm of AID.*
This was partly because the eligible countries were so poor financially and with respect to such human resources as secondary school
graduates qualified to proceed to higher training that they had to
begin with relatively small institutions. Moreover, the United
States had a large number of new countries over which to spread
a small quantity of aid resources. Administratively, it was a
much simpler and less time-consuming process to have the field
mission include small capital items in their annual grant program
submissions to Washington, have these approved at the regional
bureau level, and then let the mission director negotiate the
requisite project agreement, subject to certain guidelines from
Washington, than it was to steer a loan proposal through various
stages of the approval process and then negotiate a loan agreement,
with Washington calling the tune at every step.[23]

(4) Pre-investment/feasibility surveys. Another category
comprises grants for engineering and planning studies, often called
feasibility surveys, designed to lay the groundwork for capital
projects. The engineering component of such a study normally
stops short of preparation of working drawings, final specifications,
and other contract documents, but furnishes preliminary plans and
cost estimates which, together with data obtained from demand
analyses and projections, form a basis for tentative conclusions on
the viability of a proposed project and a decision as to whether to
proceed with it. For large-scale projects, such feasibility surveys
may cost upwards of a million dollars. For a country in a comparatively strong financial position, financing a feasibility survey
out of domestic resources presents no more difficulty than financing
anything else without foreign aid. Thus, as with the other categories,
the primary criterion for grants for feasibility surveys is the benefiting country's total resource position and its debt-servicing
capacity. Moreover, foreign financing of feasibility surveys is not
handled exclusively via grants. The World Bank, IDA, the Inter-
American Development Bank, and AID have all made loans for such
surveys.

The institution that has done the most financing in this area
is the United Nations Special Fund, recently merged with the U.N.
Technical Assistance Board into the United Nations Development
Program. From the Fund's inauguration in 1959 until the end of
1966, it had authorized financing in the amount of over $150 million
for nearly 200 "pre-investment" surveys and feasibility studies,

_____
*However, in response to increased pressures on it to pro-
mote private enterprise in less developed countries the Agency's
Washington headquarters told the mission to Nigeria in 1963 to
state a minimum of approximately $300,000 in literature prepared
for Nigerian businessmen.

77 of which had been completed and 31 of which, according to the
United Nations, had stimulated sizable follow-up investment.[24] For
each project, a specialized agency associated with the United Nations
is chosen as executing agent, meaning that it administers the survey
and recruits the personnel for it or else contracts with a private firm
to do the work. In several projects, the World Bank has been the
executing agency. Some of the Fund-supported surveys, particularly
those executed by the Bank, are wholly concerned with individual
capital projects (e.g., the Niger Dam project in Nigeria) for which
overseas finance has been requested. In most of these cases, the
survey report has served or is intended to serve as a basis for obtaining financial commitments from foreign aid sources. In other
cases, such as nation-wide surveys of a country's natural resources
or one segment of them, or surveys of a particular geographical
region or economic sector to determine its development potenti-
alities, the project is designed to uncover preliminary leads on
specific activities that might lead to fundable projects.

Drawing on its accumulated earnings, the World Bank has engaged in some direct grant financing of what it calls "project and
sector studies." Through fiscal 1967, it had allocated about $13
million to such studies, although the rate of spending from the
Bank's own resources diminished after fiscal 1966 as a result of
an agreement with the U.N. Development Program making that
agency's funds more readily available to finance studies of projects
in which the Bank complex is interested. The Bank's present policy is to finance itself the foreign-exchange costs of only those
studies that require external financing of no more than $200,000.[25]

There is a definite rationale for grant financing in this area,
apart from the primary criterion mentioned above. All agencies
in the development financing field have repeatedly had to contend
with the eagerness of political leaders and private promoters in the
underdeveloped areas to rush ahead with large capital projects before sufficient data-gathering and planning work has been done to
warrant reliable conclusions on the over-all costs and benefits of
such projects. Aid sources regularly advise applicants for capital
assistance to invest more time and money in the engineering and
economic planning groundwork of a project. Even after they have
been advised to call in competent engineering and other consultants
for a thorough study of a project, applicants frequently try to scrape
by in a hurry by using their own staff or hiring a few individuals
to do this work. Their reluctance is based partly on the added time
it takes to bring in outsiders for a thorough survey and partly on the
apparent high cost of a contract with a reputable engineering firm,
especially a foreign one (where local consultants lack the competence to do the job). The result of a half-baked survey is usually
further delays and frustrations, on the part of both the applicants
and the aid sources, which are normally anxious to move rapidly
once they have adequate data to document a project's feasibility
and the desirability of their financing it. On the other hand, if a

capital source can dangle the carrot of grant financing of part or all of a proper feasibility study before the applicant, the latter will more readily agree to the study. In the process of its execution, the applicant is almost certain to learn of facts, such as inter-relationships between the proposed project and other economic sectors, that point to optimal decisions different from preliminary decisions that had already or would have been made in the absence of such information. Thus, by providing grant financing for a feasibility survey, an aid source may be able to further the applicant's education in the advantages of careful economic analysis and planning.

If an aid source wants to change some aspects of the execution of a project or its operation when completed as proposed by the applicant, helping to finance a feasibility survey gives it further leverage to do so. Particularly when, as is usually the case, the desired changes point toward making a project more economic, foreign engineering and economic consultants retained jointly by the aid source and the applicant (this being the normal procedure) are likely (or can easily be persuaded) to recommend these very changes in their report. The aid source can then say that its statutes, by-laws, or what-not allow it to proceed with financing only if the project is executed in an economic manner as recommended by the consultants. This strategic consideration is likely to be most important for national aid sources sensitive to charges of interfering in the internal affairs of an underdeveloped country, although even the staff of an organization such as the World Bank finds itself in bargaining situations with would-be borrowers where it welcomes the supporting opinion of a "neutral" third party. I have personal knowledge of a project in which an underdeveloped country applied to a national lending agency for a loan to build a road and connecting bridge. The applicant wanted to place the bridge at the site of a village whose inhabitants had been promised it by a government minister. However, the lending agency opposed this on the strictly technical and economic grounds that the proposed site marked the widest and flattest spot in the river for miles around. When foreign engineering consultants, hired for a feasibility survey financed by the aid source, reported that a bridge sited 6 miles upstream at a narrower place in the river with higher elevations on both sides would cost nearly $1/2 million less, the aid source told the host government that it (the aid source) could not finance any bridge at the first site. The government then agreed to the second site with no public complaint.

NOTES TO CHAPTER 10

1. Robert E. Asher, Grants, Loans, and Local Currencies: Their Role in Foreign Aid (Washington, D.C.: Brookings Institution, 1961), p. 134.

2. International Bank for Reconstruction and Development, Articles of Agreement (Washington, D.C., April, 1960; reprint), Article 1, p. 1.

3. International Development Association, Articles of Agreement and Accompanying Report of the Executive Directors (Washington, D.C., January 26, 1960), Article V, Sec. 1(c), p. 10.

4. U.S. Export-Import Bank of Washington, Report to the Congress for the Twelve Months Ending June 30, 1960, p. xii.

5. The Act for International Development of 1961 (P.L. 87-195, 87th Cong., 1st Sess.).

6. U.S. Senate, Committee on Foreign Relations, Hearings on the Act for International Development of 1961 (87th Cong., 1st Sess., June 6, 1961), Part I, p. 248.

7. Tad Szulc, New York Times, May 12, 1961.

8. Albert O. Hirschman, The Strategy of Economic Development (New Haven, Conn.: Yale University Press, 1958).

9. U.S. Department of Commerce, U.S. Business Investments in Foreign Countries (Washington, D.C.: Government Printing Office, 1960), p. 91. The category of "other" industries includes little if any social overhead-type investment, since agriculture and finance and insurance comprise between 80 and 90 per cent of it. It should be noted that a significant share of investment in directly productive activities, especially petroleum and other extractive industries, involves the creation of social overhead-type facilities to serve the productive plant in the absence of an adequate existing network of such facilities.

10. International Bank for Reconstruction and Development, Annual Report, 1966-67 (Washington, D.C., 1967), p. 66. The definition of less-developed countries used in making this calculation encompassed only Cyprus, Spain, and Yugoslavia of the Bank's European borrowers.

11. U.S. Senate, Committee on Foreign Relations, loc. cit.

12. IBRD, Annual Report, 1966-67, p. 13.

13. IDA, op. cit., p. 7.

14. Inter-American Development Bank, First Annual Report (Washington, D.C., 1960), p. 13.

15.   U.S. House of Representatives, Subcommittee on Appropriations, Hearings on Foreign Operations Appropriations for 1962 (87th Cong., 1st Sess.), Part 2, p. 133.

16.   U.S. Agency for International Development, Program Coordination Staff, Principles of Foreign Economic Assistance (Washington, D.C., 1963), pp. 15–16.

17.   U.S. House of Representatives, Subcommittee on Appropriations, op. cit., p. 13.

18.   U.S. Senate, Committee on Foreign Relations, Hearings on an Act to Authorize Membership of the United States in the Inter-American Development Bank (86th Cong., 1st Sess.), 1959.

19.   U.S. Senate, Committee on Foreign Relations, Report on the Mutual Security Act of 1960 (86th Cong., 2nd Sess.), p. 11.

20.   The Act for International Development of 1961, p. 439.

21.   U.S. Agency for International Development, Proposed Foreign Aid Program, FY 1968: Summary Presentation to the Congress (Washington, D.C., 1967), p. 75.

22.   The Act for International Development of 1961, p. 428.

23.   However, the Foreign Assistance Act provides that "No agreement or grant which constitutes an obligation of the United States Government in excess of $100,000 . . . shall be made for assistance . . . if such agreement or grant requires substantive technical or financial planning, until engineering, financial, and other plans necessary to carry out such assistance, and a reasonably firm estimate of the cost to the United States Government of providing such assistance, have been completed." (Act for International Development, p. 442). Thus, most of the small capital grants to which the discussion in the text refers have required detailed engineering studies, sometimes performed by outside consultants.

24.   United Nations Development Programme, Pre-investment and Productivity (New York, 1967; Sales No. 67. IID.5), p. 8.

25.   IBRD, Annual Report, 1965–66 (Washington, D.C., 1966), p. 18.

CHAPTER **11** DISPLACEMENT OF HARD-
TERM BY EASY-TERM
TRANSFER TECHNIQUES

In this concluding chapter, we will try to shed some light on the general problem of competition among various techniques of capital transfer and specifically on the question of how far the provision or mere availability of techniques on other than the hardest terms results in displacing harder techniques from roles in which the latter are optimal.

When different forms of capital transfer are available for the same end-use and acceptance of one does not prejudice the future availability of others, in theory the recipient maximizes his future income by choosing that form which imposes the least servicing burden on him. Thus, when all four categories into which we have divided capital transfer for the convenience of this study are available for a given end-use, grants will be chosen in preference to soft loans, hard loans, and private investment; when all but grants are available, soft loans will be chosen in preference to hard loans and private investment; and, when only hard loans and private investment are available, the former will be chosen in preference to the latter. In practice, of course, all forms of capital transfer are not likely to be available for a specific end-use. This is shown by the discussion in Chapter 10 on secondary criteria for allocating different forms of capital transfer; it is also shown by evidence to be presented below on coordination of aid sources designed to reduce competition among transfer techniques.

Even if all forms of transfer were available for a given end-use, institutional factors associated with the different techniques, especially between various forms of public capital and private equity investment, would require that other considerations be taken into account in deciding which one to accept. Thus, an important difference between accepting public aid for an industrial project and inviting private investors in to do the job is that, in the first case, the government must provide the management for the project and take all risks connected with it, whereas, in the second case, the private investors relieve the government of all or part of this burden. Governments in many less-developed countries, vaguely committed to a "socialist pattern of society," are willing to accept a certain number of such burdens, but most recognize limits to their managerial resources and draw a line beyond which they will not attempt to socialize their economies.

INDIRECT VERSUS DIRECT COMPETITION
AMONG TRANSFER TECHNIQUES

At this point it is useful to recall what was said in Chapter 8 about the distinction between end-uses of foreign capital and the net economic impact of such capital. We noted there that the least common denominator of the impact of all forms of foreign capital is that, subject to certain qualifications, they add initially to the total quantity of real resources available to an economy. And because a large proportion of resources is mobile, acceptance of X amount of public foreign capital for one end-use may enable an equal amount of domestic resources to be transferred to a different end-use, for which private foreign equity capital would otherwise be required. Thus, even where different forms of capital transfer are not available for the same end-uses in the sense of specific projects, they may still be competitive, with the easier displacing the harder ones. This is the essence of the argument made by sophisticated analysts who oppose most forms of public foreign aid on the ground that such aid unavoidably interferes with movements of private capital that would otherwise be available to carry the brunt of the development effort and would be much more likely to help the underdeveloped countries achieve their growth targets than public capital inflows.[1]

Another school of thought takes the more limited position that public foreign capital offers serious competition to, and displaces, private foreign investment only when it is available directly for the same type of project, i.e., investment in local private enterprise. Criticism of public capital exporters on this ground has been made within the community of public financing institutions. Thus, Robert Garner, prime mover behind the International Finance Corporation and its president for seven years after the organization's birth in 1955, told the 1961 annual meeting of the IFC's Board of Governors in his retirement address:

> Despite the usual provisions in the laws and
> regulations of public institutions, that in fin-
> ancing purely private enterprises (without
> government guarantee) they are not to com-
> pete with private investment capital, the fact
> is that they do. By giving low cost credits to
> one business firm they deter other borrowers
> from seeking funds in the private capital mar-
> kets.[2]

At the preceding year's meeting, Garner expanded on the latter point thus:

> It seems obvious that public funds can supply
> the requirements of only a small part of the
> sound business enterprises in the developing
> countries. The lucky few can increase their

profits and thus have an advantage over the
many to whom public funds are not available.
Furthermore, and even more important, it
makes other businessmen reluctant to pay
the higher rates necessary to attract private investment capital. Many of them delay
projects in the hopes of eventually obtaining cheaper
government funds, thus retarding sound expansion
and obstructing the increased flow of private funds
into these countries. Cheap public credits may
well in the long run retard rather than advance
the pace of private economic development.[3]

With respect to competition among different forms of public
capital transfer, officials of soft loan agencies assert they are constantly on guard against situations in which their loans may be displacing hard finance. In 1963 AID's Washington headquarters sent a
message to all field missions stating that AID had heard reports of
specific situations in which underdeveloped countries turned down
"reasonable" credit offers from Western Europe and Japan in the
hope of financing the same items via AID 3/4 per cent-40-year
loans. The message indicated that these situations had generally
arisen without AID knowledge and suggested that would-be U.S.
suppliers might have been responsible for assuring the local
governments that AID soft loans would be available to finance the
purchase of U.S. goods and services.* The message went on to
stress that AID loans were not intended to be used for promoting
U.S. exports in competition with other free-world suppliers, such
promotion being the proper function of the Export-Import Bank.
It noted some exceptional situation in which AID finance might be
offered even though other credit offers were forthcoming but
emphasized the missions' basic responsibility to keep a weather eye
out for such alternative offers, inform host governments that AID
finance would normally not be available in such situations, and explain to them why it was in their own interest to help maximize the
availability of capital from different sources.

ARE COMPETITION AND DISPLACEMENT
EVER JUSTIFIABLE?

Before we look further into the facts of displacement among
the different techniques of capital transfer, it is appropriate to ask
whether all competition in any form or degree is to be regarded as
inconsistent with the fundamental goals of capital transfer to the

---

* I found in Nigeria that this was standard operating procedure on the part of U.S. firms. Nigeria was host to an unending
parade of U.S. salesmen trying to use the soft terms on AID loans
as talking points in their negotiations with the government, and
some of them spent considerable time trying to persuade the AID
mission to support their plea against AID's policy of deferring to
other credit sources.

underdeveloped areas. This, of course, raises the prior question as to what the fundamental goals are. The goals vary between different agencies of capital transfer--the private foreign investor is normally interested in maximizing his profits, whereas most national public lending agencies are motivated, on the one hand, by a concern to maximize their countries' exports, and, on the other hand, by the main objective of multilateral public aid sources, which is to promote world peace and order by enabling the less-developed countries to progress economically in a manner that maximizes the probability that they will safeguard their own independence vis-à-vis Sino-Soviet imperialism.

Professor Milton Friedman would argue that this latter purpose can be served only by allowing the private investor full scope to advance his own goal under competitive conditions and that public foreign aid is basically incompatible with either goal. I have already suggested, and will argue further below, that private foreign investment cannot possibly provide the full required amount of foreign capital resources on terms that will satisfy certain basic constraints. On the other hand, I accept the argument that, for a variety of reasons, including the human resource contribution that accompanies it, private foreign equity investment can give a greater impetus to economic growth than it is being permitted to do in many less-developed countries. Still, this is a subsidiary question of development strategy. As far as the fundamental goal of resource transfer is concerned, this study accepts as its basic premise the objective of multilateral aid agencies,viz., to help the underdeveloped countries achieve a politically acceptable rate of economic growth in a noncoercive environment.

In order to decide whether and how far displacement of one technique of capital transfer by another may be permissible, it is useful to give a simple algebraic formulation to the fundamental goal. We assume that the goal translates into a requirement for a given amount of net foreign capital inflow, denoted by C, over a certain period of time. C has two components, private investment (P) and public foreign aid (A). (The exercise could just as easily be carried out between two different components of public aid.)

Moreover, service payments on P and A are subject to constraints such as the four underlying our models in Chapters 5-9. We assume that the constraints work out to yield an amount, Q, which is the maximum permissible total of service payments on P and A in one or more given future years.

Each of P and A has minimum service rates attached to it. In the case of P, the minimum rate, which we will denote by r_1, is the rate of earnings on private capital, that the foreign investor will have to be guaranteed or given reason to believe he can attain, in order to induce him to make the investment. In the case of A, the minimum rate, which we will call r_2, is the most favorable average debt service rate including both amortization and interest available on capital that various public aid sources are willing to furnish the developing country. In much of this study, we have treated r_2 as a dependent variable to be solved for in the light of economic conditions in the borrowing country and the value attached to the ruling constraints. In practice, however, aid sources have set minimum terms on the various types of aid they are willing to provide. Because they also put ceilings on the amounts of such aid they are ready to transfer to any one country, it is possible to conceive of a set of minimum weighted average terms associated with each alternative level of total net aid which may be provided to a given country. We now have a system of two inequalities:

(1) $P + A \geq C$, and

(2) $r_1 P + r_2 A \leq Q$,

where C, r_1, r_2, and Q are predetermined. We want to find the maximum amount of private investment, independent of the complementary flow of public aid (which is to be found as a residual from the total net capital requirement after subtracting private investment), that is compatible with the foregoing inequalities.

Such a value of P is determined within the system if and only if r_2 is less than r_1, i.e., the rate of private earnings is greater than the weighted average ratio of annual debt service on public aid to the original value of the aid. Assuming that the rate of private earnings is no less than .10, for which we found evidence in Chapter 2 (for industries other than petroleum), a public loan at 6 per cent and 15 years or 5 per cent and 14 years (assuming level payment method and no grace period in either case) generates a higher annual debt service/loan value ratio than private investment earning 10 per cent. This is, of course, due to the amortization requirement attached to the public loans. But the weighted average debt service/aid value ratio applicable to the entire flow of public aid today is considerably lower. Assuming that the weighted average terms on all external debt incurred in 1965 by 40 countries covered in World Bank statistics apply to all less-developed countries--and, since the sample of 40 receives the bulk of the aid flow, this is a reasonable assumption--the weighted average debt service/loan value ratio, under the level payment system, on all loans extended in 1965 will be .041 during the average 5-year grace period and .095 thereafter. Since, according to DAC data, loan and grant or grant-like resources are now flowing to less-developed countries in virtually equal amounts, these ratios are effectively halved.

Having shown r_2 to be less than r_1, we now convert the inequalities to equalities (in order to find a maximum value for P), divide through by $-r_2$ in equality (2), add the two equalities together and obtain

$$P = \frac{C - \dfrac{Q}{r_2}}{1 - \dfrac{r_1}{r_2}}$$

Under the stated conditions, a level of private capital inflow in excess of the foregoing value for P means either that the constraint on service payments will be violated or that less public capital can be provided on the indicated average terms than is required to make up a total capital inflow of C.

The implication of this result for the normative problem of competition among techniques of capital transfer is that we may conceive of situations in which it is perfectly justifiable for public capital sources to compete with and undercut private sources in order to serve the fundamental goal of international capital transfer to developing countries. The question then is: How likely are such situations to arise in practice? This depends primarily on how relevant the constraints on foreign investment service obligations are to private foreign investment. In other words, we must consider whether there is an effective limit on Q, the capacity to service total foreign capital inflow, private investment included.

The independence constraint, or at least the variant of it that defines financial independence as that point where cumulative net resource transfer ceases rising more rapidly than the benefiting country's GNP, certainly applies to private foreign investment as far as the less-developed countries are concerned, and this is also accepted by most public aid sources, for reasons noted in Chapter 6. The governments of many less-developed countries doubtless hope that public aid sources will continue providing capital until a more stringent criterion of independence vis-à-vis private capital inflow is satisfied, namely, that the absolute value of the total private commitment stops growing. These countries want to limit their amount of foreign equity, private or public, and prefer to finance their development insofar as possible by means of debt capital (or best of all, outright grants). On the other hand, aid sources generally prefer to maximize the role of foreign private investment, for two reasons, apart from the desire to minimize the residual requirement for public capital. First, they believe that private capital brings along with it a combination of management, technical know-how, and incentives that greatly enhance a project's chances for success while exercising a healthy influence on other enterprises and sectors of the economy; and second, they feel that the cultivation of close ties between business interests in their own countries and the developing nations is likely to further the non-Communist world's political and commercial interests in the less-developed areas.

The basic factors underlying the debt service ratio constraint also apply to private investment, inasmuch as balance-of-payments crises are just as likely to jeopardize remittances of private earnings or repatriation of private capital as public debt service jeopardy, because the government of a less-developed country would sooner protect its balance of payments by creating obstacles for private remittances than by defaulting on obligations to foreign governments and multilateral institutions. Curbs on remittances of private earnings have been a frequent occurrence in Latin America; in Chapter 2, we noted the Brazilian decree of 1963 denying foreign exchange for remittances in excess of 10 per cent of the value of net investment of overseas capital, excluding reinvested earnings. To be sure, conventional measures of the debt service/export ratio exclude remittances on private investment, partly because a large share of such remittances are not fixed obligations in a strict sense and partly because of lack of data. But if remittances of private earnings stand in a "significant" proportion to a country's foreign-exchange receipts, especially where the enterprises concerned are not direct earners of foreign exchange, it is inevitable that they will attract accusations of "bleeding" the local economy and become the object of attempted controls, which will, in turn, have far-reaching repercussions throughout the economy of a type not conducive to growth.

The end-use and gross outflow constraints are probably as applicable, if not more so, to private as to public foreign investment. Private equity investment almost by definition follows a strict project approach, and private debt capital is rarely available to finance diffuse import requirements such as are covered by many public nonproject aid loans. In Chapters 2 and 9, we saw how quickly the inflow of earnings and dividends on private foreign investment builds up to exceed gross new capital outflow.

Despite the apparent relevance to private capital flows of our major constraints, it is difficult to imagine a private foreign investor taking the initiative in generating a directly productive enterprise in which he is willing to put an equity contribution that is substantial in relation to the total capital requirement only to have a public aid agency intervene and offer to provide easy-term capital to the less-developed country concerned as a substitute for the private investor's equity on the ground that payment of a 10-20 per cent return to the investor would violate certain constraints. Such intervention by a public agency would be more likely in a social overhead project budgeted in a less-developed country's development plan, where the only private finance available was in the form of high-interest, medium-term debt capital. The range between these two extremes of proffered private participation is a wide continuum, and many complex borderline situations can be envisaged. For example, on the side of equity investment, there is the problem of evaluating the proffered participation--if it seems small in relation to concessions the investor is demanding in order to secure a degree of protection against competitors that is uneconomic for the economy as a whole, public aid sources might be less reticent to move in. Another question concerns the specific industrial sector involved-- private equity capital has underwritten public utility investment in the past, although, as we saw in Chapter 10, its role in this field is vanishing in comparison to the input of public capital. The readiness of public aid sources to move into this area without avidly canvassing the field for possible foreign private participants in every power or telecommunications project contains an element of acknowledgment of political realities as well as application of our constraints.

On the other hand, it is mainly private debt investment in industry that Robert Garner accused public lending institutions, in the foregoing quote, of sometimes undercutting. It is likely that his accusation was directed partly at the Development Loan Fund, 32 per cent of whose lending through March 31, 1961, was in aid of industry.[4] In theory, public lending agencies are likely to be less careful to avoid competing with private debt investment than with private equity, because private loan investment makes less of a qualitative contribution to industrial development, involves less risk, and is more likely to run afoul of our constraints.*

PUBLIC AID AS A NET BOOSTER OF PRIVATE FOREIGN INVESTMENT

Although it is clear that there are situations in which public foreign aid competes with and displaces private foreign investment, it is not at all clear that public aid serves on net to reduce the flow of private capital to the underdeveloped areas as compared with the movement that would take place in the absence of public aid. There

---

*These considerations do not, of course excuse the practice, criticized by Garner, whereby public capital is placed in the hands of private end-users on terms below those prevailing on private money markets for similar transactions. To the extent this criticism is valid, public capital sources are failing to make adequate use of the two-step lending procedure, whereby the benefit of easy terms on public foreign aid accrues to the local government and the economy as a whole rather than to an individual private borrower.

are a number of ways in which all forms of public capital transfer, rather than displacing private foreign investment, actually facilitate it.

(1) Expanding the market. In a general way, public foreign aid gives its most powerful assist to private foreign investment by enabling underdeveloped countries to increase their real per capita income more rapidly than they could without such aid. The higher incomes mean more rapid growth of internal demand for goods and services that could be produced locally with the help of private foreign capital. Thus, foreign aid helps underdeveloped countries indirectly to surmount the barrier of inadequate demand which is so often a major deterrent to foreign private investment in facilities producing for local markets. Moreover, by financing the purchase of local inputs for aid projects and generating income in the economy's exchange sector, "local cost" expenditures out of aid funds give a short-run impetus to demand for products of local facilities in which private foreign capital may be involved.

(2) Provision of essential social overhead facilities. In order to function profitably, every productive enterprise depends on a variety of social overhead services on both the supply and demand sides, i.e., transportation, communications, power, water supply, health, education, and housing. For most enterprises, especially those of the relatively small size permitted by domestic (as opposed to export) market conditions in the majority of underdeveloped countries, it is not economical to install more than a small portion of the relevant social overhead facilities themselves; rather, they depend on outside agencies to do it. We have already seen why the creation of most of these facilities by private foreign investment is out of the question. Moreover, underdeveloped countries are as a rule unable to generate internally the necessary capital for as large a quantity of social overhead facilities as are required to support the target rate of increase in production. By making possible a net increase in these facilities, foreign public aid helps to establish the preconditions for directly productive investment, including private foreign investment. I have observed at close quarters a number of examples in Nigeria and East Africa of the consummation of a foreign private investment depending on the construction of social overhead facilities, which construction in turn depended, at least in the foreseeable future, on the availability of foreign public loans or grants.

(3) Encouragement of official policies favorable to private investment. Investment in an underdeveloped economy by a national or international public aid source lends an aura of protection to private foreign investors, who know that the agencies will apply pressure to secure fair treatment for them all and will be around to bail the country out of economic difficulties that might otherwise lead it to create difficulties for foreign investments. The World Bank usually regards equitable treatment of foreign private

investors as a condition of eligibility for Bank loans, and the United States is required by law to suspend aid to any country that expropriates U.S. private investments and fails to agree to prompt and effective compensation. The Kennedy Administration initially opposed the mandatory character of this provision of the Foreign Assistance Act, added in 1962 as the "Hickenlooper Amendment," preferring instead that the President should be allowed to waive it at his discretion, but, in 1963, Secretary of State Dean Rusk told a Congressional committee that the administration no longer had a quarrel with the amendment. In the meantime, the United States had invoked it in the case of Ceylon, which nationalized American-owned petroleum distribution facilities and then engaged in what the U.S. Government regarded as procrastination with respect to negotiating a fair settlement. It is possible that the apparent change in the administration's attitude was based partly on apprehension over the foreign policy implications of the President's waiving the aid cut-off requirement in some cases and not others. The strategy of leaving the administration's hands tied may have seemed the most effective one in the circumstances. Some months after the Ceylon episode, the Goulart Administration in Brazil agreed to an acceptable settlement in regard to some U.S.-owned properties nationalized by one of the Brazilian state governments. Doubtless, the realization that it would be next to impossible to induce Congress to retreat under such pressure regardless of how anxious the administration was to continue aid motivated the Brazilians to reach a prompt settlement. (On the other hand, in Ceylon, it took a transfer of political power to the former Opposition to change the policy toward foreign oil interests and lay a basis for the resumption of U.S. public aid in fiscal 1966.)

On the other side of the protection coin, public aid sources inevitably develop a sizable stake in the economic progress of underdeveloped countries they have aided over a number of years. When these countries encounter balance-of-payments difficulties and their governments come under pressure to control profit remittances and imports of raw materials or intermediate goods by foreign private interests, the aid agencies take these foreign-exchange demands into account in estimating emergency aid requirements. Moreover, in a broader sense, most businessmen actually engaged in exporting capital do not accept the argument of the pure free-enterprise theorists that public foreign aid leads on the whole to a slowdown in growth and greater ease of Communist penetration over the situation that would prevail if underdeveloped countries were forced to rely wholly on private capital markets for overseas finance. Rather, they agree that a commitment by public aid sources to furnish capital over a number of years to assist a country's development is more likely than not to result in a net increase in resources available for investment, more rapid economic growth, and a reduced probability of Communist takeover, partly because of the higher growth rate and partly because the presence of non-Communist public capital exerts a variety of political influences in favor of the developing country's following a non-Communist course. Thus, participation of non-Communist public aid sources in financing a country's development offers increased security to private foreign investors interested in the country.

(4) Direct financial support and provisions of attractive vehicles for private investment. Public lending agencies provide direct support to private foreign investment by (a) supplying a critical margin of finance to projects undertaken by private foreign equity capital, as well as by (b) furnishing a vehicle for private loan capital via participations in the agencies' loans for public and private sector projects. Under (a), the World Bank, International Finance Corporation, Export-Import Bank, and AID (the latter following in the footsteps of its predecessor, DLF) have all invested in projects in which private foreign investors were providing a greater or lesser proportion of the equity. Both AID and Eximbank generally prefer to have private foreign equity involved in directly productive projects to which they make loans and often insist that prospective local borrowers go to considerable lengths to attract such foreign participation.

The World Bank's Articles of Agreement specify that one of the purposes of the Bank is "to promote private foreign investment by means of guarantees or participations in loans and other investments made by private investors." However, as a result of private investors' understandable reluctance to venture outside a limited group of industries in less-developed areas, the Bank has found itself called upon to take the initiative in supplying capital. Thus, rather than finding opportunities for itself to participate in financing arranged on the initiative of private interests, it is more often the Bank that has encouraged private interests to participate in its loans.

Direct involvement of private institutions in World Bank financing in less-developed countries takes either of two forms: (1) participations in new Bank loans, whereby private investors agree to purchase specified maturities among the borrower's promissory notes as these are issued following disbursement of the loan capital, and (2) sales of old loans, whereby private investors purchase promissory notes out of the Bank's existing holdings. In order to launch the loan-selling operation, the Bank tacked its own guarantee onto a number of the early participations and sales. Published figures do not indicate to what extent this procedure was followed in regard to loans in less-developed countries, but no Bank guarantee has accompanied any participations or sales made after 1955-56, and, out of a total of $69 million worth of transactions with recourse on the Bank, involving loans to all areas, only $2.0 million had not matured by June 30, 1967.

As of June 30, 1967, the Bank had sold $713 million worth of early maturities of its loans to less-developed countries. Some $407 million worth of these maturities had already matured or been prepaid, so that total outstanding private participations in Bank loans to less-developed countries amounted to $305 million. This is slightly below a level of $309 millions achieved already in 1963, so that in the last four years there has been no net additional outflow of private capital by means of this vehicle. Of the $305 million outstanding in 1967, $204 million constituted obligations guaranteed by the Belgian, British, and French governments in connection with loans contracted on behalf of territories which at the time of signing were colonial dependencies. Such obligations are no less secure than those issued by the governments in question for domestic financing, and private purchases of them say little about the readiness of private debt capital to share the World Bank's risks. On the other hand, outstanding private participations of $101 million in obligations guaranteed only by the governments of independent less-developed countries represented an advance over the corresponding 1963 total of $67 million. In its 1966-67 Annual Report, the Bank attributed the stagnation of over-all participations to "the upward movement of interest rates on competing securities and the restriction on overseas investments from some capital-exporting countries."[5]

Even without the Bank's guarantee, a participation in a World Bank loan or purchase of a Bank-held note is about as safe an investment in an underdeveloped country as any private foreign lending institution could hope for. Because of the Bank's pace-setting role in international development finance and its dependence on private foreign markets for most of its own funds, the powers supporting the Bank will do everything possible to prevent defaults occurring on loans held by it. Much of the inviolability of Bank-held loans rubs off on notes purchased by private investors out of the same loans. In addition, private financial institutions have developed a fair degree of confidence in the procedures followed by the Bank to ensure that the projects it finances are technically and economically sound and can be expected to generate more or less directly the financial (though not necessarily foreign-exchange) resources required to service the relevant loans. Thus, the limited extent to which private loan capital has taken advantage of the prime investment opportunities presented by World Bank loans in the underdeveloped areas suggests that there are strict limits to the amount of such capital available for investment in these areas even under favorable conditions.

In addition to direct participations and sales, the World Bank has promoted a number of joint lending operations in which a placement with one or more private financial institutions is made coincident with and for the same purposes as a Bank loan. Such an operation was the occasion of the first direct Indian borrowing in the U.S. capital market. In March, 1957, the First Boston Corporation arranged a credit of $11.2 million from five U.S. commercial banks for the purchase of jet aircraft by Air India International, and the World Bank made a simultaneous loan of $5.6 million for the same purpose. The Bank agreed to defer repayment of its credit until the last two years of the total nine-year maturity, so that the private credits could be repaid first.[6] The Bank has characterized this type of operation as playing "a useful part in encouraging private capital to invest in projects of high economic priority in less-developed countries."[7]

The International Finance Corporation, Export-Import Bank, and Inter-American Development Bank have followed the World Bank's example and raised portions of the capital required for their current loan disbursements by means of participations and sales. Such transactions are particularly important to the IFC, whose principal objective is to enhance the role of private enterprise, both domestic and foreign, in the development effort. Ideally, each of its own investments is supposed to act as a spearhead for private capital, and the sooner such capital is forthcoming to reduce or even replace altogether IFC's commitment in an operation, the better IFC likes it. IFC's 1966-67 Annual Report describes sales of investments as

> . . . the most important single source of replenishment of IFC's funds . . . over 25 per cent of IFC's total commitments have been revolved in this way, and as of June 30, 1967, IFC had obtained the participation of other investors in more than half the commitments it has made. . . . Through sales of investments to other institutions, the Corporation has demonstrated the possibilities of opening up channels for portfolio investment in private industry in the developing countries.[8]

Banks, investment companies, pension funds, mutual funds, and insurance companies have all purchased parts of IFC investments. In absolute amounts, sales of loan and equity investments through fiscal 1967 totaled $42.1 million, while about $18.0 million out of a total of $25.1 million in IFC stand-by and underwriting commitments had been taken over by others. The report notes that investments in four countries--Mexico, Brazil, the Philippines, and Colombia--have attracted 55 per cent of the purchases from IFC's portfolio.

The Export-Import Bank has long been receptive to applications by U.S. banks for participations in its loans, and, in March, 1960, it instituted new procedures whereby it took the initiative in seeking such participations. In just over four years, up to the end of fiscal 1966, the Bank had sold six issues of guaranteed Participation Certificates, of which $1,385 million worth was still outstanding; however, given the Eximbank guarantee, purchases of these involve participation in Eximbank as a U.S. Government corporation rather than in the provision of capital to less-developed countries on a risk-sharing basis. On a much smaller scale, the Bank also regularly transfers loan commitments to commercial banks, etc., and sells participations in specific loans. The Bank's published data do not indicate how much of this activity relates to its commitments in less-developed areas.

The Inter-American Development Bank was able to sell participations in early maturities of its loans from the start of its operations in 1961. According to Robert Cutler, then U.S. Executive Director of the IDB, "Our bank is able to sell short-maturity participations because the World Bank has made the market."[9] After hearing Cutler describe the participation of U.S. commercial banks in IDB loans, Congressman Otto Passman characteristically missed the point by grumbling, "I wish those banks had become as interested before we passed this authorization."[10] It was, of course, precisely the opportunity of taking the early maturities in a loan arranged by a U.S. Government-backed public lending institution that induced the banks to make their contribution. Through 1966, cumulative sales of participations in IDB loans were $28.7 million.

It cannot be proven statistically beyond any doubt that present-day public foreign capital movements are responsible, on net, for more private capital movement to less-developed countries than would take place in the absence of public aid. This is because, as is the case with most problems in economics, the system of relationships is underidentified--that is, we do not have observations on private capital movements to a given country during a given period both with and without public foreign aid, and international and inter-temporal comparisons involve too many imponderables to yield universally acceptable conclusions. Nevertheless, I am convinced that the considerations outlined above place the weight of the impact of foreign aid on the side of furthering private capital movements, rather than curbing them.

DISPLACEMENT AMONG CATEGORIES OF PUBLIC AID

The next question to be considered is that of competition among forms of public capital transfer located at different points along the spectrum. Because hard and soft loans are frequently made for the same types of end-uses, the problem of potential competition raises itself more openly in regard to soft loans than grants, which are provided for more restricted nominal purposes except in countries where immediate political objectives predominate. However, because of the mobility of resources, grants may be just as competitive with hard loans; to the extent a country receives P.L. 480 grant aid to cover agricultural imports it would have had to purchase anyway, it should require less hard loan aid to attain the same developmental goals.

In the popular debate concerning the advisability of soft loans, the fear has often been expressed that soft loans, like "bad money" under Gresham's Law, would quickly drive hard-lending institutions, dispensing "good money," out of business. Speaking before the Special Senate Committee to Study the Foreign Aid Program on behalf of the "Citizen Advisers on the Mutual Security Program" appointed by President Eisenhower in 1956, Benjamin Fairless states: "We feel that the 'soft loan' principle undermines real loans. Why should one country get a loan on a so-called soft basis, as against a sister country getting a hard loan? The first thing you know, the drift will be to all soft loans. We want to stop it."[11] A less drastic prognostication was offered at about the same time by Professor Edward S. Mason:

> Among the contenders [in offering development aid]
> will be foreign private investment, dollar loans from
> Export-Import Bank and the World Bank, govern-
> mental local currency, or "fuzzy loans" and grants.
> Under these circumstances it may be difficult to pre-
> serve that degree of "hardness" in the provision of
> capital that the stage of development of a particular
> country justifies.[12]

If the use of soft loans as a major instrument of international development finance posed a serious threat to the continued operations of hard lenders, one would have expected top officials of institutions such as the World Bank to know and worry about it. Yet the Bank's professional leadership was in the forefront of the movement to give respectability to soft lending and establish a soft loan arm within the Bank itself. As we saw in Chapter 3, in 1951, then Bank President Eugene Black was already pointing to the need for techniques of capital transfer to the underdeveloped areas other than "loans which have a reasonable prospect of repayment."[13] By 1961, having guided the International Development Association into existence, Black was calling upon national lending agencies to produce an "aid mixture (with) a larger component of funds on a grant basis or on terms comparable with IDA's."[14] Far from fearing that the expansion of soft lending would undercut their own operations, officials of the World Bank and Export-Import Bank regarded it as absolutely necessary to protect them. The reason for this was that, in the absence of a good supply of soft loans and grants, the only way for less-developed countries to obtain the foreign capital they required to achieve their target rates of growth would be to contract debt on terms that would rapidly carry their debt service/export ratios above prudent levels. At such high levels, the countries in question would probably still be able to obtain privately financed or government-backed short- and medium-term export credits, but the more of these they obtained, the greater the jeopardy to which existing loans of public lending institutions would be exposed, and the less creditworthy these countries would be for further loans from such institutions.

The role of soft loans in keeping underdeveloped countries' debt service obligations under control, and the resultant feelings of relief among officials of hard-lending agencies, are brought out in the following exchange between President Linder of the Export-Import Bank and Congressman Passman in the 1961 hearings of the latter's subcommittee:

> Mr. LINDER. The Indians are the most careful people I know in respect of not increasing their liabilities to the Export-Import Bank in particular, or generally, I think, beyond what they believe conservatively is their capacity to pay.

> Mr. PASSMAN. They do not have to do so, because they can get possibly four or five times as much through these other sources, such as DLF and the others, the foreign relief programs. They can get sufficient money from these sources to satisfy these loans.[15]

There is no doubt that governments of most developing countries would like to get as much foreign aid as they can on the easiest terms available. Thus, if a developing country could obtain soft loans and grants to the full extent of its desire for foreign capital, forms of capital transfer on harder terms might well be nosed out of the picture. But the World Bank leadership and U.S. Government policy-makers saw no difficulty in avoiding this problem through, on the one hand, inevitable limitations on the availability of easy-term capital appropriated out of public tax funds, and, on the other hand, arrangements for coordinating lending operations among sources of hard and soft loans. The fact that easy-term capital was in limited supply would force the administrators of these funds to ration them among eligible borrowers, and the establishment of coordinating machinery would enable hard loan agencies to take first pick of projects presented for overseas financing. Thus, a developing country would have little direct influence on the decision of how much easy-term aid it should receive. Rather, external capital sources, by explicit or implicit coordination, would determine an optimum mixture of different aid forms for the country, and rejection by the country of all or part of the hard loan component of this mixture would in no way increase the easy-term finance available to it.

COORDINATING PUBLIC AID FROM
HARD- AND EASY-TERM SOURCES

The machinery that now exists for coordinating hard and soft public finance is quite impressive. In the cases of the World Bank and IDA, and the Inter-American Development Bank with its Fund for Special Operations and Social Progress Trust Fund, soft-lending operations are merely additional windows in organizations that also deal in hard loans. With an arrangement of this type, the determination of how much hard and soft finance will be provided and what projects will be financed at the different windows is made internally within a single lending organization. In the case of the U.S. Government, the responsibility for assigning Eximbank loans and different forms of AID finance to particular countries and projects is more diffused, although coordinating machinery exists and operates actively. The ruling principle is that Eximbank has first refusal on any capital project presented to AID. The Bank takes a potential borrower's debt-servicing capacity into account in deciding whether to exercise its option and, on this ground, lets AID pick up a number of projects that meet Eximbank's project criteria. However, Eximbank does not like to enter into advance agreements with AID, explicit or implicit, on what proportion of total U.S. aid to a country will be in the form of soft versus hard loans, and it frequently decides to take a project that several offices in AID, including the country mission, want to finance via a soft loan. The Secretary of State can overrule the Bank and give a project back to AID if he considers it in the national interest to do so, but this rarely, if ever, happens. The AID leadership values cordial relationships with Eximbank too highly to appeal to higher authority when the Bank feels strongly that it should handle a particular project. As a rule, once Eximbank has agreed to finance a project, it will not defer to AID even if the would-be borrower decides to accept finance and procurement from a European source in preference to the Bank. (Such an instance occurred during my tour of duty in Nigeria. Eximbank is sometimes at a competitive disadvantage in relation to European hard lenders because of its policy of tailoring maturities on its project loans to the expected life or pay-out period of the equipment to be purchased thereunder, whereas a European public source may be willing to finance a variety of items of varying economic life-expectancy out of a single line of credit extending as long as 20 or 25 years.)

As for the mechanics of coordination between AID and Eximbank, AID is supposed to forward expeditiously to Eximbank documentation on any loan application it receives directly or through a country mission. Regular weekly meetings are held between representatives of the two agencies, normally involving both policy- and working-level staff members on both sides. The participants discuss allocation of projects between the agencies, although the ultimate decision on allocation is usually made internally within Eximbank. However, AID representatives at these meetings may present arguments in favor of AID's handling a project and are sometimes able to influence Eximbank's decision by such tactics as pointing to forthcoming projects that are likely to be more attractive to the Bank than current ones. In any case, AID cannot begin what it calls "intensive review" of a loan application until Eximbank has formally waived its option.

Coordination within single lending institutions or governments does not rule out competition among unrelated aid sources. However, machinery also exists for coordinating the operations of different sources. Since all free-world capital-exporting nations belong to the World Bank-IDA-IFC complex and have their own executive directors in it or, in the case of smaller nations, share in electing executive directors, there are automatic channels of coordination between national lending agencies, on the one hand, and the international complex on the other. In the case of the United States, this coordination is expedited through the National Advisory Council on International Monetary and Financial Problems, established by the Bretton Woods Agreements Act of 1945. Statutory members of the Council are the Secretaries of the Treasury (chairman), State, and Commerce, the Chairman of the Board of Governors of the Federal Reserve System, the President of Eximbank, and the Administrator of AID. Through the Secretary of the Treasury, the U.S. executive directors in the World Bank complex, the Inter-American Development Bank, and the International Monetary Fund participate in the work of the Council. One of the Council's purposes is to

> . . . coordinate, by consultation or otherwise, so far
> as is practicable, the policies and operations of the
> representatives of the United States on the Fund and
> the Bank, the Export-Import Bank of Washington and
> all other agencies of the Government to the extent that
> they make or participate in the making of foreign loans
> or engage in foreign financial, exchange or monetary
> transactions.[16]

Weekly meetings of the Council discuss pending loans by the various U.S. and international agencies on the basis of summary papers on the loans prepared and distributed beforehand.

The most notable recent development in the aid coordination field is the proliferation of formal machinery whereby bilateral and multilateral sources providing aid to a particular country meet regularly, usually under the chairmanship of the World Bank, to evaluate jointly the country's requirements and recent performance and achieve some degree of coordination (which varies considerably from one situation to the next) in their respective aid policies vis-à vis the country. Frequently, the Bank prepares extensive documentation for such meetings, assembling data that most individual aid sources are in no position to gather for themselves. When the coordinating machinery has the title of a "consortium," which applies to India, Pakistan (both under World Bank sponsorship), Greece, and Turkey (these two organized by OECD), it has the objective of securing pledges of specific amounts of assistance from its members in order to make up an agreed total resource package. On the other hand, "consultative groups," which are the more common type of arrangement, are, in the DAC's words, "rather more forums for discussion than vehicles for positive action."[17] The World Bank leads nine of these, involving varying combinations of 18 capital-supplying countries (including Taiwan in the group for South Korea and Kuwait in the one for Tunisia), and is laying the groundwork for more still (I observed at close range some preparations for a group concerned with the three East African countries as a unit). The IDB sponsors a consultative group for Ecuador. According to the above-quoted DAC report, "More than 30 per cent of the net flow of official disbursements is related to consortia and consultative groups." Recently, the growing debt burden of less-developed countries has been a central object of concern to consultative groups, which have had to examine closely the distribution of vehicles of capital transfer on different terms among the different bilateral and multilateral components of the resource flow.

The World Bank's 1966-67 Annual Report notes that the Bank has "for some time . . . been experimenting with arrangements for combining its own loans with bilateral export credits in such a way as to bring about the most economical procurement of goods and services and the financial terms most appropriate to the projects and the developing countries concerned."[18] In June, 1967, the Bank convened multilateral discussions on such questions in regard to two Latin American countries. To coordinate policies of aid sources with respect to Latin America, the Inter-American Development Bank hosts a biweekly meeting of officials from the Latin American sections of the World Bank, International Monetary Fund, Export-Import Bank, and AID. Finally, in addition to the formal coordination machinery, national lending agencies engage in frequent ad hoc consultation with each other and with the World Bank in regard to lending activities in specific countries.

All these coordination procedures do not lead to a complete absence of competition among various lending agencies and forms of capital transfer. There is fairly active competition among national lending agencies with respect to financing exports of certain types of equipment for which the world market is aggressively (though not perfectly) competitive. According to my experience in Africa, this applies to such items as railroad locomotives, power generators, and telecommunications equipment. On the other hand, many national lending agencies cannot offer soft loans to

finance such items, with the result that the competition is often
carried out by means of variations in interest rates and maturities
within the range of hard finance, differences in price and quality
with respect to different makes of equipment, bribery of host
government officials by manufacturers, etc. Earlier in this
chapter, we noted the efforts AID makes to ensure that its soft
loans do not compete with credit offers of other countries that AID
considers to be on "reasonable" terms. In come less-developed
countries, any additional loans on even the most lenient hard terms
would carry the countries' debt service ratios into unsafe territory,
so that AID might occasionally find that its own terms were the only
"reasonable" ones. I am not personally familiar with situations in
which this has occurred, although it is a fully justifiable policy
under the criteria developed in this study.

I have been informed of one instance of competition among
public capital sources in which the World Bank itself was the culprit.
For several years after its inception in 1957, the International Finance Corporation, a Bank affiliate, had considerable difficulty in
launching operations in India. IFC's first two investments in India
were subsequently canceled; its first disbursements in India took
place only in 1963. I am told that the basic reason for this slow
performance was that the Indian Government preferred private
Indian firms to satisfy their foreign-exchange requirements by
drawing on credits involving service payments to the original lender
(i.e., foreign-exchange obligations) at lower interest rates and
longer maturities than is the case with IFC. Such credits have been
available since 1955 in the form of World Bank Loans to the
Industrial Credit and Investment Corporation of India, Ltd. (ICICI).
Through June 30, 1967, the Bank had lent $140 million to ICICI for
relending to local private industry. A two-stage procedure is
followed, whereby private firms repay ICICI on harder terms than
ICICI repays the Bank. Thus, the terms from the viewpoint of the
end-user are similar to those of IFC and ICICI loans, but the Bank
loans to ICICI offer more favorable terms from the viewpoint of
India's balance of payments.

In this case, since IFC's operations are necessarily on a
small scale in relation to the World Bank's (cumulative IFC oper-
ational investments and underwriting commitments in all countries,
net of cancellations and terminations, were only $210 million at the
end of fiscal 1967), the Indian Government presumably figured that
it stood to incur at most a marginal foreign-exchange loss by dis-
couraging the use of IFC credits. Doubtless, if the IFC had been
set up to provide a volume of resources commensurate with the
Bank's contribution and it was clear to the Indian Government that
the potential IFC contribution represented a net additional supply of
foreign exchange, the Indians would probably have encouraged it
from the start.

ADDITIONAL STRATEGY TO PREVENT
UNWANTED DISPLACEMENT

In general, if a government seriously interested in promoting its country's development believes that a potential transfer of capital on hard terms represents a substantial net additional contribution to resources available for development, which cannot be replaced by a transfer on softer terms if it is rejected, then, unless there are strong political or ideological objections, the government will ordinarily choose to maximize available external resources by accepting the transfer on hard terms. Ensuring that the government concerned looks on the hard-term transfer in this light involves two elements of strategy on the part of aid sources: first, they must make clear that potential transfers on soft terms will not be reduced to the extent hard-term capital is accepted; and, second, they must make clear that such transfers will not be increased to the extent legitimate offers of hard-term capital are rejected. Perhaps the most useful way of communicating these points is for aid sources to give the impression of willingness to provide an amount of easy-term capital that is more or less fixed in the short run. This is one of the ends served by advance commitments of aid for two or more years of a multiyear development plan. In Chapter 10, we noted an instance in which the Nigerian Government on its own initiative suspended negotiations with AID for a 3/4 per cent, 40-year loan to purchase U.S. railway track when the United Kingdom offered a loan on hard terms for the purchase of British track, stating that this loan would be supplemental to the current U.K. commitment to the Nigerian development plan. The Nigerians felt that by accepting the British offer they were maximizing resources available for the plan. (It was also noted in Chapter 10 that there were some doubts whether this would be the net effect of the Nigerian decision, in view of the difficulties being encountered in finding eligible projects to absorb the U.S. commitment.)

On the other hand, where different forms of public capital transfer are included under the same commitment but not identified with separate amounts, there is a danger that the host government will assume it can maximize the proportion of easy-term finance within a given aid total by rejecting hard-term transfers proffered by the relevant source. To use another Nigerian illustration, some elements in the Nigerian Government were concerned that agreeing to medium-term Eximbank credits to local private business ventures might, if these were "charged" to the total U.S. aid commitment of $225 million, reduce the amount of U.S. aid available to the public sector. The issue was not raised in acute form during my tenure in Nigeria because of the minimal amount of such lending that took place during the first 18 months of the plan, i.e., only

a single $2 million credit. But, in anticipation of future develop-
ments, the AID mission suggested to Washington that the United
States not regard such loans as coming under the over-all aid commitment, to avoid giving the Nigerians an incentive to disapprove
them. However, Washington rejected this suggestion on the
ground that the commitment had merely been intended to state an
over-all magnitude of resources the United States would make
available to the 1962-68 Plan, and Eximbank credits were no less
U.S. resources than AID grants and loans. In my view, some formula along the lines proposed by the mission should be used in such
cases to avoid misunderstandings and provide a positive incentive
for governments of less-developed countries to encourage direct
foreign loans to private enterprise.

NOTES TO CHAPTER 11

1.   A cogent elaboration of this argument may be found in three
sources: "American Private Enterprise, Foreign Economic Development, and the Aid Programs," a paper prepared for the Special
Senate Committee to Study the Foreign Aid Program by the American Enterprise Association, Inc., included in Compilation of Studies
and Surveys prepared under the direction of the Special Committee
to Study the Foreign Aid Program (85th Cong., 1st Sess.); testimony
before the Senate Special Committee on behalf of the American
Enterprise Association by Milton Friedman and W. Glenn Campbell,
1957; and Milton Friedman, "Foreign Economic Aid," Yale Review, Summer, 1958.

2.   International Finance Corporation, Summary Proceedings,
1961 Annual Meeting of the Board of Governors (Washington, D.C.,
1961), p. 15.

3.   IFC, Summary Proceedings, 1960 Annual Meeting of the
Board of Governors (Washington, D.C., 1960), p. 5-6.

4.   Clive S. Gray, "The Spectrum of International Capital
Transfer to the Underdeveloped Countries" (Unpublished Ph.D.
dissertation, Department of Economics, Harvard University, 1964),
p. 708.

5.   International Bank for Reconstruction and Development,
Annual Report, 1966-67 (Washington, D.C., 1967), p. 18. Data on
participations outstanding in 1967 were computed from the
Bank's Statement of Loans--June 30, 1967 (Washington, D.C., 1967);
1963 data from its 1962-63 Annual Report (Washington, D.C., 1963),
Appendix K.

6.   IBRD, Twelfth Annual Report: 1956-57 (Washington, D.C.,
1957), pp. 14, 30, 63.

7.   Ibid., p. 14.

8.   IFC, 1966–67 Annual Report (Washington, D.C., 1967), p. 7.

9.   U.S. House of Representatives, Subcommittee on Appropriations, Hearings on Foreign Operations Appropriations for 1962, (87th Cong., 1st Sess.), Part 2, p. 131.

10.   Ibid., p. 128.

11.   U.S. Senate, Foreign Aid: Report of the Special Committee to Study the Foreign Aid Program (85th Cong., 1st Sess.).

12.   Edward S. Mason, "Competitive Coexistence and Economic Development in Asia," in International Stability and Progress: United States Interests and Instruments (New York: American Assembly, June, 1957), p. 93.

13.   From an address in Chicago, January 10, 1951. Cited by Gerald M. Alter, Capacity of Underdeveloped Countries to Service Foreign Capital Inflows (Washington, D.C.: IBRD, July 22, 1953; Preliminary draft, mimeograph), p. 2.

14.   IBRD, Summary Proceedings, 1961 Annual Meetings of the Board of Governors (Vienna, September, 1961), p. 12.

15.   U.S. House of Representatives, Subcommittee on Appropriations, op. cit., p. 72.

16.   22 U.S.C. 286b.

17.   Organization for Economic Cooperation and Development, Development Assistance Efforts and Policies, 1967 Review (Paris, 1967), p. 134.

18.   IBRD, Annual Report, 1966–67, p. 9.

MATHEMATICAL APPENDIX

MATHEMATICAL APPENDIX

(1) Definition of terms used in Part II models:

Y_1 = a measure of national income in the first year of the period under consideration. Gerald Alter uses net geographical national product, Dragoslav Avramovic gross domestic product.

D_n = cumulative resource transfer from abroad at the end of year n, net of any repayments of principal. Referred to in text as "debt," although it may be (and frequently is) understood to include inflow of equity capital.

D_o^a = ratio of pre-existing foreign debt to Y_1.

S_o^a = ratio of aggregate domestic savings to national income in first year.

K = incremental capital/output ratio, i.e., ratio of domestic investment in one year to the increase in national income between that year and the following one.

r = target annual rate of increase of national income.

s = annual rate of increase of aggregate domestic savings.

s' = marginal aggregate savings ratio.

s'' = marginal per capita savings ratio.

p = annual rate of net population increase.

i = weighted average rate of return payable on new foreign capital inflow. Chargeable in year n on D_{n-1}.

i_1 = weighted average rate of return payable on pre-existing debt ($D_o^a Y_1$).

M_o^a = ratio of aggregate imports to national income in first year.

M = ratio of aggregate imports to national income when assumed constant.

X_o^a = ratio of aggregate exports to national income in first year.

X = ratio of aggregate exports to national income when assumed constant.

m = annual rate of increase of aggregate imports.

x = annual rate of increase of aggregate exports.

A_1 = weighted average annual amortization rate on pre-existing debt ($D\ddot{o}Y_1$).

DSR = predetermined limiting value for the debt service/export ratio.

a = weighted average annual amortization rate on new foreign capital inflow. Chargeable in year n on D_{n-1}.

N = annual requirement for resource inflow net of interest and amortization payments on pre-existing debt.

C = DSR times exports in a given year n, less service payments due in that year on pre-existing debt. It may be regarded as residual debt-servicing capacity in year n.

z = the proportion of new aid that can be extended in the form of loans generating service payments in and before year n; 1-z is the proportion that must be extended in the form of grants or loans generating no service payments by year n.

k = the proportion of annual (1) investment or (2) import expenditures eligible for financing via external resource transfer under the end-use constraint.

Time variables

t_1 = year in which domestic savings first equals or exceeds investment.

t_2 = year in which rate of increase of debt is reduced to same level as rate of increase of GDP, i.e., r.

t_3 = year in which rate of increase of debt equals zero.

t_x = year in which rate of increase of debt is reduced to same level as rate of increase of exports.

t_m = year in which rate of increase of debt is reduced to same level as rate of increase of imports.

(2) (a) = Expression for debt on Alter assumption of constant marginal per capita savings ratio:

$$D_n = Y_1 \left\{ \frac{Kr-s''}{r-i}[(1+r)^n-(1+i)^n] - \frac{a}{p-i} \, So-s'' \, [(1+p)^n-(1+i)^n] \right\}.$$

(b)   Expression for debt on Avramovic assumption of constant marginal aggregate savings ratio:

$$D_n = Y_1 \left\{ \frac{(Kr-s'}{r-i}[(1+r)^n-(1+i)^n] - \frac{S_0^a-s'}{i}[(1+i)^n-1] \right\}.$$

(c)   Expression for debt on Gray assumption of constant aggregate savings growth rate:

$$D_n = Y_1 \left\{ \frac{Kr}{r-i}[(1+r)^n-(1+i)^n] - \frac{S_0^a}{s-i}[(1+s)^n-(1+i)^n] \right\}.$$

(Note: the remaining formulae in this Appendix assume a constant aggregate savings growth rate.)

(3) Expressions for debt assuming constant growth rates of imports and exports:

(a)   Imports increase at same rate as GDP, exports more rapidly:

$$D_n = Y_1 \left\{ \frac{M}{r-i}[(1+r)^n-(1+i)^n] - \frac{X_0^a}{x-i}[(1+x)^n-(1+i)^n] \right\}.$$

(b)   Exports increase at same rate as GDP, imports more slowly:

$$D_n = Y_1 \left\{ \frac{M_0^a}{m-i}[(1+m)^n-(1+i)^n] - \frac{X}{r-i}[(1+r)^n-(1+i)^n] \right\}.$$

(4) Equation for iterative derivation of t_3, year in which debt is maximized, on assumption that all capital inflow bears return of i:

$$\frac{Kr}{r-i}[r(1+r)^{t_3}-i(1+i)^{t_3}] - \frac{S_0^a}{s-i}[s(1+s)^{t_3}-i(1+i)^{t_3}] = 0.$$

(5) Assuming that debt bearing a positive return is maximized in year t_3, and that residual capital requirement is financed by grants and/or zero-interest loans:

(a)   Expression for debt bearing positive return:

$$D_n = Y_1 \left\{ \frac{S_0^a}{s-i}\left[\frac{s(1+s)^{t_3}}{i(1+i)^{t_3-n}} - (1+s)^n \right] - \frac{Kr}{r-i}\left[\frac{r(1+r)^{t_3}}{i(1+i)^{t_3-n}} - (1+r)^n \right] \right\}.$$

(b)   <u>Definition of t_L, year in which first loans made bearing positive return:</u>

$$\overset{a}{S_o}_{s-i}\left[\frac{s(1+s)^{t_3}}{i(1+i)^{t_3-t_L}}-(1+s)^{t_L}\right]-\frac{Kr}{r-i}\left[\frac{r(1+r)^{t_3}}{i(1+i)^{t_3-t_L}}-(1+r)^{t_L}\right]=0,$$

$$t_L < t_3.$$

(c)   <u>Expression for grants and zero-interest loans required through t_3:</u>

$$G = Y_1\left\{K\left[(1+r)^{t_L}-1\right]-\frac{\overset{a}{S_o}}{s}\left[(1+s)^{t_L}-1\right]\right\}.$$

(6) (a)   <u>Expression for that part of debt in year n derived from debt contracted before year 1:</u>

$$(1+i_1)^n \overset{a}{D_o}.$$

(b)   <u>Relationship in year t_3 of earnings on initial debt to earnings on new debt, assuming all debt bears a positive return of i:</u>

$$i_1(1+i_1)^{t_3}\overset{a}{D_o} = \frac{\overset{a}{S_o}}{s-i}\left[s(1+s)^{t_3}-i(1+i)^{t_3}\right]-\frac{Kr}{r-i}\left[r(1+r)^{t_3}-i(1+i)^{t_3}\right].$$

(c)   <u>Expression for grants and zero-interest loans in residual capital requirement variant, including annual earnings on pre-existing debt.</u>

$$G = Y_1\left\{K\left[(1+r)^{t_L}-1\right]-\frac{\overset{a}{S_o}}{s}\left[(1+s)^{t_L}-1\right] \quad t_3 i_1 \overset{a}{D_o}\right\}.$$

(7)   <u>Method used to compute compound annual rate of growth of savings and other variables:</u>

The compound rate of growth is given by $g = (b-1)100$, where

$$\frac{b^n+1}{b+1} = \frac{\sum\limits_{t=1}^{n} P_t b^{t-1}}{\sum\limits_{t=1}^{n} P_t}, \text{ P being the variable whose growth}$$

is being measured. Out of all sets of estimated ("dummy") P's conforming to a straight-line geometric growth path and summing to the total of the actual P's, the sum of the squared absolute deviations between actual and estimated P's is at a minimum in the set generated by the above g. A principal advantage of the technique is that no observed value of P (e.g., savings) carries greater weight in determining the rate of growth than any other observed value of P by virtue of its location in time (although the least squares technique employed here does cause weight to be correlated with magnitude). Thus, the method reduces distortions caused by selecting individual years as terminal points. The method was devised by Boris P. Pesek.[2]

(8) Formula for maximum value of i which borrowing country can pay and still approach any independence constraint asymptotically:

$$\frac{Krs - S_o^a r}{Kr - S_o^a} \; .$$

(9) Expression for t_2, year in which rate of increase of debt is reduced to the same level as the rate of increase of GDP, assuming all debt bears a positive return of i:

$$t_2 = \frac{\log \left[\dfrac{Kr(s-i) - S_o^a(r-i)}{S_o^a(s-r)} \right]}{\log(1+s) - \log(1+i)} \; .$$

(10) Expression for t_x, year in which rate of increase of debt is reduced to the same level as the rate of increase of exports:

(a)   Need for debt determined by investment-savings gap (iterative solution required):

$$\frac{Kr}{r-i} \left[(r-x)(1+r)^{t_x} - (i-x)(1+i)^{t_x} \right]$$
$$- \frac{S_o^a}{s-i} \left[(s-x)(1+s)^{t_x} - (i-x)(1+i)^{t_x} \right] = 0.$$

(b)   Need for debt determined by import-export gap, imports increase at rate r, exports more rapidly:

$$t_x = \frac{\log \left[\dfrac{M(i-x) - X_o^a(i-r)}{M(r-x)} \right]}{\log(1+r) - \log(1+i)} \; .$$

(c)   Need for debt determined by import-export gap, exports increase at rate r, imports more slowly:

$$t_x = \frac{\log \left[\dfrac{X(m-i) - M_o^a(r-i)}{M_o^a(m-r)} \right]}{\log(1+m) - \log(1+i)} \; .$$

(11) Expression for weighted average annual amortization rate (equal annual principal installment or net value methods) or reciprocal of final maturity (level payment method) applicable to new debt, subject to debt service ratio constraint, with the interest rate fixed at i:

$$a = Y_1 \frac{DSR \cdot X_0^a (1+x)^{t_x} - (i_1 + a_1)D_0^a(1+i_1)^{t_x}}{D_{t_x}} - i.$$

(12) Equation for derivation of interest rate, sum of interest and amortization rates, or proportion of aid that must be extended in form of either grants or loans generating no service charges before target date, subject to debt service ratio constraint:

$$\frac{[1 + (i+a)z - \frac{iz}{2}]^{n-1}}{(1 - \frac{iz}{2})^n} = \frac{N + C}{N}.$$

(Note: this formula assumes a one-year grace period for repayment of loan principal; also, in any year interest is payable on only half the new gross inflow in that year.)

(13) Equation for derivation of the constant annual growth rate of imports implied by a given cumulative import-export gap (assuming zero interest on foreign debt) through year t and a given constant annual growth rate of exports (x):

$$\frac{(1+m)^t - 1}{m} = \frac{D_t/Y_1 + \frac{X_0^a}{x}[(1+x)^t - 1]}{M_0^a}.$$

(Whereas the left-hand expression is the formula for the amount of an annuity of unit value per period after a term of t periods at a rate of interest of m per period, m can be read immediately from ordinary interest tables.)

(14) Expression for weighted average annual amortization rate (equal annual principal installment or net value methods) or reciprocal of final maturity (level payment method) applicable to new debt, subject to end-use constraint, with the interest rate fixed at i:

(a) Eligible expenditures a proportion of investment:

$$a = Y_1 \frac{Kr\,[k-(1+r)^{t_2}]+S_0^a(1+s)^{t_2} - (i_1+a_1)D_0^a(1+i_1)^{t_2}}{Dt_1} - i.$$

(b) Eligible expenditures a proportion of imports:

$$a = Y_1 \frac{kM - Kr(1+r)^{t_m}\quad S_0^a(1+s)^{t_m} - (i_1+a_1)D_0^a(1+i_1)^{t_m}}{Dt_m} - i.$$

(15) Equation for deriving year n in which annual net inflow of private resources becomes negative, assuming rate of return i exceeds rate of growth of net inflow q:

$$(1+q)^{n-1} = \frac{i\,[(1+q)^{n-1} - 1]}{q}.$$

(Whereas the right-hand side of the equation represents i times the formula for the amount of an annuity at rate q, the formula can be solved iteratively for n-1 (and thus n) very simply by multiplying i times a range of annuity values corresponding to a given i and then comparing the results with a compound interest table.)

(16) Equation for maximum weighted average interest rate chargeable if net resource outflow in year n is to be no less than amount B, where the growth rate of gross outflow q is less than the full service rate, $\frac{i}{1-(1+i)^{-n}}$, but greater than i. (The net outflow of loans in year 1 is given by L_1):

$$\frac{i}{1-(1+i)^{-n}} = \frac{(1+q)^n - \frac{B}{L_1}}{\frac{(1+q)^n-1}{q}}.$$

(Whereas the left-hand side of the equation represents the formula for an annuity whose present value is 1, i is obtained easily from interest tables.)

NOTES TO MATHEMATICAL APPENDIX

1.   Taken from Dragoslav Avramovic et al., Economic Growth and External Debt. Economic Department, International Bank for Reconstruction and Development (Baltimore: The Johns Hopkins Press, 1964), Mathematical Appendix prepared by S. Shahid Husain, p. 190. A slight difference between the above rendering of this expression and its original version arises from Husain's assigning zero instead of 1 to the first year of the period.

2.   Boris P. Pesek, "Economic Growth and Its Measurement," Economic Development and Cultural Change, IX, No. 3 (April, 1961), pp. 295-330, Essays in the Quantitative Study of Economic Growth, presented to Simon A. Kuznets on the occasion of his 60th birthday.

BIBLIOGRAPHY

BIBLIOGRAPHY

PUBLIC DOCUMENTS; OFFICIAL REPORTS

United States

The Act for International Development of 1961. P.L. 87-195 (87th
    Congress, 1st Sess.), September 4, 1961, Sec. 201 (b), p. 2.

American Enterprise Association, Inc. "American Private Enter-
    prise, Foreign Economic Development, and the Aid Programs."
    Included in Compilation of Studies and Surveys prepared under
    the direction of the Special Committee to Study the Foreign
    Aid Program. (85th Cong., 1st Sess.) Washington, D.C.:
    Government Printing Office, 1957.

Berenson, Robert L.; Bristol, William M.; and Straus, Ralph I.
    The Accumulation and Administration of Local Currencies--A
    Report to the Director of ICA, August 5, 1958. ICA, 1958.

Gray, Clive S. Non-A.I.D. External Assistance to Nigeria. Air-
    gram of U.S. AID Mission in Nigeria to AID/Washington,
    February 1, 1962.

Mason, Edward S. et al. The Problem of Excess Accumulation of
    U.S.-Owned Local Currencies. Findings and Recommendations
    submitted to the Under-Secretary of State by the Consultants
    on International Finance and Economic Problems, April 4, 1960.
    Washington, D.C.: Department of State, 1960 (mimeograph).

McGlauflin, Arthur M. Alternative Sources of Financing for Pro-
    posed A.I.D. Capital Projects. Airgram of AID/Washington to
    all AID overseas missions, April 16, 1963.

President's Committee to Study the United States Military Assist-
    ance Program (The Draper Committee). Composite Report.
    Washington, 1959.

President's Task Force on Foreign Economic Assistance, The
    Act for International Development--A Program for the Decade
    of Development: Objectives, Concepts, and Proposed Program.
    May 23, 1961.

_____. The Act for International Development--A Summary Presentation, June, 1961. (Department of State Publication 7205, General Foreign Policy Series 169, released June, 1961.)

U.S. Agency for International Development. Press releases announcing AID loans, 1961-68.

_____. Proposed Foreign Aid Program, FY 1963 (1964; 1965; 1966; 1967; 1968): Summary Presentation to the Congress. Washington, D.C., 1962, 1963, 1964, 1965, 1966, 1967.

_____. A Study on Loan Terms, Debt Burden and Development. Washington, D.C., April, 1965 (reprinted March, 1966).

_____. U.S. Overseas Loans and Grants and Assistance from International Organizations: Obligations and Loan Authorizations, July 1, 1945-June 30, 1966. Special Report prepared for the House Foreign Affairs Committee. March 17, 1967.

_____, Executive Secretariat. "Renegotiation Provision in A.I.D. Loan Agreements." Policy Determination No. 2, May 8, 1962.

_____, Office of the Controller. Status of Loan Agreements as of June 30, 1967. (Report No. W-224.)

_____, Office of Program Coordination. Gross National Product--Growth Rates and Trend Data, by Region and Country. (Report No. RC-W-138.) Washington, D.C., March 31,1967.

_____. Far East--Economic Growth Trends. Washington, D.C., September, 1966.

_____. Latin America--Economic Growth Trends. October, 1966.

_____. Near East and South Asia--Economic Growth Trends. September, 1966.

_____. Operations Report. Various quarterly issues, 1962 through 1967.

_____, Program Coordination Staff. Principles of Foreign Economic Assistance. Washington, D.C., 1963.

U.S. Department of Commerce, Office of Business Economics. Foreign Investments of the United States, 1953.

_____. Annual article variously entitled "Foreign Investments, 1965-66 . . . " or "International Investments of the United States in 1966 . . . " in Survey of Current Business, August, 1961-64, September, 1965-67.

_____. U.S. Business Investments in Foreign Countries. A
Supplement to the Survey of Current Business, Washington,
D.C.: Government Printing Office, 1960.

U.S. Department of State. Highlights of President Kennedy's New
Act for International Development. (Department of State Pub-
lication 7211, General Foreign Policy Series 170, released
June, 1961.)

_____. Report to Congress on the Mutual Security Program
for the Fiscal Year 1958; 1959; 1960; 1961. (Department of
State, General Foreign Policy Series.)

_____. Summary Presentation, Mutual Security Program.
Various years, 1957 through 1960.

U.S. Development Loan Fund. Annual Report. 1959, 1960.

_____. The Development Loan Fund. February, 1960
(pamphlet).

_____. Legislative History of the Development Loan Fund.
1958 (mimeograph).

_____. Terminal Report. Washington, D.C., January, 1962.

U.S. Export-Import Bank of Washington. "Credits authorized
1934 to 12-31-60, inclusive, classified by purpose." Table
printed on separate sheet, 1961.

_____. Export-Import Bank of Washington, 1934-59: Twenty-
Fifth Anniversary Review. Washington, D.C.: Government
Printing Office, 1959.

_____. Report to the Congress for the Twelve Months Ended
June 30. Various years, especially 1960 through 1966.

U.S. House of Representatives. Agricultural Trade Development
and Assistance Act of 1954 and Amendments. Washington,
D.C.: Government Printing Office, 1966.

_____, Committee on Agriculture. Report on Public Law 480.
Published as a House Document, semiannually for the periods
July 1, 1954-December 31, 1954, through January 1, 1964-June
30, 1964, and annually from December 31, 1964, onward.
Titled "Food for Peace" beginning in 1962.

_____, Committee on Foreign Affairs. Citizens Foreign Aid Committee: Report on the Mutual Security Program, and Comments Supplied by Department of State, Department of the Treasury, Department of Defense and International Cooperation Administration. (86th Cong., 1st Sess.) Committee print, April 27, 1959.

_____. Criticisms of the Foreign Aid Program and Comments Supplied by The Department of State, the International Cooperation Administration and the Department of Defense. (86th Cong., 1st Sess.) Committee print, June 12, 1959.

_____. Hearings on the Foreign Assistance Act. Various years, 1961 through 1967.

_____. Hearings on the International Development and Security Act of 1961. (87th Cong., 1st Sess.) 1961.

_____. Hearings on the Mutual Security Act of 1958; 1959; 1960.

_____. Report on the Mutual Security Act of 1958; 1959; 1960.

_____, Subcommittee of the Committee on Appropriations. Hearings on Foreign Operations Appropriations. Various years, 1961 through 1967.

U.S. International Cooperation Administration. Operations Report. Various quarterly issues, 1958 through 1961.

U.S. Senate, Committee on Appropriations. Hearings on Foreign Assistance and Related Agencies Appropriations. Various years, 1961 through 1967.

_____, Committee on Foreign Relations. Hearings on an Act to Authorize Membership of the United States in the Inter-American Development Bank. (86th Cong., 1st Sess.) 1959.

_____. Hearings on the Food for Peace Bill. Various years, 1959 through 1967.

_____. Hearings on International Development and Security, 1961. (87th Cong., 1st Sess.) 1961.

_____. Hearings on the Mutual Security Act of 1958; 1959; 1960.

_____. Report on the Mutual Security Act of 1958; 1959; 1960.

_____, and U.S. House of Representatives, Committee on Foreign Affairs. Legislation on Foreign Relations with Explanatory Notes. (86th Cong., 1st Sess.) Committee print, December, 1959.

_____, Special Committee to Study the Foreign Aid Program. Compilation of studies and surveys prepared under the direction of the Special Committee to Study the Foreign Aid Program. (85th Cong., 1st Sess.) 1957.

_____. Foreign Aid: Report of the Special Committee to Study the Foreign Aid Program. (Report No. 300, 85th Cong., 1st Sess.) May 13, 1957.

_____. Hearings. (85th Cong., 1st Sess.) 1957.

International Organizations

Abs, Hermann J.; Franks, Sir Olivers; and Sproul, Allan. Bankers' Mission to India and Pakistan. (Letter to Eugene R. Black, dated March 19, 1960; IBRD print.)

General Agreement on Tariffs and Trade. International Trade 1965. Geneva, 1966.

Inter-American Development Bank. Agreement Establishing the Inter-American Development Bank. Washington, D.C., 1965.

_____. Annual Report. Washington, D.C., 1960 through 1967.

_____. IDB--This Is the Inter-American Development Bank. Washington, 1967 (pamphlet).

_____. Inter-American Development Bank--Activities: 1961- 1966. Washington, D.C., 1967.

_____. Proposal for an Increase in the Resources of the Inter- American Development Bank. Report of the Board of Executive Directors to the Board of Governors. Washington, D.C., April, 1967.

_____. Social Progress Trust Fund Agreement. Washington, D.C., 1964.

International Bank for Reconstruction and Development. Annual Report. Washington, D.C., 1950 through 1967 (beginning with 1963-64, covers International Development Association as well).

_____. Articles of Agreement. Washington, D.C., April, 1960 (reprint). Economic Development. Washington, D.C., 1951 .

_____. Some Techniques of Development Lending. Washington, D.C., September, 1960 (pamphlet).

_____. Statement of Loans--June 30, 1964; 1965; 1966; 1967. Washington, D.C., 1964 through 1967. Published separately from annual report beginning with 1964.

_____. Summary Proceedings, Annual Meetings of the Board of Governors. Washington, D.C., 1956 through 1967, except Vienna, 1961.

_____. The World Bank in Asia. Washington, D.C., October, 1960.

_____. The World Bank in Latin America. Washington, D.C., March, 1960.

_____. World Bank Loans at Work. Washington, D.C.: various issues.

_____, Economics Department. External Medium- and Long-Term Public Debt--Past and Projected Amounts Outstanding, Transactions and Payments: 1956-1975; 1956-1976. Washington, D.C., October 14, 1966; December 4, 1967.

International Development Association, Annual Report. Washington, D.C., 1960-61, 1961-62, and 1962-63 (beginning with 1963-64, merged with annual report of IBRD).

_____. Articles of Agreement and Accompanying Report of the Executive Directors. Washington, D.C., January 26, 1960.

_____. Statement of Loans--June 30, 1964; 1965; 1966; 1967. Washington, D.C., 1964 through 1967. Published separately from annual report beginning with 1964.

International Finance Corporation. Annual Report. Washington, D.C., 1956-57 through 1966-67.

_____. Articles of Agreement. Washington, D.C., July 20, 1956.

_____. Summary Proceedings of the Annual Meetings of the Board of Governors. Washington, D.C., 1957 through 1967.

International Monetary Fund. International Financial Statistics. Various monthly issues.

Organization for Economic Cooperation and Development. Development Assistance Efforts and Policies in 1961. Paris, September, 1962.

_____. Development Assistance Efforts and Policies--1963 (1964; 1965; 1966; 1967) Review. Paris, 1963 through 1967.

_____. The Flow of Financial Resources to Countries in Course of Economic Development in 1960. Paris, February, 1962.

_____. The Flow of Financial Resources to Less-Developed Countries, 1956-1963; 1961-1965. Paris, 1964, 1967.

_____. Geographical Distribution of Financial Flows to Less-Developed Countries, 1960-64; 1965. Paris, 1966, 1967.

Organization for European Economic Cooperation. The Flow of Financial Resources to Countries in the Course of Economic Development, 1956-59. Paris, 1961.

United Nations Department of Economic and Social Affairs. Foreign Capital in Latin America. New York, 1955.

_____. Handbook of International Trade Statistics. Prepared for the U.N. Conference on Trade and Development, Geneva, 1964.

_____. International Flow of Long-Term Capital and Official Donations, 1959-61. New York, 1963.

_____. World Economic Survey. New York, 1963 through 1966.

_____ and Statistical Office. Yearbook of International Trade Statistics, 1965. New York, 1967.

United Nations Development Programme. Pre-Investment and Productivity. (Sales No. 67.IID.5.) New York, 1967.

United Nations Secretary-General. The Capital Development Needs of the Less Developed Countries. New York, 1962.

United Nations Special Fund. Annual Report. New York, 1963 through 1966.

United Nations Statistical Office. Monthly Bulletin of Statistics. Various issues.

Other

Government of the Federation of Nigeria, Federal Office of Statistics. Digest of Statistics. Lagos, various quarterly issues.

_____, Ministry of Economic Development. National Development Plan, 1962-68. Lagos, 1962.

Government of France, Ministry of Foreign Affairs, French Economic Assistance in West and Equatorial Africa 1948-1958-- A Decade of Progress. New York: French Embassy Press & Information Service, November, 1958.

Government of India, Planning Commission. Second Five Year Plan, 1956: Summary. New Delhi, 1956.

_____. Third Five Year Plan. New Delhi, 1961.

_____. Third Five Year Plan--Draft Outline. New Delhi, June, 1960.

Government of Pakistan Planning Commission. Second Five Year Plan (1960-65). Karachi, June, 1960.

Great Britain. Colonial Development Corporation. Annual Report. London, 1961 through 1966.

Great Britain. Colonial Office. Colonial Development and Welfare Acts. (Report to Parliament.) February, 1959.

BOOKS: UNPUBLISHED DISSERTATIONS

Alter, Gerald M. "Savings and Investment Aspects of Raising Income Levels in Underdeveloped Countries." Unpublished Ph.D. dissertation, Department of Economics, Harvard University, 1954.

Asher, Robert E. Grants, Loans, and Local Currencies: Their Role in Foreign Aid. Washington, D.C.: Brookings Institution, 1961.

Ashworth, William. A Short History of the International Economy, 1850-1950. London: Longmans Green, 1952.

Avramovic, Dragoslav, assisted by Ravi Gulhati. Debt Servicing Capacity and Postwar Growth in International Indebtedness. Baltimore, Md.: The Johns Hopkins Press, 1958.

_____, and Associates. Economic Growth and External Debt. Economic Department, International Bank for Reconstruction and Development. Baltimore, Md.: The Johns Hopkins Press, 1964.

_____, and Gulhati, Ravi. Debt Servicing Problems of Low-Income Countries, 1956-58. Baltimore, Md.: The Johns Hopkins Press, 1960.

Black, Eugene R. The Diplomacy of Economic Development. Cambridge, Mass.: Harvard University Press, 1960.

Feis, Herbert. Europe: the World's Banker, 1870-1914. New Haven, Conn.: Yale University Press (Council on Foreign Relations), 1930.

Foreign Policy Clearing House. Strategy for the 60's (Summary and Analysis of studies prepared by 13 Foreign Policy Research Centers for the United States Senate). Washington, D.C., 1961.

Gray, Clive S., "The Spectrum of International Capital Transfer to the Underdeveloped Countries." Unpublished Ph.D. dissertation, Department of Economics, Harvard University, 1964.

Imlah, Albert H. Economic Elements in the Pax Britannica. Cambridge, Mass.: Harvard University Press, 1958.

Jenks, Leland H. The Migration of British Capital to 1875. New York: Alfred A. Knopf, 1938.

Kuznets, Simon. Capital in the American Economy—Its Formation and Financing. Princeton, N.J.: Princeton University Press (National Bureau of Economic Research), 1961.

Lewis, Cleona. America's Stake in International Investment. Washington, D.C.: Brookings, 1938.

Little, I. M. D., and Clifford, J. M. International Aid: A Discussion of the Flow of Public Resources from Rich to Poor Countries with Particular Reference to British Policy. London: George Allen and Unwin Ltd., 1965.

Mikesell, Raymond F. The Economics of Foreign Aid. Chicago, Ill.: Aldine, 1968.

Paauw, Douglas S. Financing Economic Development, the Indonesian Case. Glencoe, Ill.: The Free Press (Center for International Studies, M.I.T.), 1960.

Salant, Walter S., and Associates. The United States Balance of Payments in 1968. Washington, D.C.: Brookings Institution, 1963.

Shonfield, Andrew. The Attack on World Poverty. New York: Random House, 1960.

Vanek, Jaroslav. Estimating Foreign Resource Needs for Economic Development. Theory, Method, and a Case Study of Colombia. New York: McGraw-Hill, 1967.

Wolf, Charles, Jr. Foreign Aid; Theory and Practice in Southeast Asia. Princeton, N.J.: Princeton University Press (RAND Corporation), 1960.

ARTICLES; PAPERS; SPEECHES; PERIODICALS;
NONOFFICIAL REPORTS

Alter, Gerald M. Capacity of Underdeveloped Countries to Service Foreign Capital Inflows. Washington, D.C.: IBRD, July 22, 1953. (Preliminary draft, mimeograph.)

_____. "The Servicing of Foreign Capital Inflows by Under-developed Countries," in Economic Development for Latin America, proceedings of Round Table of the International Economic Association, Rio de Janeiro, August 18-26, 1957 (New York, 1961).

Baldwin, David A. "The International Development Association: Theory and Practice," Economic Development and Cultural Change, Vol. X, No. 1 (October, 1961), pp. 86-96.

Black, Eugene R. "Finance for the Growth of India," Commerce (Bombay), December, 1958. (IBRD reprint.)

_____. Speech to the Institute of Bankers, London, December 1, 1959. Washington, D.C.: IBRD, 1959.

_____. Speech to United Nations Economic and Social Council, April 7, 1960. (IBRD mimeographed release.)

Brand, Vance. Speeches as Managing Director of the Development Loan Fund, 1959-61. (Mimeographed releases of the DLF.)

Cleveland, Harlan. "The Convalescence of Foreign Aid," American Economic Review: Papers and Proceedings of the 71st Annual Meeting of the American Economic Association, December, 1958, Vol. XLIX, No. 2 (May, 1959).

_____. "The Fits and Starts of Foreign Aid," The Reporter, April 16, 1959, pp. 25-29.

Coffin, Frank M. "Some Thoughts on Policy-Making in A.I.D." Speech before Conference on Foreign Aid, Trade, and Investment, Washington, D.C., May 4, 1962. (AID mimeographed release.)

_____. Speeches as as Managing Director of the Development Loan Fund, 1961. (Mimeographed releases of the DLF.)

Cooper, Richard N. A Note on Foreign Assistance and the Capital Requirements for Development. Prepared for the U.S. Agency for International Development. Santa Monica, Calif.: The RAND Corporation, February, 1965 (Memorandum RM-4291-AID).

Davis, John H. "Agricultural Surpluses and Foreign Aid," American Economic Review: Papers and Proceedings of the 71st Annual Meeting of the American Economic Association, December, 1958, Vol. XLIX, No. 3 (May, 1959).

Diamond, William. "Economic Problems of Foreign Trade and Investment in Underdeveloped Countries," Ohio State Law Journal, Vol. 17, No. 3. (IBRD reprint.)

Domar, Evsey D. "The Effect of Foreign Investment on the Balance of Payment," in Domar (ed.), Essays in the Theory of Economic Growth. New York: Oxford University Press, 1957.

Friedman, Milton. "Foreign Economic Aid," Yale Review, Summer, 1958.

Iliff, Sir W. A. B. "The World Bank and the Sterling Area," National Provincial Bank Review (England), February, 1958. (IBRD reprint.)

International Road Federation. World Highways. Articles in various issues.

Lieftinck, Pieter H. External Debt and Debt-Bearing Capacity of Developing Countries. (Princeton Essays in International Finance, No. 51.) Princeton, N.J.: Princeton University Press, 1966.

Mark, Louis, Jr. "The Favored Status of the State Entrepreneur in Economic Development Programs," Economic Development and Cultural Change, July, 1959.

Mason, Edward S. "Competitive Coexistence and Economic Development in Asia," in International Stability and Progress: United States Interests and Instruments. New York: The American Assembly, 1957.

_____. "Foreign Money We Can't Spend," Atlantic Monthly, May, 1960, pp. 70-86.

Mikesell, Raymond F. "Coordinated Lending," International Development Review, Vol. III, No. 2 (June, 1961).

Morgenthau, Hans J. "A Political Theory of Foreign Aid," American Political Science Review, June, 1962, pp. 301-10.

Nehru, B. K. "A Rational Approach to Foreign Assistance," International Development Review, Vol. II, No.2 (October, 1960).

Nurick, Lester. "The World Bank, the International Finance Corporation and Foreign Investment," Federal Bar Journal, October, 1959. (IBRD reprint.)

Nurkse, Ragnar. "International Investment Today in the Light of Nineteenth Century Experience," Economic Journal, December, 1954.

Ohlin, Göran. Foreign Aid Policies Reconsidered. Paris: Development Centre of the Organization for Economic Cooperation and Development, 1966.

Overseas Development Institute. British Aid--1: Survey and Comment. London, 1963.

_____. British Aid--2: Government Finance. London, 1964.

_____. British Aid--3: Educational Assistance. By Peter Williams. London, 1964.

_____. British Aid--4: Technical Assistance. By Peter Williams. London, 1964.

_____. British Aid--5: Colonial Development. London, 1964.

_____. German Aid. By John White. London, 1965.

_____. Investment and Development. By Sir Leslie Rowan, J. H. Loudon, Sir Jock Campbell, Arthur Gaitskell, and William Clark. London, 1965.

_____. Japanese Aid. By John White. London, 1964.

Pesek, Boris P. "Economic Growth and Its Measurement," Economic Development and Cultural Change, Vol. IX, No. 3 (April, 1961), pp. 295-330. Essays in the Quantitative Study of Economic Growth, presented to Simon Kuznets on the occasion of his 60th birthday.

Pincus, John A. "The Cost of Foreign Aid," Review of Economics and Statistics, November, 1963, pp. 360-67.

Qayum, A. "Long Term Economic Criteria for Foreign Loans," Economic Journal, June, 1966, pp. 358-69.

Rosenstein-Rodan, P. N. "International Aid for Underdeveloped Countries," The Review of Economics and Statistics, Vol. XLIII, No. 2 (May, 1961).

Schelling, Thomas C. "American Aid and Economic Development: Some Critical Issues," in International Stability and Progress: United States Interests and Instruments. New York: The American Assembly, 1957.

Schmidt, Wilson E. "The Economics of Charity: Loans Versus Grants," Journal of Political Economy, August, 1964, pp. 387-95.

Society for International Development. Summary of symposium on soft loans at 2nd Annual Conference of SID, Washington, D.C., March 11-12, 1960. International Development Review, Vol. II, No. 1 (May, 1960).

_____. Survey of International Development. Various issues.

Stanford Research Institute. Significant Issues in Economic Aid to Newly Developing Countries. Palo Alto, 1960. (mimeographed staff paper.)

Szulc, Tad, New York Times, May 12, 1961.

Viner, Jacob. "International Finance in the Postwar World," Journal of Political Economy, April, 1947.

Walinski, Louis J. "B. K. Nehru's 'Rational Approach,'" International Development Review, Vol. III, No. 1 (February, 1961).

Wood, C. Tyler. "Problems of Foreign Aid Viewed from the Inside," American Economic Review: Papers and Proceedings of the 71st Annual Meeting of the American Economic Association, December, 1958, Vol. XLIX, No. 3, (May, 1959).

Woods, George D., "Address to the Board of Governors and Concluding Remarks," September 25, 1967. Washington, D.C.: IBRD, 1967.

ABOUT THE AUTHOR

Clive S. Gray, since January, 1968, a member of the Harvard Advisory Group in the Departamento Administrativo de Planeación, Government of Colombia, Bogotá, has been professionally involved with capital transfer to less-developed nations on the sides of both source and recipient nations. As an economist with the U.S. Agency for International Development mission to Nigeria during 1961-63, he helped to plan the build-up of U.S. aid following the U.S. Government's decision to commit $225 million of assistance to Nigeria's 1962-68 Development Plan. Subsequently, as an economic adviser in Kenya's Ministry of Economic Planning and Development during 1964-67, Mr. Gray assisted in the preparation of Kenya's 1966-70 Development Plan as well as in designing projects for overseas aid and negotiating assistance for them.

He has published articles in African journals on the relationship between trade and monetary aspects and on the methodology of economic planning in East Africa.

Mr. Gray received his M.A. degree in political science from the University of Chicago and his Ph.D. in economics from Harvard. He has also studied at the universities of Frankfurt/Main and Delhi.